The Sociology of Community Action
Monograph 21
Editor Peter Leonard
Contents

Introduction

The Sociology of Community Action.   Peter Leonard   5

History, Ideology and Practice

Social Theory and the Historical Construction
of Social Work Activity: The Rôle of Samuel
Barnett.   Diana Leat   21

The New Towns: A Philosophy of
Community.   Brian Heraud   39

Community Work and Political Struggle:
the Possibilities of Working on the
Contradiction.   Paul Corrigan   57

Whose Grass Roots? Citizens, Councillors
and Researchers.   Jon Davies   75

Case Studies in Community Action

Socio-Political Correlates of Community
Action: Conflict, Political Integration and   Neil Gilbert and
Citizen Influence.   Harry Specht   93

Bread and Justice: The National Welfare
Rights Organization.   Hilary Rose   113

Community Action, Quasi-Community Action
and Anti-Community Action.   Norman Dennis   143

Community Action in a Glasgow Clearance
Area: Consensus or Conflict?   Sydney Jacobs   165

Chaucer House Tenants' Association: A Case
Study.   David Thomas   185

Gosford Green Residents' Association: A Case
Study.   John Benington   205

University of Keele, Keele, Staffordshire.

Note

Manuscripts to be considered for publication in the form of
Monographs of the Sociological Review and contributions to be
considered for inclusion in the *Sociological Review* should be sent to
Professor Ronald Frankenberg, Managing Editor.

ISBN 0 904425 00 2

Printed and bound in Great Britain
by J. H. Brookes (Printers) Limited, Hanley, Stoke-on-Trent, Staffs.

Sociological Review Monograph 21

Notes on Contributors

J. Benington
Project Director, Coventry Community Development Project.

P. Corrigan BSc
Lecturer in Sociology, University of Warwick.

J. Davies BA, MA, DPSA
Lecturer in Social Studies, University of Newcastle upon Tyne.

N. Dennis BSc
Senior Lecturer in Social Studies, University of Newcastle upon Tyne.

N. Gilbert PhD
Associate Professor, School of Social Welfare, University of California, Berkeley.

B. Heraud BSc, PhD
Principal Lecturer in Sociology, Polytechnic of North London.

S. Jacobs BA, PhD
Research Officer, Race Relations Board, London.

D. Leat BSc, PhD
Lecturer in Sociology, City University, London.

P. Leonard BSc, MSc
Professor, Department of Applied Social Studies, University of Warwick.

H. Rose BA
Professor, School of Applied Social Studies, University of Bradford.

H. Specht PhD
Professor, School of Social Welfare, University of California, Berkeley.

D. Thomas BA, MPhil
Lecturer in Community Work, National Institute for Social Work, London.

Cover design by Cal Swann FSIA

INTRODUCTION:
THE SOCIOLOGY OF COMMUNITY ACTION

Peter Leonard

The Purpose of the Monograph

'Community action' is a term which has substantial currency in the rhetoric of debate about housing, planning and welfare operations of the State, of their relationship to the private market, and their impact on various sections of the population. Community action as a form of collective response to specific social issues is seen by some as a disruptive and unhelpful challenge to effective planned change; by some as a more sophisticated means by which working class areas are manipulated by a new group of bourgeois professionals; by yet others as an effective way of increasing local control over bureaucracy and developing a consciousness of the possibilities of collective power. With community action as an idea and a practice so central to current controversy, it seems important to explore both the idea and the practice from various standpoints.

The intention behind this monograph when it was planned was that it should explore community action, and the context within which community action takes place, from a standpoint which was *primarily* sociological. It is probably important to clarify this. The emphasis here is on the primary focus so far as analysis is concerned, and is not intended to suggest that other analyses, drawing on the disciplines of economics, political science, or psychology (especially social psychology) are not equally valid, depending upon the questions the investigator is asking and the level of analysis, from macro to micro, that he is interested in. In fact, the writers in this book themselves occasionally draw on other disciplines in seeking understanding and explanation. The editor is not of the view that there should develop a sub-branch of the discipline of sociology called 'the sociology of community action', but that sociology should make its distinctive contribution eventually to a multidisciplinary approach. At this point, however, a specific focus on community action within a monograph series concerned broadly with sociology was considered useful.

The monograph was planned to draw upon two primary sources of contribution. Sociologists were to provide historical and theoretical papers on a number of issues relating to community action, whilst community activists themselves were to supply empirical studies which could offer some understanding of the processes involved. This book is the result of the struggle to achieve these objectives, a much delayed process which illustrates, perhaps, the problematic nature of this area of study and practice: namely, the reluctance of practitioners to write about and reflect upon their practice, and of theoreticians to concentrate attention on some of the central issues of this type of social action. Although the process of producing the monograph has involved considerable struggle and delay, the result should be of substantial interest to both academics and activists (and some activists are also academics). The editor's commitment in working to produce this book has been not simply in order to increase knowledge about community action as an end in itself, an interesting theoretical exercise; it has been undertaken in order to contribute to more effective community action by analysis of its specific objectives, context and processes.

This monograph does not contain an extensive discussion of the range of definitions of community action, for this discussion can be found elsewhere, for example in the work of the Gulbenkian Community Work Group (1973). Nor does it provide a single overview of alternative approaches to the functions and context of community action within the social structure. Instead, the monograph provides a number of related theoretical and empirical papers which should contribute to answering some of the following central questions:

1. What are the historical and structural contexts within which particular forms of community action take place?
2. What are the social processes involved in community action as it proceeds, including the various definitions of the situation by the participants involved?
3. What is the outcome of various forms of community action: who benefits, who loses, and what are the unintended consequences in general?

The Context of Community Action

The focus of attention in this book is on a range of activities undertaken by community groups in relation to issues that affect them. Whilst the term community action might include any movement by any minority group to achieve change, it has come to be associated particularly with protest and conflict strategies. As the Gulbenkian

Group suggests, current usage now tends to emphasise 'the collective nature of community action, the poor (or deprived) taking action on their own behalf, a location in a neighbourhood, and objectives framed in terms of overcoming political powerlessness' (1973:40). Although most contributors to the monograph have addressed themselves directly to such forms of community action, scope has been allowed for wider issues and definitions to be included so that certain historical, ideological and practice questions can be dealt with in a broad context.

Before we examine specifically the contributions made to the monograph, we shall explore some of the factors which have recently increased the interest and commitment of academics and practitioners in the development of community action strategies. My own professional background and interests lead me to focus attention on factors related to the problematic nature of Welfare State processes at the local level, the ideology which underpins such processes, and their effects on both welfare consumers and welfare staff. In brief I am suggesting that:

1. The operations of the Welfare State at the local level (especially the personal social services) have been largely dominated by a particular set of assumptions, explanations, values and interests which we might term a 'welfare ideology'.

2. This ideology, which emphasises the helping of individuals, families or communities who suffer from problems, is under increasing critical pressure both from alternative explanations and ideologies, and from a material reality which contradicts the ideology.

3. As the ideological crisis in welfare provision deepens, those engaged in its processes, including social workers, teachers, and community activists, are struggling to forge a new framework for theory and practice which includes the development of new kinds of community action.

If, as Marsh (1964) maintains, 'the social services are those provided by the community for no other reason than that of maintaining or improving individual well-being', then we can probably rely on the good-will of local politicians, bureaucrats and professionals. Such a view is implicit in the 'welfare ideology'.

The Welfare State in general and the personal social services in particular are usually seen within the 'welfare ideology' as primarily benign and altruistic in purpose; even the controlling functions are in people's best interests. Less attention is given to the ways in which

7

social services, including housing and planning, enable a sufficiently disciplined, healthy, and motivated labour force to be delivered and maintained for the purpose of economic production. It is assumed that by delivering specific services to individuals and groups (the disadvantaged, poor, deprived and handicapped) the State can even up their life chances. Casualties are seen essentially (in spite of verbal reservation) as incidental problems which could be solved provided more social service, housing and financial resources, better planned and distributed, and more precisely directed were made available. Such an approach does not envisage the possibility that deprivation and poverty might be fundamental to the social structure rather than incidental.

Behind this traditional view of the purpose of the Welfare State lies an institutional definiton of the nature of the problems to be faced, which emphasises individual, family, or community pathology. Attention is devoted to individual and group defects (the 'problem' is primarily in them) and so the response of the Welfare State must often be to remove or ameliorate these defects. The fact that personal social services, in particular, are organised primarily to deliver individual services (attempts in some local authorities to develop statutory community action strategies has met with great political resistance) is both the result of a pathology model of problems and serves to reinforce such an institutional definition.

This pathology model is central to at least some versions of the idea of a 'cycle of deprivation'. It is an idea which has a long history and which often involves accounts of the poor and the 'problematic' which change little over the years. Consider this statement made in 1947 by C. P. Blacker in his Eugenics Society study of 'Problem Families': 'A problem family is one that lives in squalor and is content to do so. It apparently suffers from domestic and possibly social ineducability. Its members may be distinguished by lack of character and by mental backwardness, sometimes associated with relatively numerous children, child neglect, intemperance, etc.' (Blacker 1947.) Now compare it with Sir Keith Joseph's statement about single mothers: '. . . a high and rising proportion of children are being born to mothers least fitted to bring children into the world and bring them up . . . They are producing problem children, the future unmarried mothers, delinquents, denizens of our borstals, sub-normal education establishments, prisons, hostels for drifters.' (Joseph 1974.)

The point about such accounts of the poor and deprived is that

they repesent the thinking associated with the idea of family transmitted pathology. Sir Keith Joseph was responsible (while Secretary
for Social Services) for stimulating research into what he described
as the 'phenomenon of transmitted deprivation', whereby the carriers
of poverty are seen as the families themselves, whose children are
poorly socialized (lacking love, stimulus and discipline) and who therefore grow up with behaviour patterns which lead to further poverty.
Thus, on the basis of Department of Health and Social Security
finance, the Social Science Research Council is dispensing funds directed to research about the cycle of deprivation and about how social
services can be utilized to break the cycle. Inevitably, focus is placed
on the supposed inadequacies and inabilities of poor people rather than
on wider economic and political structures.

One further feature of the welfare ideology concerns the issue of
responsibility. A liberal humanitarian ethos pervades the social services
which, while it focusses on individual and community pathology does
not (or tries not to) blame the individual directly. Given the over-
whelmingly determinist view of man's behaviour which the social
sciences, especially sociology and psychology, have often supported, to
hold an individual responsible for his actions would be intenable. The
welfare client is mostly seen as not being able to help his condition; he
is driven by forces both internal and external beyond his control—
genetic inheritance, early childhood, family experiences, and current
social conditions. Of course, in practice, the attitude to individual
responsibility is an ambiguous one, but nevertheless the determinist
view has two consequences of some importance. In the first place it
tends to deprive the welfare client of moral status. His behaviour is
analysed in terms of the determinants upon him and insufficient account is given of behaviour as a result of intentions. For example,
some kinds of delinquency may represent a response to property relations in society. Reduction of moral status of the welfare client frequently leads to a devaluing of the accounts of his circumstances
which the client himself might give. His account of the world as
divided between 'Us' and 'Them' may well be an accurate reflection
of his experience of exploitive relationships and institutions in both the
work place and in the welfare agency. Secondly, the determinist view
tends to see the clients as acted upon rather than acting. The social
service organizations and the welfare officials *act* and the client is the
object of the action.

Such features of the dominant welfare ideology are clearly in conflict with many of the assumptions underlying community action. Further, it is the experience of this ideology as a practice, which in reaction, has contributed to the development of community action itself. Obviously, such a reaction has occurred among members of local communities who are expected to be passive in the face of the operations of the local Welfare State. It has also, however, effected those who are employed to operate the welfare system. Academic critiques of the dominant welfare ideology and alternative explanations of social problems have their place, but for the social worker, for example, who experiences the stress, the frustration and the pain of working with the most deprived and oppressed in society, it is the *material reality* of their clients' circumstances which affects them most profoundly. It is this which contributes most to the sense of despair which seems so widespread among at least certain groups of social workers. The new structures of social services have been developed but they seem not only to fail to meet the material reality of many of their clients, but positively to contribute to their oppression by services which only ameliorate, pacify and turn away anger. But just as some welfare clients by means of community action are organizing in various ways to confront social welfare bureaucracies, so also are some social workers in writing and in organization, beginning to argue for alternatives to the welfare ideology and the traditional welfare response. Community action is seen as one such alternative, and at present the most promising one.

History, Ideology and Practice

The first section of contributions to the monograph examines some specific issues which throw light on the historical context within which community action has developed and the problems and possibilities which it now faces.

The first two papers do not focus attention directly on community action in a narrow sense, but explore some of the ideological influences which affected interest in 'community' as an idea and in understanding the relationship between individual responsibility and poverty in Victorian society. It is this latter issue which is Diana Leat's concern in her paper on the social theory of Samuel Barnett. Given the widespread assumptions that are made about the ideology of individual responsibility which the Charity Organization Society and its supporters are assumed to have held, it is valuable to have a detailed analysis of the ideas of a major figure in the early years of social work. She argues that Barnett was substantially more sophisticated sociologically in his analysis of poverty than any of his social work contempories. In spite of his adherence to some of the major ideological assumptions of his Victorian fellow reformers, he nevertheless sees individual responsibility as mediated through the harshness of the culture of poverty. He appears to see the value of improving health and educational provision as a means of improving working class character—a clear understanding of the significance of state intervention as a means of securing, in Marxist terms, the reproduction of labour. Leat also shows us that Barnett could understand that the development of certain personal characteristics of the poor (dependence and servility) was a product of interpersonal interaction, rather than being inherent in the individual.

Leat argues that Barnett's conception of the way in which poverty should be attacked rests on a community-based politically oriented approach to social work in which the settlement would be a major instrument. The settlement would, she argues 'combine the short-term immediate alleviation of individual misery with a long-term assault on the structural conditions giving rise to poverty'. Had Barnett's ideas about social work had greater impact, a consensus-oriented, liberal reformist community work might have developed to a greater degree as a counter-balance to the individualistic casework approach which came to dominate social work. But there were other, more influential factors operating at the turn of the century and beyond which need further exploration, including the poor law administration, the development of Fabianism and the growing power of medical and pseudo-medical models of pathology.

Brian Heraud, in his paper on New Towns, also explores developments which originate in the nineteenth century. In a study of the influences which contributed eventually to the establishment of New Towns after the second world war, he raises some important questions about the idea of community as an ideology. As other contributors to the monograph also suggest, 'community' is an ideological construct with a variety of origins serving a multitude of purposes. It has its origins in critiques of the modern city and the powerlessness, alienation and conflict which it generates especially among certain sections of the working class.

The central issue to which Heraud addresses himself is the contradiction between the growth of urbanization and its consequences on the one hand, and government policy in New Town development on the other. Why did government not attack the problem of the large cities directly, rather than side-step it by seeking solutions in the creation of new 'communities'? The answer, Heraud suggests, lies in the long ideological preparation of planners and others stemming from the Garden City movement, an anti-urban literary tradition, and responses to the increasing power of the urban proletariat. A major purpose in the creation of New Towns, as in other urban planning developments, is to be found in its use in reducing and controlling class conflict by the attainment of 'social balance' and by separation from the more deviant forms of working class politics which exist in the large cities. Heraud shows that much within the ideology of community is part of a conservative literary tradition of anti-urbanism, but he also suggests that at the same time it contains contrary elements deriving from a socialist, albeit medievalist, literature. It is interesting to compare this analysis with that of Paul Corrigan's which follows. Although in both papers the point is made that the idea of community and its use in planning can contribute to the reproduction of labour and the control of conflict, in Corrigan's case the basic question is asked—who has the crucial power? Although there were the contrary ideological elements which Heraud identifies, the material power of the ruling class has enabled it to express its dominant ideology in many different guises, from public health legislation, through education, to community development projects and New Towns. An important issue which Heraud touches on, and which is exercising some community activists in the field, is the extent to which concern with local community problems diverts attention from wider structural issues. Such has been the effect (and intention?) of the Home Office Community Development Projects, as C.D.P. workers, in their developing analysis, are beginning to show (see Coventry C.D.P. 1975).

The remaining two papers in this section both examine directly some practice issues for community activists. Paul Corrigan's approach is to argue that what community workers need most, at present, is a theory which will help them to locate themselves structurally. From a Marxist perspective he proceeds to answer the question—why does the State need community workers? His answers in some ways parallel those of Heraud in their emphasis on ruling class fear of working class communities and the need to control or destroy them. Corrigan, however, follows through his analysis by examining in detail the rôle of the community worker as part of the ideological state apparatus intent on preserving those elements in working class communities beneficial to economic production and social control and on eliminating deviant and dangerous elements.

This analysis does not, however, lead Corrigan to the view that community workers have no choice but to operate in an oppressive way. He suggests, in fact, that providing they have an ideological base that they can use in their day-to-day practice, they will be able to operate for the working class. Although those entering community work are, partly because of their origins and partly because of the material reality which surrounds them, beginning to see their work in terms of class struggle, such an analysis can sometimes be completely immobilizing. It is because of this that Corrigan is intent on developing a Marxist analysis which has practical application. He starts this process of building a practice theory by looking at the issue of intervention or non-intervention in working class communities. His answer in terms of political strategy rather than bourgeois morality only begins to tackle the problems and a great deal more work would obviously need to be done to make the argument both fully convincing and practically specific. However, the start is made and if developed could have substantial consequences for community work education and practice.

The final paper in this section, by Jon Davies, confronts some of the issues in community action practice and research which do not usually appear in the literature. He argues that writing about community action can, in effect, obscure the problems involved in the development of the literature. The differences of interest and values of politicians, researchers and activists which Davies explores are not, however, just significant in the *accounts* of community action—they pose substantial problems in the development of the *practice* of community action itself.

Of particular importance in Davies' account is the politically vulnerable position of the researchers who 'too easily internalize a self-imposed veto' on political partisanship. In spite of his concern for the researchers, however, Davies' contribution to *the sociology of the sociology* of community action stems also from his experience of the rôle of local politician and his at least partial identification with the councillor's experience of 'a bloody sociologist sneaking round my ward causing trouble'. He shows that there are a number of structural factors effecting the rôle of the local councillor which is bound to make him suspicious of and hostile towards community action. These rôle constraints, emanating as they do from the nature of the political system at local level, enable us to place into context the relationships between community activists and councillors as revealed in the later case studies in this monograph of Norman Dennis, Sidney Jacobs and David Thomas. What becomes clear in reading Davies in relation to the case studies is that those engaged in community action need to take full account of the structural position of local councillors; an understanding of the importance of party loyalty, of professional rivalry between politician and community activists, and of the tension between central policy-making and ward representation, is essential if effective strategies are to be developed. What is ineffective is to write-off local politicians as of no significance in the struggle for more local control; they may be mobilized on its behalf, but at least the basis for their opposition must be understood if it is to be properly battled with.

Case Studies in Community Action

This main section of the monograph consists of a number of specific accounts of community action which enable us to begin to understand the social processes involved and their consequences.

The first two papers provide us with useful comparative accounts of U.S. experience in the field of community action. Neil Gilbert and Harry Specht's study of the Model Cities programme touches on a major problem which confronts community activists—does participation with and political integration into the established power structure lead inevitably to tokenism and the eventual political neutering of the community activity? This is an extremely difficult question to answer and the authors recognize that in attempting to explore it they are faced with a large number of conceptual and empirical problems. Clearly, the idea of 'community participation' is part of a rhetoric which can cover a wide range of political objectives.

For Gilbert and Specht, a manageable question is whether citizen participation improves the *effectiveness* of policies and programmes, and it is to this question that they give their attention. The authors recognize that their methodology, based as it is on the accounts of bureaucrats and professionals rather than citizens, is open to objection, but it enables some very rough measures to be made. The answers appear comforting to the liberal or moderately radical professional, for

14

Introduction

they suggest that citizen-dominant programmes are the least effective, staff-dominant programmes rather better, and that those where citizens and professional influence are balanced are the most effective. The study raises a number of theoretical and research problems, not least concerned with the criteria that Gilbert and Specht use measuring positive programme outcome—quality, speed, efficiency, co-ordination and implementation. An important issue here is whether citizen participation and influence should be seen primarily as a means by which programme effectiveness might be improved, or whether such influence might not also be seen as a means to other ends, an experience which provides an education preparatory to wider political struggles.

Hilary Rose acknowledges the importance of this aspect of the process of participation in her account of the National Welfare Rights Organization. In chronicling its rise and decline she argues that evaluation must include the growth of self confidence amongst those who have experienced the oppression of poverty and racism. Rose's paper gives rise to a number of important questions which centre on the attempt, represented in this monograph, to account for differences in the perspectives and achievements of different community activities. It shows, in the case of the N.W.R.O., the extent to which basic social and political structures are questioned and identifies, as an important political objective of powerful elites, the possibilities inherent in community action as an establishment response to disaffection; the incorporation of the urban poor, 'maximum feasible co-option'. The paper raises therefore, in a fresh form, the question which haunts most community activists; is community action which is limited to *local level* operation, rather than contributing to a national campaign, simply an inexpensive means of adjusting people to the imperatives of the economic and political structure? In her analysis of the range of problems which N.W.R.O. experienced, Hilary Rose explores the relationship between the professional community workers and the local indigenous leadership. This relationship is seen as a contradiction between centre and periphery, one which had momentous implications in making N.W.R.O. a structured pressure group rather than a mass movement. The overall analysis of this paper demonstrates the need, as the author expresses it, of locating community action within a general theory of class if the structural context is to be more fully understood. In this she parallel's Corrigan's argument in the earlier paper in the monograph, an argument clearly expressed also in the recent work of Community Development Projects.

The next two papers in this section focus on a much smaller canvas; they are accounts of community action in the field of housing redevelopment. The first, by Norman Dennis, is an example of the failure of community action at a very local and small-scale level. Dennis gives us a detailed account of the delay, the prevaracation, the supression of material and the distortion of meeting minutes which was involved in a process which ensured the defeat of a group of local residents by the local authority. It is an account which raises a number of important issues. Like Jon Davies, Norman Dennis is a local councillor and his paper highlights the ambiguities in the rôle of the councillor with regard to redevelopment. The dilemma is clearly that of whether, as a councillor, to get to the central levers of power in the party caucus and thereby hope to influence overall housing and planning policy, or to remain an *ombudsman* at the ward levels, a lonely voice dependent on constituency backing. Dennis' experience appears to be similar to that of Davies', namely that an effective politician cannot continuously emphasise local ward needs; identification with a local community appears to be self-defeating. Although the process of community action may, as we have seen, be important in developing political knowledge and skills at the local level, the absence, as in this case, of concrete achievement must be compensated by the learning of bitter lessons about the resourcefulness of local government structures when faced with the inconvenient demands of local communities.

Sidney Jacobs's study of a small part of Glasgow slum clearance provides another, though more successful, example of the struggle of a small group against the massive bureaucratic structures of a local authority housing department renowned for its lack of effectiveness and its insensitivity. In his account of this struggle, Jacobs argues that the local residents had effectively no choice about the strategies they were bound to use. Whereas much of the conventional literature of community work suggests that collaboration and bargaining strategies are also available as options in achieving community goals, Jacobs maintains that how strategies are defined is a function of the social context of the definer. Thus, those who are powerless have no real choice between conflict and consensus (collaboration, bargaining) strategies, for the powerless are not in a position to negotiate.

Jacobs further argues that consensus models of community action function to legitimate many existing strategies and structures. These arguments are important attempts to explore the ideological basis of conventional wisdom, especially in the field of professional community work training. It suggests once more that an understanding of community action depends on locating it within the class structure so that its relationship to economic exploitation can be revealed. Given this class location, Jacobs is naturally concerned about the rôle of the professional community worker. Apart from anything else, his presence can be utilized to support an account by elite groups of community action as caused by 'trouble makers'; seen in Davies' words once more as 'sneaking round my ward causing trouble'. But Jacobs seems also to demonstrate the need for some professional support to community groups. His account of the problems of continuing to operate with a constituency which is declining because of re-housing, links with a similar account by David Thomas in the monograph. In both cases the problem of maintaining morale and momentum was one which the professional worker might help with.

David Thomas' account of the struggle of Chaucer House against the London Borough of Southwark is, among other things, valuable as another view of the relationship of the local councillor to the local community. Once again, we see the perception by the local resident and the community activist of the councillor, because he is more interested in 'Town Hall affairs' than in his local constituency, being someone who cannot effectively be used as a resource. It was on the basis of a realization of the need to find alternatives to ineffective local representation that the Chaucer Home strategies were based. At the same time, the experience of stigma accelerated the consciousness of the residents about the need for action. Thomas provides a detailed account of the objectives and strategies involved in various stages in the action, and is particularly useful in analysing the rôle of the professional community worker. In particular, he shows how a professional worker can assist in helping individuals to operate collectively, to identify their targets and to work on a broad base of issues. He analyses the sources of power in community action at the local level as existing in the collectivity, its leadership and its consciousness of the futility of individual action. At the same time the Association's analysis of its local authority opponents enabled it to understand that the continued existence of Chaucer House affected the material interests of various sections within the local authority; rivalries and tensions *amongst* local authority staff and councillors were seen as an important factor in the situation.

The final paper in the monograph provides both a parallel and a contrast with the other accounts of small-scale community action. As a detailed record it compares with David Thomas' paper; but the contrast between this account and others lies in the fact that it describes and analyses a relatively 'non-crisis' situation for the participants. The paper places this particular piece of activity within the context of the Coventry C.D.P. in general and argues that the problems which communities face in Coventry must be understood against a background of the operations of local capitalism. This is, of course, part of a general thesis which some C.D.P.'s are developing; an attempt referred to earlier, to locate community issues more firmly within an analysis of social class and economic structure.

The value of this particular local account lies in the opportunity it has provided for those involved, both the residents and the professional worker, to reflect on 12 months of activity and to try to draw lessons from it. Within the context of the broad aims and methods of the Coventry C.D.P. in the field of information and intelligence, technical and administrative support, community organization and adult education we are able to see some of the problems involved in their implementation.

Although it is clear that the community action of the Gosford Green Residents' Association brought some specific material benefits to those involved, the most interesting part of the analysis concerns the development of the political consciousness of the Association and, in particular, its committee. The lessons learned at both tactical and strategic level seem to have been important: the realities of power and leadership, the importance of political discipline and collective responsibility, and the deepening understanding of the local authority system. Above all, perhaps, is the consciousness of the significance of taking initiative, of *acting* rather than simply responding, being *acted upon*. This account, with its frank, self-critical reflections, should enable both sociologists and community activists to increase their understanding of the processes involved and of the problems which face the community worker in deciding on the objectives and methods of his intervention.

Conclusion

This monograph has attempted to contribute to both the development of general sociological perspectives on community action and to the accumulation of detailed accounts and analyses of community action as a social process. It is clear that this represents only an early stage, alongside other efforts elsewhere, in the establishment of a structurally located theory of community action. Such a theory would benefit both sociologists and community activists, and should be developed in partnership.

The monograph raises a number of theoretical and practical issues which suggest some of the lines on which future work might develop. This work includes:

1. An analysis of community action within the context of a range of macro-structural factors. This would include specifically the political economy of the Welfare State and the ways in which the economic structure in general, both public and private market, affects communities and neighbourhoods. Such an analysis would be the basis of a fuller understanding of the relationship of community action to the class structure and its potential as an additional form of working class politics.

2. Study of the ideologies of those involved in community action, both local residents and 'outside' professional activists. There is a substantial literature on the different models of community action on the consensus conflict continuum; are these models available in the way the literature often suggests or are the options much more closed as a consequence of the relative powerlessness of many community groups? In general, work needs to be done, as we have seen, on the relationship of different strategies of community action to different models of society, and the ideologies which these represent.

3. Exploration of the knowledge, skills and processes involved in effective community action. In particular, there is a need to understand more fully the effects of specific kinds of professional intervention on outcome. Whilst this raises the spectre of the evaluation of *results*, and the great theoretical and methodological problems which this is bound to involve, such evaluative attempts, as we have seen in some of the papers in the monograph, are essential if deeper understanding of the process of community action is to be gained. Such an analysis of process would benefit from both structural and phenomenological perspectives; the former in identifying the micro as well as the macro political and economic variables operating on the participants, and the latter providing better understanding of the

subjective meaning which a form of action has to those involved in it.

References

Blacker, C. P. (1947), *Problem Families*, Eugenics Society.

Coventry Community Development Project (1975), Final Report, 'Prosperity and the Persistence of Inequality', obtainable from C.D.P. Information and Intelligence Unit, Mary Ward House, Tavistock Place, London, WC1H 9SS.

Gulbenkian Community Work Group (1973), *Current Issues in Community Work*, Routledge and Kegan Paul, London.

Joseph, K. (1974), speech reported in full in *The Times* newspaper, Monday, 21st October.

Marsh, D. (1964), *The Future of the Welfare State*, Longmans, London.

SOCIAL THEORY AND THE HISTORICAL
CONSTRUCTION OF SOCIAL WORK ACTIVITY:
THE ROLE OF SAMUEL BARNETT

Diana Leat

There are histories of social work, but there has as yet been little attempt to provide a sociological analysis of the historical construction of social work activity.* If the nature and form of the activity are viewed as socio-historically constructed rather than the 'natural' unfolding or recognition of objective truths their construction becomes a problem to be investigated. This article does not claim to represent such an analysis. The task here is the more modest and menial one of making a start on the preparation of the ground, of weeding out some of the more misleading conceptions serving to obscure our view of the early forms of social work activity.

One approach for the sociologist wishing to analyse the social processes involved in the construction of social work as a social activity would be to begin by consulting the available histories of social work, and, more generally, social welfare. The analyses in such texts generally share two features in common. First, a central rôle in the development of social work is allotted to the Charity Organisation Society and second, the principles and practices of the COS, and thus in large measure the principles and practice of social work in general as it developed in Britain, are related to the prevailing social and economic philosophy. The development of social work in nineteenth century Britain and the particular form taken by social work activity is to this extent treated as unproblematic. Put crudely the argument runs as follows: given the common sense knowledge and philosophy of social and economic problems in nineteenth century Britain the particular form, the principles and practices assumed by the COS follow logically; the COS constituted the main, if not the only, available model of institutionalised social work activity and thus the particular form assumed by social work in Britain in this century is similarly predictable.

The suggestion in this article is that a consideration of the work of Samuel Barnett raises important doubts concerning the adequacy of the analysis outlined above. Barnett's writings highlight the obvious but often over-looked fact that the nineteenth century common sense body of knowledge concerning the aetiology and solution of social problems was not entirely consistent and homogeneous; his practice and influence suggest that there was a alternative available approach to social problems and their solution, other than that constituted by the COS, *within the sphere of social work itself*. The development of Fabian philosophy in the latter part of the nineteenth century clearly constituted one such alternative approach. But to a large extent this represented a rejection of social work and a 'creating of political solutions'. This did not constitute an available alternative approach *within* social work. Myopic concentration on the rôle of the COS in the development of institutionalised social work and the tendency to consider Barnett only in the context of his membership of the COS has led to an oversimplified analysis of both the development of social work in Britain and of Barnett's rôle in this process.

The Charity Organisation Society, or as it was originally known the Society for Organising Charitable Relief and Repressing Mendicity, was established in 1869, born of a mixture of fear, paternalistic concern and a complex, if inadequately simplistic, theory of society and social problems. Perhaps the most central premise upon which the COS rested was that charity, far from preventing or treating the problem it sought to solve, was in fact creating or, at the least exacerbating it. At the first meeting of the Society the Earl of Derby summed up this principle from the Chair when, noting that pauperism was increasing more rapidly than either charity or wealth, he suggested:

> 'It admits, to my mind, of only one explanation: By want of proper supervision and control, by excessive laxity, and absence of discrimination between the deserving and undeserving, we are pauperizing, year by year, an increasing number of our people' (Charity Organisation Society 1870: 5-6).

The cause of pauperism was thus seen to lie in the system—not in the social or economic system *per se* but in the system of indiscriminate alms-giving which had the effect of creating thriftlessness and dependence in those who received it. The system must therefore be altered, to provide not indiscriminate alms but 'true charity'. 'True charity' which by definition treated only those thought worthy of help far from encouraging thriftlessness and dependence would strengthen character, encourage independence and help to preserve the family

22

as the fundamental unit of society. 'Charity is a social regenerator . . . We have to use charity to create the power of self help' (Loch: 1882).

Although the system was seen to be at fault by reorganising the system of alms-giving it was not thought that one could completely eliminate the problem. The *real* root of the problem and thus its ultimate solution was seen to lie in the individual lack of self-dependence. Lack of self-dependence was considered to be at the heart of pauperism and since self-dependence is possible for all men the individual who does not attain this happy state is to be held responsible for his failure and assisted in making good this deficiency. Any arrangement which militates against achievement of the goal of self-dependence was thought to merely exacerbate the problem and should therefore be checked. The problem of pauperism was thus defined as essentially a problem of character not of circumstance and its solution was seen to consist in the confrontation of the individual with his responsibility for self-dependence.

Such principles alone do not, however, necessarily lead to the conclusions derived from them by the COS. The practical implications of a stress upon individual responsibility are dependent first, upon the interpretation of the nature and scope of individual responsibility and second, upon an analysis of the factors which might militate against or weaken individual responsibility. It was not the doctrine of self-dependence and self-help in itself which led the COS to under-emphasise structural solutions to the problem of pauperism but rather their particular interpretation and analysis of the nature and social bases of both individual responsibility and of the factors producing its diminution. The failure to recognise that the principles and precepts of social and moral theories must be interpreted to provide recipes for action and that any given principle admits a variety of interpretations has led some social work historians to adopt an over-simplified analysis of the homogeneity of the origins of social work. The tendency is to lump together all those who preach the 'same' principles without considering the interpretive meaning of those principles in terms of practical action.

The principle of maximisation of self-dependence is not logically incompatible with structural solutions to social problems if the analysis of factors serving to weaken or prevent self-dependence is seen to include structural factors. Indeed the COS, as noted above, recognised that 'the system' might be in part responsible for a lack of self dependence. But the structural factors isolated related to the organisation of alms-giving and the analysis was not extended to include more basic structural aspects of the wider social and economic system. A further structural factor defined by the COS as a source of social problems was the geographical separation of rich and poor. It was this geographical gulf between rich and poor which was seen to be one cause of the disequilibrium between charity and the Poor Law manifested in the phenomenon of 'indiscriminate almsgiving'.

It is clear therefore that the COS did not define structural factors as irrelevant in the aetiology and solution of the problem of pauperism. Their analysis of the rôle of such factors was, however, limited. The primary assumption was not that the basic structure of society led to social problems but rather that imperfections or temporary imbalances in the system did so. Apart from a few minor alterations to these superficial blemishes on the face of society the problem lay in the individual. The individual must be adjusted to the system rather than *vice versa*. The notion that social conditions might prevent the individual's fulfillment of his responsibilities is:

> 'a vain and idle hypothesis. The social conditions *will* permit them; for their very efforts to do so will make them steady and efficient workers, whose services will be valued by the community.' (Bosanquet, H. quoted in Woodroofe 1968: 34.)

It followed from this that State intervention must be kept to an absolute minimum. This minimum included the maintenance of the Poor Law, based upon the principles of 1834, but very little else.

Barnett's definition of the major social problems of the late nineteenth century is in many respects not significantly different from that of the COS or any other of his contemporaries. Like them he accepted that pauperism was *the* problem of the day and that all other problems—drink, idleness, crime—were either causes or results of pauperism. Prior to the surveys of Booth, and later of Rowntree, knowledge of the extent of the problem and its causes was based upon relatively unsystematic and inadequate data. Mayhew's *London Labour and the London Poor*, Thomas Beames' *Rookeries of London* and other works, such as Hyndman's survey, tended to be rejected as journalistic sensationalism. The lack of such basic factual material did not, however, deter either the COS or Barnett from theorising about the causes, consequences and potential cures for pauperism.

Barnett differs from the then dominant approach to social problems not in his definition of the problem *per se* but rather in his analysis of its causes. He also diverges from mainstream approaches in his emphasis upon the necessity for adequate knowledge of the problems and in the means advocated for obtaining such knowledge. This is not to suggest that other bodies considered investigation and fact-finding an irrelevant or unnecessary exercise. Much of the work carried out at this time is quite clearly aimed at providing such information—though it should be remembered that the COS emphasis upon the importance of investigation to secure adequate knowledge of the case in hand, was based upon the desire to expose fraudulent claims rather than upon any sociological or even pseudo-sociological theory of the social causation of problems. It is therefore ironic that such activities should now be claimed as the beginnings of casework! Apart from any difference in the underlying theory or legitimation of the necessity of obtaining fuller knowledge of the poor there is a difference in method between Barnett's approach and that of others.

Whereas most bodies, including the COS, relied mainly, though not exclusively, on information obtained by interviews and visits Barnett stressed the crucial importance of what we would now call participant observation. Writing in 1897 after the publication of the first volumes of Booth's study and at a time when statistical information was more and more becoming available Barnett emphasises that facts and figures alone are not enough if the social meaning of the problem is to be understood. In taking part in the everyday life of the community, in the streets, in the schools, in the clubs, on committees:

> 'the residents in a settlement learn what are the interests of working people, what their opinions, what their order of thought, what their language. Their minds are changed by the atmosphere they breathe. They take in knowledge much they do not tabulate; they absorb thought as air;' (Barnett 1897: 279).

That Barnett was not content with what amounted to fairly crude questionnaire techniques and insisted instead on the method of participant observation through the Settlement perhaps explains his divergence from dominant theorising about the nature and aetiology of social problems.

Starting out from the currently accepted definition of pauperism as the major problem of the day Barnett also in part accepts the dominant theory of the social and economic necessity of poverty. Along with many others of his day he regards the existence of suffering as a necessary and indeed in many ways potentially beneficial feature of social life. Similarly, he shares in the common-sense knowledge of his milieu in defining individual and family responsibility as desirable and to be encouraged wherever and whenever possible. Lack of individual and family responsibility is likewise defined as contributory to if not constitutive of most of the major social problems, including pauperism. But the fact that Barnett shares with his contemporaries these basic principles of common knowledge should not be taken to imply that he subscribes to other parts of the body of everyday knowledge of his time. Nor should agreement in principle be taken to signify agreement in practice. As already noted theoretical principles, bodies of abstract knowledge, do not automatically translate themselves into practical recipes for action but must rather be interpreted and 'worked' by social actors. To assume as does, for example, Stedman Jones that Barnett's statement: 'Our aim is to decrease sin not suffering' implies any simple theory of pauperism as an expression or result of working class immorality, and an equally simple policy of moral control or regeneration as a solution, is to overlook the interpretive work to be done in understanding social meaning. Barnett *does* link sin and pauperism but, as he makes perfectly clear, sin has many manifestations. He certainly does not regard it as the exclusive prerogative of the poor—as some of his philanthropic contemporaries did.

> 'If one sentence could explain the principle of our work, it is that we aim at decreasing, not suffering, but sin . . . sin in the sense of missing the best. . . . Sin must be recognised as manifold, and anything which mars the grandeur of human life must be brought under a converting influence!' (Quoted in H. O. Barnett 1921: 76.)

Thus while it is true that few of Barnett's 'social work' colleagues would have disagreed with his basic statement, many might have taken exception both to his interpretation of the proper application of the term 'sin' and to his analysis of the relationship between 'sin', so defined and applied, and pauperism.

As noted above, Barnett explicitly and superficially accepts the then dominant common sense definition of poverty as socially and economically necessary and desirable. But where he differs from many of his contemporaries is in recognising that:

> 'Poverty is a relative term: The citizen whose cottage home, with its bright housewife and happy children, is as light in our land, is poor in comparison with the occupant of some stately mansion.' (Barnett 1888a: 143.)

and *this* is the poverty Barnett accepts as socially tolerable and perhaps desirable. One may doubt whether many late nineteenth century cottagers had either a bright housewife or happy children and yet accept the distinction between such poverty and:

> 'the poverty by which men and women and children are kept from nourishment and sent out to work weak in body and open to every temptation to drink . . . the poverty which makes men slaves to work and uninterested in the magnificent drama of nature or life!' (Barnett 1888a.)

This is the poverty that Barnett refuses to regard as socially or economically necessary. This is the poverty which is 'an evil to be cured'. Barnett therefore explicitly rejects the legitimation of poverty in terms of its necessity in motivating the poor to work—slavery to work is itself a form of poverty. His acceptance of certain types of poverty as socially desirable is rather based upon a theory of the good life as the simple life, the golden age of nature in which home comforts and the happy family abound.

Throughout his writings on social problems Barnett adopts an approach which rejects any absolute definition of poverty and directly anticipates later theories of poverty as relative deprivation. The poverty of the East End is not to be assessed in and of itself but must rather be seen in relation to the wealth of the West End. The elimination of poverty is inseparable for Barnett from the expansion of equality—rather than merely being a question of raising the poor above some hypothetical line. Equality in turn implies applying to one's neighbour's life and comfort the standards one applies to one's own life and comfort.

> 'To treat one's neighbour as oneself is not to decorate one's own house with the art of the world, and to leave one's neighbour's house with nothing but drainpipes to relieve the bareness of its wall.' (Quoted in H. O. Barnett 1921: 139.)

The ostentatious and senseless luxury of the West End insofar as it reflects and exacerbates social inequality is a social problem to be eliminated:

> 'The habit of fostering every whim or of out-doing neighbours in extravagence of furniture and food is anti-social . . . Luxury in so far that it increases the feelings which make divisions, is a greater social danger than even drunkeness.' (Barnett 1904: 31.)

In adopting such an approach Barnett expands and develops the notion of poverty well beyond its dominant definition in his own time. Poverty is not merely lacking the material, physical essentials

27

of life—a decent home, enough food, enough rest, however these are defined (and Barnett would argue that they must be assessed in relation to the standard of wealth in that society). To live in poverty is also to lack spiritual, aesthetic, creative—call them what you will —necessities of social living.

> 'The poverty which has to be cured is the poverty which degrades human nature and makes impossible for the ordinary man his enjoyment of the powers and tastes with which he was endowed at his birth.' (Barnett 1888a: 143.)

And the powers and tastes with which man is endowed at his birth include, according to Barnett, the enjoyment of art and literature, the potential for creative fulfillment in work and in leisure.

> ' . . . the best in knowledge and beauty must be within everyone's reach. Libraries, Art, Galleries, good music, University teaching, must be as near to a West End as to an East End suburb. There can be no real unity so long as the people of different parts of a city are prevented from admiring the same things . . . ' (Barnett 1904: 31).

Not only is this a significant expansion of the then dominant conception of poverty it was also at variance with contemporary common-sense ideas about the social distribution of 'human potential'. According to the common-sense body of knowledge the working class, like the subjects of imperialism, were genetically inferior. Just as they had lightweight bodies so they had lightweight brains and lacked the genetic capacity to think intelligently, appreciate good books, music and art. It was, of course, admitted that some individuals from the ranks of the working class might, under exceptionally favourable circumstances, make good this genetic deficiency. Such fairytale transformations are a not infrequent element in the working class novel of this period. Violet in Besant's *Children of Gibeon* is the daughter of a washerwoman but brought up by Lady Mildred Eldridge, a wealthy aristocrat she is indistinguishable from Valentine the daughter of a wealthy heiress. Similarly, Valentine's eventual husband, Claude, a working class boy brought up in the slums, has been subjected to Lady Mildred's philanthropy and at the end of the book possesses a first class Cambridge degree and the beginning of a career in law. (Besant: 1886). But such instances were regarded as romantic fictions —the exception that proves the rule. The idea that as a class the poor might be similarly endowed was not seriously considered. Again Barnett diverges from the common-sense knowledge of his time and directly anticipates much later theories of the social as opposed to genetic creation of intelligence. The working class:

> 'have the same ability to enjoy and to think, but they have not the means. Everyone must have been struck over and over again by the greater mental possessions of a child brought up among educated people than those of a better taught child brought up out of touch with educated people.' (Barnett 1897: 283.)

It is therefore true but misleading to suggest that Barnett accepted the dominant perception of the working class as unintelligent and inappreciative of art and literature. He accepts the description but rejects the explanation.

In his general analysis of the causes of poverty the same formula holds for the most part and this may be one reason why Barnett's work has been passed over as merely another variation on the dominant late nineteenth century theme. Barnett's acceptance of and divergence from the common-sense of his contemporaries is nicely illustrated in his discussion of the relationship between self-reliance and poverty.

As already noted one of the most frequent targets of COS criticism in the late nineteenth century was charity, Charity in general and indiscriminate charity in particular was regarded as one of the major stumbling blocks in the solution of the social problems of the day. Charity, it was alleged, was an important cause of poverty and no solution would be achieved until this was eliminated. Poverty was conceived of as essentially a problem of a lack of self-reliance; charity had the effect of increasing this lack of self-reliance leading to idleness, dependence and begging. Thus in treating the manifest symptoms, the charitable were in fact exacerbating the underlying causes. To achieve any appreciable effect in eliminating the causes of poverty it was therefore thought necessary to increase the independence and self-respect of the poor, to raise them to a level from which they could once more begin to exercise the virtues of self-reliance and self-help. Those who had slipped below this level because of their own immorality, profligacy, lack of character or whatever were held responsible for their present conditions and thus undeserving of help in the climb out of it. It was recognised, however, that the individual's powers of self-reliance might be weakened or rendered temporarily ineffective by circumstances beyond his control—illness, temporary unemployment and so on. Such circumstances were in general conceived of as purely individual, personal misfortunes or the result of minor and/or temporary injustices or imbalances in the social system. The cause of and thus the solution to poverty lay ultimately in the hands of the individual. And it was the individual upon whom attention was concentrated and with whom (or on whom) the COS and other similar bodies worked. The aim was to increase the individual's taste for hard and regular work, to promote thrift and regular saving, to encourage careful budgeting thus enabling the individual to look after himself (and his family) within the existing social and economic system.

Barnett on the whole accepts the dominant condemnation of charity as an evil to be eradicated. He concurs with the view that charity, in attempting to solve the problem of poverty, merely serves to exacerbate it. He too considers that charity merely treats the symptoms and not the cause. But again this measure of agreement should not be taken to suggest that Barnett is correctly described as a supporter of the common sense theory of poverty and the rôle of charity in its solution. The fact that Barnett made statements such as:

> 'Indiscriminate charity is among the curses of London. To put the results of our observation in the strongest form, I would say that "the poor starve because of the alms they receive".' (Quoted in H. O. Barnett 1921: 83.)

has misled some critics into looking no further at Barnett's theory, assuming it to be indistinguishable from others of his day. Barnett does not, however, reject charity *per se*. The charity he abhors is that which is:

> 'an insurance against the discontent of the poor a propitiation for the enjoyment of luxuries, or a relief to the giver'. The 'easy charity', 'the conscience money' which involves no effort or sacrifice on the part of he who gives and no interest in or feeling for the recipient, the charity which simply serves to solve the middle class conscience and paper over the problem, is what Barnett rejects. 'Gifts must be the expression of real and intelligent interest. Far then, from wishing to stand in the way of relief, I appeal for more relief . . . '(Quoted in H. O. Barnett 1921: 85).

The latter statement might perhaps have also been made by any of Barnett's contemporaries but the difference lies in the meaning given to the nature of this 'real and intelligent interest' and the type of relief appealed for.

Barnett's conception of 'real and intelligent interest' in the problems of the disadvantaged and the type of relief which he considers desirable and potentially effective cannot be separated from his analysis of the causes of those problems. Accepting the common sense knowledge of the late nineteenth century Barnett emphasises a

30

lack of character and self-reliance among the causative factors of poverty. Intelligent and effective relief is thus relief which strengthens character and makes good deficiences in independence and powers of self help. But where Barnett parts company with the dominant theories of his milieu is in his approach to the scope and nature of individual independence and self reliance. 'Character' and 'Independence' are not seen as genetic or purely individual traits but are rather conceived of as socially produced. The causal chain is thus amplified to read— poverty is caused by a lack of self-reliance, thrift, character; lack of self-reliance are individual characteristics but are in turn caused or at least exacerbated by social (structural) conditions. It is not sufficient therefore to reject charity on the grounds that it contributes to the formation and maintenance of dependency and to continue to seek a solution to the problem simply by working on the individual.

> 'The dangers of the relief which weakens self-reliance have been recognised, the kindness which removes every hindrance from the way has been seen to relax effort; but even so there is no justification for law and custom to intrude obstacles to make the way harder or to bind on life's wayfarer extra burdens.' (Barnett 1888a: 144.)

The 'intelligent' and effective solution is thus seen to lie at least in part at a structural level and will only be achieved by social rather than individual change. Indiscriminate charity is doubly dangerous insofar as it affects the individual who receives it and he who gives it, blinding both to the real root of the problem. The two questions which the social reformer must ask himself in his search for a solution to the problem of poverty are therefore: How is character to be strengthened? and How are the obstacles imposed by law and custom to be removed? And insofar as law and custom affect the development of character these two questions are inseparable:

> 'Character largely depends on health and education. Children born of overworked parents; fed on food which does not nourish . . . cannot have the physical strength which is the basis of courage.' (Barnett 1888a: 144.)

Development of character is therefore not simply a matter of individual moral quality but is rather dependent upon social conditions which facilitate or hinder it. Whether or not Barnett's analysis of the relationship between character, courage and sufficient food would find much support today is debatable but that he comes closer than many of his contemporaries to a sociological rather than a moral or individualistic theory of social problems is undoubted.

In line with this analysis the solution to the problem of poverty is conceived of not in terms of moralising casework or individual, temporary, material or psychological support but rather in terms of social structural change.

> 'They who would really serve their neighbour's needs by a gift must bring the latest knowledge of human nature to bear on the applicant's character, *and treat it in relation to the structure of society . . . they must be students of society and of the state.*' (Barnett 1888a: 233.)

Barnett's own analysis of society and the State led him to conclude that the development of character and the elimination of poverty could only be achieved by a fairly radical revision of the distribution of social and economic benefits and advantages in favour of the poor. That such a suggestion today appears to be tautologous does not detract from the fact that it was considered socialistic nonsense rather than self-fulfilling common sense amongst many of Barnett's contemporaries. Such redistribution is not to be conceived of in terms of the usual individual charitable hand-outs but must rather involve a redefinition of rights; structural revision rather than individual readjustments. To improve the health (and thus the character) of the poor Barnett rejects the then usual solution of charitable distribution of treatment and/or material financial aid to individuals or families. Rather, he suggests, health should be recognised as a right of the working class, a social rather than individual responsibility requiring social provision. Not only must provision be made by means of public health measures to improve the standard of housing, airspace and water in working class areas, but in individual cases of illness:

> 'Medical relief and direction should be a right, not a favour grudgingly given through Relieving Officers.' (Barnett 1888a: 145.)

But equalisation of the chances of the poor in obtaining health care must be supplemented by a similar redistribution of the benefits of education if the problem of poverty is to be solved. Lack of education, for Barnett, is the major factor in the generation of problems. It is education which more than any other single measure will solve the problem of poverty and allow the poor to claim for themselves the right of self-direction so long denied. It is education which will create a more equal and just society in which no man is forced to be dependent on any other.

Barnett does not accept that the Education Act of 1870 has done very much to redistribute the benefits of education. The rich and the poor child may both have the opportunity to attend school, but the mere provision of schools will not eliminate poverty and class division if those schools do not provide comparable education.

To the middle class reformers of the late nineteenth century it seemed apparent that schools could do little to improve the characters of children whose parents were singularly lacking in all of those qualities deemed admirable by the middle class. And in any case it was the responsibility of the parents, not the school, to cultivate character. In this way the middle class congratulated themselves on the upbringing of their own children and provided further justification for the view that poverty could only be eliminated by the creation of self-reliant, independent parents sensible of their responsibilities to their children. The middle class individual and not the system of education was responsible for the success of his (middle class) children and thus *mutas mutandis* the working class parent was to blame for the failure of his children.

As previously noted Barnett accepts the common sense definition of character and self reliance as a necessary prerequisite for the elimination of poverty, but he rejects the view that character development or socialisation is a purely individual matter. That middle class children have more 'character' he accepts; that this 'character' prevents them becoming poor he accepts; where he diverges from the dominant body of knowledge is in his insistence that possession of such character is not a result of genetic superiority nor of the superiority of middle class home socialisation, but is rather the result of unequal distribution of education benefits enjoyed by middle class over working class children. The schools of the richer classes are better staffed and better equipped; they recognise their responsibility in developing character and set themselves to produce

'self reliant men and women, wanting perhaps, in sympathy and moral thoughtfulness, careless perhaps of others poverty, not always intelligent, but strong in qualities which keep them from poverty.'

It is not some genetic deficiency, immorality or inadequacy in working class parents which prevents their children from developing similar characteristics: the difference lies in the inequality of the education system. The remedy lies therefore not in individual improvement *per se* but in an equalisation of the system which will thereby provide the opportunity for individual improvement.

33

'The teachers in our elementary schools must therefore be more in number, have more time to know their pupils and feel more responsible for each individual.' (Barnett 1888a: 146.)

Alterations in the health and education systems will do much, according to Barnett, to improve the character of the working class and thus go some way towards eliminating the problem of poverty. But these measures alone are not sufficient. Such measures create or extend the possibility of independence; what is also required is the destruction of obstacles to working class independence. Poverty and lack of self-reliance is not, according to Barnett, the result simply of individual failing or inadequacy. It is in part the result of laws and customs which create insurmountable obstacles in the path of the working class. Laws and customs as much as individuals create poverty. Once this is recognised it must also be recognised that the solution to the problem of poverty cannot be found in work with individuals but must also involve changes in the social system of law and custom which produces poverty. The land laws, for example, were once functional but

'times have changed and now these laws, instead of making wealth, seem to help in making poverty. The country labourer . . . sees land all around him which is serving the pleasures of the few, and not the needs of the many; he is shut out from applying his whole energy to its development for he cannot hope to get secure tenure of a small plot.'

In the city the same situation applies:

'because so large a portion of profit must go to the owner who has done no share of his work, his wages must be reduced.' Thus 'Law, with good intention, created the obstacle which he could not surmount. Law could remove the obstacle.' (Barnett 1888a: 148.)

Barnett's sociological sophistication (relative to his social work contemporaries) in analysing the causes of poverty does not, however, stop short here. He proceeds to analyse the rôle of custom in the creation and maintenance of poverty. Accepting that the poor lack self-reliance, that they appear to seek and rely on a position of dependence on others, he adopts a (primitive) version of labelling theory to explain this. The poor are not naturally servile, dependent and cringing; such behaviour is created in the process of interaction with those who label them as such.

'It is by custom that the poor are treated as belonging to a lower, and the rich to a higher class: that employers expect servility as well as work for the wages they pay; that property is more highly regarded than a man's life; that competition is held in a sort of way sacred . . . Many

34

> a man is . . . hindered in the race because he meets with treatment
> which marks him out as an inferior. He is discouraged by discourtesy,
> or he is tempted to cringe by assertions of inferiority.'

It follows from this that:

> 'greater courtesy; a wider recognition of the equality in human nature;
> a more set determination to regard all men as brothers.'

must be listed among the cures for poverty. Charitable gift-giving to
individuals can only exacerbate the problem because:

> 'it is not only gifts which demoralise; it is the attitude of those who
> think that gifts are expected of them, and of those who expect gifts.
> Gifts are only safe between those who recognise one another as equals.'
> (Barnett 1888a: 149).

The implications of such a theory could of course be hard and
Barnett, like the COS, was quite capable of refusing help on the
grounds that it would demoralise and weaken the self-respect of the
recipient. But he did at least attempt to be consistent in his treatment
of the poor. When critics alleged that the settlements placed too much
stress on entertainment, attempting to save the poor by pictures,
parties and pianos, Barnett replied:

> 'If we refuse a coal ticket because we wish to treat the people with
> respect, it is only right that we should invite them to meet as friends.'
> (Quoted in H. O. Barnett 1921: 152.)

And his refusal to take the people of Whitechapel to the mansions
and homes of those wealthy benefactors who failed to treat them as
equals, as important and personal guests, must have exasperated and
bewildered the self-congratulatory Lord and Lady Bountiful.

The Settlement was an instrument designed in accordance with the
analysis of poverty outlined above. Its aim was a combined attack on
the various causes of poverty. Demonstration of the individual human
equality of rich and poor at the level of day-to-day interaction was to be
allied with attempts to redress the social structural imbalance in social
justice. A detailed discussion of the aims and work of Settlements
is beyond the scope of this article. It is sufficient merely to point out
that through the Settlement Barnett hoped to combine the short-term
immediate alleviation of individual misery with a long-term assault
on the structural conditions giving rise to poverty. An increase in
courtesy, understanding and recognition of human equality between
rich and poor; a more equitable distribution of art galleries, music,
education, decent housing, parks, health care, access to legal redress

Diana Leat

and the promotion of working class power and skills in determining and fighting for community reforms were among the many hoped for results of the Settlement.

The suggestion in this article is that the available explanations of the construction of social work activity at the turn of the century are over simplified. Social work's apparent rejection of, for example, Fabian philosophy and practice as an approach to the solution of social problems may be explained away in terms of the latter's implicit denial of social work. But rejection of the community-based politically oriented approach to social work exemplified in Barnett's work cannot be so easily accounted for. The construction of social work activity thus remains a problem to be investigated and Barnett's work and influence in this process would seem to be a particularly fruitful point at which to begin. At a time when one to one casework is increasingly being rejected in favour of a more critical community based social work much of his writing repays more careful scrutiny. In particular perhaps we should do well to take note of his distrust of the cult of the expert, the power of professionalism and his emphasis upon the aim of all social work (whether casework or communiy work) as its own extinction.

* See, for example,

Jorns, A. (1931), *The Quakers as Pioneers in Social Work*, Macmillan, London.

Lubove, R. (1966), *The Professional Altruist; The Emergence of Social Work as a Career*, Harvard University Press.

Mowat, C. L. (1961), *The Charity Organisation Society*, Methuen, London.

Owen, D. (1965), *English Philanthropy 1660-1960*, Oxford University Press.

Rooff, M. (1972), *One Hundred Years of Family Welfare*, Michael Joseph, London.

Seed, P. (1973), *The Expansion of Social Work in Britain*, Routledge and Kegan Paul, London.

Woodroofe, K. (1968), *From Charity to Social Work*, Routledge and Kegan Paul, London.

Young and Ashton, E. T. (1956), *British Social Work in the 19th Century*, Routledge and Kegan Paul, London.

References Cited

Barnett, S. A., quoted in Mrs. H. O. Barnett (1921), *Canon Barnett: His Life, Work and Friends*, John Murray, London, p. 76.

36

Barnett, S. A. (1888a), 'Poverty: Its Cause and Cure' in Canon and Mrs. S. A. Barnett, *Practicable Socialism*, Longmans Green & Co., London, p. 143.

Barnett, S. A. (1888), 'Charity Up to Date' in *Practicable Socialism, op. cit.*, p. 233 (my emphasis).

Barnett S. A. (1897), 'Settlements or Missions' in *Towards Social Reform*, T. Fisher and Unwin, London, 1909, p. 279.

Barnett, S. A. (1904), 'Class Divisions in Great Cities', in *Towards Social Reform, op. cit.*, p. 31.

Besant, W. (1886), *Children of Gibeon.*

Charity Organisation Society, (1870), Meeting of the Society for Organising Charitable Relief, March 30th, 1870, pp. 5-6.

Loch, C. S. (1882), *The Charity Organisation Reporter*, 13th July, 1882.

Woodroofe, K. (1968), *From Charity to Social Work*, Routledge and Kegan Paul, London.

THE NEW TOWNS: A PHILOSOPHY OF COMMUNITY

Brian Heraud

---

1. *Introduction*

The new towns, in their origins, conception and development, provide an important context in which to review the concept of community and the strategy of community action at the inter-organizational and local planning level. The concern in this review is not so much to confront the realities embodied in the concepts of community and community action, that is to ask such questions as 'to what extent have planners been successful in creating communities in new towns?', although the exploration of these issues may be justifiable sociological concerns. Rather, my concern will be to discuss the new towns and their advocates in terms of the 'philosophy of community' that they represent, and to attempt to uncover some of the ideological roots of such a philosophy, as a contribution to the general purpose of the monograph. Certainly, one of the concerns of the article it is to revive, in the context of discussion of the new towns policy, the question that Dennis (1968) posed some years ago; 'why should the idea of (neighbourhood) community be so much more popular than a realistic appraisal of the idea would lead one to expect?'

One of the major rationales for the new towns and of much planning activity today, as well as of the Garden Cities of the past, lies in the concept of community and the critique of the development of the modern city which this suggests. Essentially, this aspect of the case for new towns involves the claim that the modern city (including its suburban areas) has evolved to a size and scale which has destroyed or at least diminished for the majority of the population the sense of identity with community in its physical or spatial aspect. Man as an individual in large urban areas has, it is argued, become dominated by forces which oppress and diminish him in relation to his immediate environment. Stein (1957), one of the first new town advocates in the United States, argues that 'man is submerged in the colossal

39

human swarm, his individuality overwhelmed, his personality negated, his essential dignity is lost in crowds without a sense of community.'

It is an important aspect of the main argument in this article that such views originated during the 19th century, in particular in Britain. Ebenezer Howard, one of the most important original advocates of the Garden City (and eventually new town) idea, saw the city as it had developed during the 19th century as an essentially temporary phenomenon related to an earlier phase of industrialization (Howard 1898). His views went some way beyond the usual critique of the 19th century city, with its range of physical and social problems.

The Garden City concept was based on the view that the city of the immediate past had played an important function in promoting technological and industrial change, for example by providing for the concentration of population in one place. With the growth of rapid transit systems, urban concentration was no longer a necessity for further economic growth, and the next stage of industrialization would require new urban forms. Again, the 19th century city was not only redundant economically, but led to impersonality, anonymity and alienation that was damaging to man's real need for smaller social groups (such as the family) and for community life. For Howard 'the crowded cities have done their work . . . they are in the very nature of things entirely unadapted for a society in which the social side of our nature is demanding a larger share of recognition.' (Howard 1898). In Howard's view such cities would inevitably give way to a new form of urbanism, of which the Garden City would be the key element.

If the modern city denied man community life because of its scale and character then, the Garden City and (later) new town advocates argued, new settlements on a much smaller scale would create the conditions necessary for such community life. Howard in fact defined the Garden City as a town 'designed for healthy living and industry of a size that makes possible the full measure of social life, but not larger.' (Howard 1898). What he advocated were towns of 30,000 population at low densities where each family would have a house with a garden, each town to be surrounded by an agricultural green belt. There were a variety of other elements to Howard's scheme, including the vesting of the ownership of land in trustees whereby increases in land values would accrue to the community rather than individual owners.

The scheme was not confined to the planning of individual Garden Cities. While the individual Garden City would be the basic unit for work and living Howard suggested that a number of such cities be arranged in clusters of eight with a total population of 240,000, linked by rapid transit, so that people could have the dual advantages of living in small towns with the benefits of city life within reach. Cities of the size of London could gradually be reduced in size and density and also take on the characteristics of the Garden City.

The new towns also embody the dual aspects of Howard's scheme. New town advocates stress both the 'intra-community' aspects of the policy, that new towns can recreate community life based upon the physical organization of a socially balanced and occupationally self contained population, and the 'inter-community' aspects, where the rôle of the new towns is in organizing and accommodating urban and suburban expansion and the growth of the city in general. (Clapp 1971.) Both these arguments make use of the idea of community, either directly or indirectly, as a basis for advocacy. This is particularly important in the case of intra-community aspects, where the assumption is that community is based upon a particular spatial entity and that a physical organization of such an entity from the ground up would give rise to social interaction and community identity between the inhabitants of such a place.

Although the latter assumption is never very clearly stated by new town advocates and planners, this formulation at least brings the concept of community as used in the new town context into the heart of the broad sociological controversy over the meaning of community. As Bell and Newby (1972) have suggested, in reviewing Hillery's (1955) work on the many attempts to find definitions and criteria for community, the majority of discussants include (in ascending order of importance) the three components of area, common ties and social interaction in their definitions, all of which appear central to the use of the term in the new town context.

Howard's scheme for Garden Cities proved to be the basis for the new towns that followed, both for the detailed plans that it offered and, after a long campaign by those who supported the scheme, for the hold it eventually took upon planners and government officials in Britain. Less than fifty years after the publication of Howard's book the new towns became one of the principle features of official urban policy in Britain (with the passing of the New Towns Act 1946), although the immediate circumstances of post war Britain were also an important contributing factor to the realization of the plan (Rodwin 1956). The new town idea has also been adopted as official policy in a number of other industrialized societies, most notably in the United States (Merlin 1971).

But here lies the paradox. The essentials of Howard's scheme lay in an antipathy to big city life and the evils to which he thought it gave rise, although he was never opposed to cities as such. Yet during the century preceding the publication of Howard's book Britain had been transformed from a rural to an urban society. 72 per cent. of the population of England and Wales was classified as urban by 1891. Moreover, a marked feature of this development was the increasing concentration of population in the largest cities; not only was Britain highly urbanized but it was a 'big city' society.[1] Given this situation, it is something of a puzzle that the idea of the movement of big city population to small towns and suburbs came to be so readily adopted as a solution to city problems, by comparison to a direct concentration on the problems of the cities themselves. As Petersen comments 'the notion that no solution to urban problems is possible within the framework of the metropolis . . . is on the face of it unreasonable. There is . . . no clear, rational line from urban problems to this "solution" ' (Petersen 1968).

There have been various attempts to explain this paradox. Certainly, Howard's ideas had the support of important figures such as Osborn and Mumford and later of a pressure group, the Town and Country Planning Association. But the Garden City movement and its pressure group was probably not effective alone in bringing about the fruition of this policy, for there were contradictions built into the functions of the movement and it had a limited appeal to influential people (Foley 1962). Instead, it can be argued that it was 'only in the context of a long ideological preparation that this extra-ordinary realization of the New Town myth could have been brought about' (Petersen 1968).

Here a number of contrasting aspects of that ideological preparation are discussed, firstly that deriving from the social and economic conditions of 19th century Britain and secondly that deriving from the literary tradition of the time. Finally, the functions of this ideology, in particular the concept of community which appears basic to all aspects of the ideology, are discussed in terms of the rationalization of contemporary planning activities.

2 Social and Economic Conditions in 19th Century Britain

Perhaps the most influential explanation put forward by urban sociologists for the success of the Garden City philosophy, of which the idea of community is an integral part, is that it represents a characteristic 'anti-urbanism' deriving in particular from the social and economic circumstances of 19th century Britain (see Glass 1955). The city was identified with the mass of the working class following the substantial population movements to towns and cities during the course of the 19th century and there was a fear, particularly in the early part of the century, of a working class revolution. The urban middle classes either segregated themselves in their own parts of the city or moved away from the city. Rural living was not only some kind of guarantee of security, but also an avenue of social advancement and status, particularly if this was associated with property owner-ship. In this sense, the middle class were emulating the mode of living of the aristocracy and landed gentry. However, these groups were not divorced from town life, because they were the industrial owners and managers of the time. This somewhat parasitic fusion of the urban and rural in the life styles of the upper and middle classes also contributed to the maintenance of stability and the balance of power. But throughout the 19th century the towns grew due to the influx of the rural working class, with a concomitant increase in the social and physical problems associated with such rapid growth.

These industrial towns and cities represented, in the words of Ruth Glass, 'above all . . . a formidable threat to the established social order: the more the towns were deserted by the upper and middle classes, the more plainly were they also the barracks of a vast working class whose lessons in the power of combination had already begun, and whose sporadic riots were the portents of latent insurrection' (Glass 1955).

However, by the last two decades of the 19th century this threat seemed less intense. One factor was that the working class had them-selves begun to join to some extent in the move to the suburbs where, according to Glass, their radicalism was tamed. The flight from the cities should not be exaggerated here, for clearly any very large movement was impracticable. The importance of this movement was ideological rather than physical; as Glass comments 'all strata of

43

society take an active part in it, and since the turn of the century none of them has spoken plainly against it' (Glass 1955).

The ideological influence of the anti-urban movement also fell heavily upon the urban reformers and planners of the 19th century, as well as their successors in the 20th, and resulted in the belief that one of the most important remedies for urban ills lay in the development of model communities, industrial villages and (later) Garden Cities. To a 19th century reformer such as Solly these developments were means by which the ills of urban working class life could be remedied, 'where they can be found employment, profitable to themselves and the community, where they can be decently housed and fairly well remunerated' (Glass 1955); to a later commentator (Glass) this was simply a means of social control, for the worker could be brought into closer contact with a paternalistic employer.

The planning ideology that has developed in the 20th century has several complex strands, but prominent amongst them was the view that great cities do not provide a basis for decent living amongst the bulk of their population (Foley 1960; Eversley 1973). From this springs the view that the best alternative is community life based upon the development of small, low density communities, either in the context of the re-planning of existing towns and cities or new towns for the control of overspill from the cities and for further growth. The ideology also gives emphasis to such ideas as the neighbourhood unit as a basis for planning and the provision of each family with access to their own garden. There are a number of other inter-related aspects of this policy, including the regional redistribution of population and employment in the country as a whole.

The town planning profession, as it developed in the 20th century, had in the Garden City movement and its supporters, a ready made image of the kind of communities that might be created, although there has always been a vocal minority within the profession arguing the alternative case for the acceptance of high density city life. In its development, town planning was clearly in competition with other interests and professions, and the identification of a specific series of ideas and programmes was an important way of gaining political and other support and attracting and recruiting manpower. But in order to make this appeal as broad as possible, town planning could not afford to take any one simple and rigid line, and commentators on the ideology of town planning direct attention more to the variety of competing ideological strands and the relationships between such elements as the key issue in such developments, rather than the monolithic nature of such an ideology. Apart from the ideology discussed so far, that of social advocacy, Foley (1960) has identified two other strands of thought in modern town planning. One concerns the provision of proper criteria for the use of land in order to reconcile competing claims amongst aspirant users (the umpire rôle), the other to provide a better physical environment in cities by means of improved housing, provision of open space and so on. These subideologies are in some aspects compatible, and probably the greatest conflict is between the neutralism of the umpire rôle and the social advocacy of the low density/de-centralization philosophy. The simultaneous availability of these alternative strands has meant that town planning has been able to call upon the maximum possible political support from all major interests and parties; on the other hand, strains exist (particularly between the umpire and the advocate rôle) which means that there are inconsistencies built into the system.

Some commentators have felt that the availability of a plurality of town planning ideologies may mean that town planning all too easily comes to reflect the interests of those power groups anxious to maintain their position and to defuse potential political conflict and therefore becomes part of the machinery of social control. Dennis (1968) argues that once the partial dispersal of working class populations from urban centres has taken place the idea of making residential estates into 'inward looking' communities would act as a further means of controlling and reducing class conflict. This would occur mainly through the involvement of potential political activists in the politically neutral and time consuming activities of Community Associations although this is not the overt purpose of such Associations. Whilst such Associations *may* help in making residential areas better places to live in, the ideology of the neighbourhood community movement is rarely questioned and in fact contains little of practical use.

A further ideological element in the popularity of the neighbourhood community idea (and most important according to Dennis) is that it directs attention away from the wider social and cultural basis of social and personal problems. Instead attention is directed to the local, community based causes of such problems, therefore providing no real challenge to established beliefs and institutions.

The political basis of the belief in local neighbourhood community

45

is, as a feature of the ideology of town planning, therefore of a conservative nature, one which accepts and justifies the existing order and ignores the existence of change and conflict.

3. *The English Literary Tradition*

The fears engendered by the economic and social facts of life in 19th century cities were also fed by a rich cultural vein, that of the literary outpourings of the poets, novelists and essayists of the period. Thus according to Petersen, one explanation for the success which the Garden City movement had in gaining acceptance of its policies 'must be that England's educated classes, the planners and legislators who made the key decisions realizing this policy, were influenced by a century of anti-urban animus. The literary works that Englishmen study in school and, as adults, read for pleasure, almost all speak with one voice, saying that cities are evil' (Petersen 1968).

The literary tradition cited here contains many complex strands and has its origins in a number of much earlier writers. Although in their different ways such writers were all committed to the community idea, the nature of such commitment varied with their overall standpoint. One type of distinction (Plant 1974) is between those writers who talk about community by restating the values of a pre-existing rural life, whether this takes them back to the village community of the latter part of the 18th century or further back to feudal society, and those who look to the idea of community as a basis for egalitarianism, socialism and social change and as an answer to problems in the present. The conservative and mainly pessimistic bias of the majority of the former group, characterized by a mainly negative reaction to the establishment of an urban-industrial society, emerged as the dominant reaction (Petersen 1968). This bias seems typical of a range of writers from the nature poets such as Wordsworth and Cowper to contemporary writers such as Eliot and Leavis (Eliot 1939 and Leavis and Thompson 1933).

In the latter case, not only is there a general concern with what is happening to culture and society through urbanization and industrialization, but there is also a strong evocation of the rural community of the past: 'the old England was the England of the organic community . . . but at the moment what we have to recognise is that the organic community has gone . . . its destruction in the West is the most important fact of recent history' (Leavis and Thompson 1933).

By destroying this kind of community, it is argued, with its close relation between living and work, industrialization has resulted in the creation of mass culture and a mass society, a standardization and levelling down in which cultural values and standards are threatened. Thus the majority of the writers so far quoted represent in their different ways a conservative ideology and perhaps none more so than Leavis with his own formulation of the 'English dream'. It should also not be forgotten that such ideologies, particularly of the earlier writers, were nourished by the beginnings of sociological theorizing. A work such as Toennies 'Community and Association' (published in 1877) expressed a theme of the decline of family-centred rural life that re-appeared in much of the literature of the period and in subsequent years. Again, sociological theories of urban/rural contrast were important in reviving the idea of community as a topic of sociological interest, as well as carrying the implication that rural and community based society was somehow to be preferred to urban based society (Redfield 1941).

But it is important not to make the error of identifying anti-urbanism and the evocation of the traditional community with any particular political orientation. In the previous section of the paper, Glass argued that anti-urbanism was associated with a fear of the industrial working class on the part of the ruling class and that such a bias was somehow typical of conservative thought. However, the city was also attacked by radical and socialist writers. The twin themes of revivalist Christianity and medieval socialism exemplify this attitude in writers of the past, in particular in the figures of Kingsley, Morris and Ruskin. Kingsley, in his critique of the city as providing few of the physical conditions necessary for a decent normal life, expounded an idea not far removed from that of the Garden City movement in the 20th century (Kendall n.d.). The medievalist socialist William Morris advocated rather similar ideas, and these have been interpreted as corresponding to some of the indications given by Marx on the Gotha programme (Henderson 1935).

But of all the medievalist socialists, by far the most important in terms of his influence on pioneers of town planning such as Geddes (and also Howard) was Ruskin (Geddes 1884). While his hatred of the city was intense, Ruskin's economic ideas were superior to those of his contemporaries. His plans for the reform of city life are quoted at some length by Howard in 'Garden cities of tomorrow', and he

47

conducted a variety of practical experiments to combat some of the evils of urban life. The following quotation from Ruskin appears at the head of chapter one of the 2nd edition of Howard; 'thorough sanitary and remedial action in the houses that we have; and then the building of more, strongly, beautifully, and in groups of limited extent . . . walled around so that there may be no festering and wretched suburb anywhere, but clean and busy streets within and the open country without, with a belt of beautiful garden and orchard round the walls . . . This is the final aim' (Howard 1902).

These figures from the past, distant though they may seem, are quoted in order to suggest that there may be important parallels between some of the intellectuals of the past, whether from left or right, and that of the Marxist version of a socialist society. In both alienation by re-fashioning them into a stronger community' (Petersen both cases there was an attempt 'to rescue individuals from urban cases, there was an attack on commercialism and profit mongering, in 1968; see also Plant 1974).

In the present, this tradition is best represented in the figures of Hoggart and Williams (Hogart 1957; Williams 1961 and 1965). The latter, for example, rejects Leavis' conception of the organic community as the natural social order and argues in a Marxist sense that the new system of production, industrialism, will provide the material conditions for the emergence of a new social order. He reformulates the 'English dream' as residing in a tradition in which the aim has always been to 'create an educated and participating democracy . . . we can achieve this only in terms of an industrial society, and the community we are building is and must be a wholly new kind of community' (Williams 1962). Essentially the community to which Williams is referring is one of co-operation, fraternity, participation, egalitarianism and a sense of membership in which the conservative idea of an elite or landed class is absent. Again, Williams's 'long revolution' implies that this new development towards a new kind of community is part of a universal historical movement in which an industrial society such as Britain may be at a comparatively early stage. The theory is thus evolutionary in type, and bears some resemblance to the views of Howard previously quoted, whilst the conception of social change involved is in some respects similar to that of Leavis in that primary emphasis is placed on the rôle of culture (Filmer 1969).

In this section it has been argued that the largely anti-urban bias of much of the literary tradition in England since the 18th century, from whatever source this has come, has influenced in an important sense the ideologies and background assumptions of many of the advocates of the Garden City movement, and later of the planners and administrators who were instrumental in developing and promoting the new towns policy. In 1899, a year after the publication of Howard's book, the Garden City Association was formed to promote Howard's ideas. This Association (which eventually changed its name to the Town and Country Planning Association), and its chief proponents (in particular F. J. Osborn) were in the crucial period of the 1930s and 1940s important in gaining acceptance by the Government of the new town idea (Buder 1969). Osborn, and the even more influential Mumford, wrote a preface and an introductory essay respectively to Howard's book when it was re-published.

The case made by Petersen for the crucial nature of the literary influence on these and other men who promoted the new town idea is not one of direct influence. In Howard's case, he was only indirectly in touch with the literature of the time and in fact was probably most influenced by the technocratic, socialist Edward Bellamy and his work 'Looking Backwards' in which he advocated co-operative national ownership of land (Rodwin 1956). In the case of Geddes the influence of a writer such as Ruskin was probably more profound. What is being argued is that the literary tradition, representing as it does some of the broader social currents of opinion, had provided a background against which these advocates, planners and administrators were themselves educated, and which continued to provide part of the dominant tradition of the society in which they later moved.

What is also at issue is the extent to which such tradition reflects in any way the lives of the great majority of people who were to be affected as a result of these policies.

4. *Community as a Sociological Charter*

Finally it is important to consider the ideological support provided by the philosophy of community for the strategies of the groups involved in the new town planning process, in particular planners and those defending their interests from planners. In general the concept of community can be seen as a code word or token for certain states of being desired by particular groups, and is part of the attempt to persuade others of the legitimacy of such aims (Alonso 1970). In this sense the term is (amongst others) a particularly powerful form of propoganda because of its ambiguous, everday meaning and the difficulty of dislodging the meaning from other forms of usage. In this sense it can be used in disguise in a variety of ways to appeal to many different audiences. As Cresswell puts it: 'in transactions between groups which threatened each other or are striving to achieve an identity it (community) is a vital emotive word . . . since the word is used as a claim both for support and for a particular state of being it is not just a version of reality but, in a condensed form, a sociological charter' (Thomas and Cresswell 1973).

For new town advocates and planners, the goals that were specified were such features as 'self containment' (people should both live and work in the town) and 'social balance' (people of different social classes should live in and mix together in the town). These specific aims were however often part of the more general and underlying argument that new towns should be communities, although this word was never defined by new town planners (Thomas and Cresswell 1973). It was assumed that if the above goals were attained, this 'community' would somehow follow, an assumption built into the terms of reference of the committee set up to plan the new towns in 1945. This has enabled planners to defend their policies, appeal for support to a number of groups involved and shield themselves from criticism (Dennis 1972). One particularly powerful argument here is based on the 'inter community' aspect of new towns. Planners have often justified their actions by claiming that they are serving the community outside the local area, that is the city or regions from which population will come. Planners can thus claim to be speaking for a 'community' which in effect cannot speak for itself, and are making claims on behalf of such a community that are very hard for rival groups to deny.[2] But this adds further power to the arm of the planner. The uses of words like 'community' as weapons of persuasion seem part of the social control function of the profession of planning, even though they may be part of the latent aspects of this structure.

In the case of the various groups defending their interests from planners in the new towns context, for example local protection societies and agricultural interests, the uses to which the word community have been put are equally ambiguous. For example, such evidence as exists suggests that such groups are not united against an external common threat, as everyday community theory would suggest, but that the 'community' in this sense contains a number of differing strategies. For example in Stevenage the main protest came from middle class newcomers who had moved to the country to escape the town life that was now being thrust upon them (Orlans 1952). The indigenous inhabitants were more divided in their loyalties, seeing some advantages (such as increased trade) in the change. At Milton Keynes, although the various farming interests united in their opposition to the loss of agricultural land, they still asked for the highest possible compensation. The area was also partly populated by overspill from urban areas and some of the support for the scheme was from those who felt that they could only gain by improved facilities (Thomas and Cresswell 1973).

However divided, these groups, like the planners with whom they were in contention, used the word community because of the power and authority it provides to persuade others of the justice of their cause.

5. Conclusion

The purpose of the article has been to explore some of the explanations of the popularity of the community concept in the context of the new towns as a contribution to the study of community as ideology. The paper has not attempted to consider the attempts by sociologists to evaluate directly the stated aims of planners in this context, such as the achievement of community in its various forms, although this is a legitimate sociological enterprise in which some progress has been made (see Ogilvy 1968 and Zehner 1971). In fact it has been argued that new towns provide a unique basis for research into various social, economic and political aspects of community and community development because of the possibility of observing the development of community relationships from their inception (Gans 1956). Thus the whole network of relationships commonly described as community may differ in a new town from more established situations because of 'its newness, its social organization and culture and its social and ecological independence' (Gans 1956). For this reason the new towns provide an important focus for research into community.

However, the purpose here has been to pay attention to the ideological bases of the planners' aims and in particular to analyse some

51

of the latent aspects of the planners involvement with community as a concept. This has been attempted on the grounds that it should not be the rôle of the sociologist to devote his entire attention to the manifest (or stated) aims of planners and others by taking planners' definitions of the situation as the entire focus for discussion or research (Rex 1974). It is even argued that the term community should not be treated in any other way than as an ideological construct and that those who are trying to formulate some scientific or descriptive meaning of community are, in whatever context, misunderstanding the logic of the situation (Plant 1974).

In the analysis of this ideology, its origins and functions, one particular argument has been briefly examined: that the economic conditions of the early 19th century gave rise to a fear of urban-based class conflict and hence to a more general fear of cities. This provided the impetus for a programme of decentralization of the working class populations of cities in which the underlying object, through such devices as the neighbourhood community concept, was to split up and divide the working class and hence lessen the threat of class conflict. Such anti-urbanism was seen not only as a deliberate turning away from the reality of modern industrial society, but also as embodying conservative political philosophies.

This interpretation of reformist attitudes has also been questioned in the course of the paper. The idea that the anti-urban tradition is necessarily one that is associated with a conservative political bias has already been criticised, in particular by reference to a variety of literary sources.

Thus the anti-urban concept does not seem to discriminate between basic political orientations. This suggests that the anti-urban category may not be particularly appropriate or useful in the analysis of human responses to urban life. This is also born out by recent evidence and discussion about those urban planners who are supposed to represent anti-urban attitudes (in particular in their espousal of the idea of community). A case in point is that of Howard, the founder of the Garden City idea. Howard has often been accused of an anti-urban bias (see Glass 1955; Rodwin 1956) and in some sense this may be true if the city is seen as synonymous with the metropolis which (to Howard) is the creator of social disorganization and alienation. But Howard basically accepted the city, was born and bred in it and was always attracted by its variety and vitality, as his early letters show (Buder 1969). Thus Osborn writes of Howard: 'he saw the city as the social place and the country as the unsocial place . . . it never occurred to him that country villages . . . had a greater sense of community than big cities. He was inherently a townsman wanting to remain a townsman when the town had married the country' (Hughes 1971).

A very similar interpretation could be made of Mumford, who has been held up as being in the centre of the anti-urban tradition (White 1964). Mumford, like Howard before him, can equally be interpreted as an enthusiast for the city, if the forces that enhance rather than destroy life and social relationships in the city prevail (Goist 1969). Mumford is critical of the development of the modern city where the human purposes which cities are supposed to serve, namely to transform power and human energy into physical, social and cultural form, are denied. The growth of the modern metropolis has, for Mumford, denied such purposes and needs. The alternative to the modern metropolis is a regional framework much on the lines suggested by Howard, in which the inhabitants of cities of different sizes obtain the advantages of metropolitan life in the context of balanced communities without the existing disadvantages of the modern metropolis. Mumford has been criticised because it is believed that the regional approach and Garden City idea are not relevant to modern urban problems, and because it is thought that his approach to the city is too organic and metaphysical (White 1964).

Thus the anti-urban category, implying as it does also a critique of the concept of community, would seem to be a somewhat misleading category in the light of this discussion (Goist 1969). Howard, Mumford and other urban planners have been discussed very largely in relation to a convenient but possibly rather meaningless label which ignores the complex nature of responses to urban life and which does not facilitate the analysis of such responses (including the recent renewal of interest in the concept of community) and the ideologies lying beneath them.

Footnotes

[1] Taking 1851 as a base year with an index of 100, by 1901 the index for population growth had risen to 254 for the 84 'great towns' but to only 169 for the rest of England and Wales; see Ashworth, W., 'The Genesis of Modern British Town Planning', Routledge, London, 1954.

Brian Heraud

² The Skeffington Report on public participation in planning states that 'we do not think of the public solely in terms of the community as it shows itself in organized groups. We regard the community as an aggregate comprising all individuals and groups within it without limitation'; Skeffington Report, People and Planning, 1969.

References Cited

Alonso, W. (1970), 'What are New Towns For?, Urban Studies, vol. 7.

Bell, C. and Newby H. (1972), 'Community Studies', Allen and Unwin, London.

Buder, S. (1969), 'Ebenezer Howard: The Genesis of a Town Planning Movement', Journal of the American Institute of Planners', vol. 35.

Dennis, N. (1968), 'The Popularity of the Neighbourhood Community Idea', in Pahl, R. (ed.), Readings in Urban Sociology, Pergamon, Oxford.

Dennis, N. (1972), 'Public Participation and Planners Blight', Faber and Faber, London.

Eliot, T. S. (1939), 'The Idea of a Christian Society', Faber and Faber, London.

Eversley, D. (1973), 'The Planner in Society', Faber and Faber, London.

Filmer, P. (1969), 'The Literary Imagination and the Explanation of Socio-Cultural Change in Modern Britain', Archiv. Europ. Sociol, vol. 10.

Foley, D. (1960), 'British Town Planning: One Ideology or Three?' British Journal of Sociology, vol. 11.

Foley, D. (1962), 'Idea and Influence: The Town and Country Planning Association', Journal of the American Institute of Planners, vol. 28.

Gans, H. (1956), 'The Sociology of New Towns: Opportunities for Research', Sociology and Social Research, vol. 40.

Geddes, P. (1884), 'John Ruskin, Economist', William Brown, Edinburgh.

Glass, R. (1955), 'Urban Sociology in Britain', Current Sociology, vol. 4.

Goist, P. (1969), 'Lewis Mumford and "Anti-Urbanism"', Journal of the American Institue of Planners, vol. 35.

Henderson, P. (1935), 'Literature and a Changing Civilisation', John Lane, London.

Hillery, G. (1955), 'Definitions of Community: Areas of Agreement', Rural Sociology, vol. 20.

Hoggart, R. (1957), 'The Uses of Literacy', Chatto and Windus, London.

Howard, E. (1902), 'Tomorrow: A Peaceful Path to Real Reform', 1898; later re-issued as 'Garden Cities of Tomorrow', Swan Sonnenschein, London.

Hughes, M. (ed.), (1971), 'The Letters of Lewis Mumford and Frederic Osborn, Adams and Dart, Bath.

Kandall, G. (n.d.), 'Charles Kingsley and His Ideas', Hutchinson, London,

Leavis, F. and Thompson, D. (1933), 'Culture and Environment', Chatto and Windus, London.

Merlin, P. (1971), 'New Towns', Methuen, London, discusses the development of the new town idea in Britain, Scandinavia, Holland, France, Poland, Hungary and the U.S.A.

Oglivy, A. (1968), 'The Self Contained New Town' Town Planning Review, vol. 39.

Orlans, H. (1952), 'Stevenage: A Sociological Study of a New Town', Routledge and Kegan Paul, London.

Petersen, W. (1968), 'The Ideological Origins of Britains New Towns', Journal of the American Institute of Planners, vol. 34.

Plant, R. (1974), 'Community and Ideology', Routledge and Kegan Paul, London.

Redfield, R. (1941), 'The Folk Culture of Yucatan', Unversity of Chicago Press.

Rex, J. (1974), 'Sociology and the De-mystification of the Modern World', Routledge and Kegan Paul, London.

Rodwin, L. (1956), 'The British New Towns Policy', Harvard University Press, Cambridge.

Ruskin, J., 'Sesame and Lilies', quoted in Howard, E. 'Garden Cities of Tomorrow', *op. cit.*

Solly, H. (1884), 'Re-housing of the Industrial Classes . . . ', cited by Glass, *op cit.*

Stein, C. (1957), 'Toward New Towns for America', Reinhold, New York; cited in Clapp, J. (1971), 'New Towns and Urban Policy', Dunellen, New York.

Thomas, R. and Cresswell, P. (1973), 'The New Towns Idea', Open University.

White, M. and L. (1964), 'The Intellectual versus the City', Harvard University Press.

Williams, R. (1961), 'Culture and Society', Penguin. London.

Williams, R. (1962), 'Communications', Penguin, London.

Williams, R. (1965), 'The Long Revolution', Penguin, London.

Zehner, R. (1971), 'Neighbourhood and Community Satisfaction in New Towns', Journal of the Amercian Institute of Planners, vol. 37.

COMMUNITY WORK AND POLITICAL STRUGGLE: WHAT ARE THE POSSIBILITIES OF WORKING ON THE CONTRADICTIONS?

Paul Corrigan

Throughout the western world, states are characterized by one of the two major symbols of control in capitalist society; the tank or the community worker. For the progressive forces in all these nations it becomes vitally important to have an analysis and a practice for struggling with these symbols and realities. It is one of the curious failings of the British left that more time is spent analysing the tank abroad than the community worker here. The lessons of Tsarist Russia are clear; at some stage revolutionaries must communicate with the Army. The Bolsheviks spent many years doing that; it would appear that the Portugese Left has similarly been politically engaged. The simple political fact that this tactic is based on is that it takes more than a tank to control a society, it takes a man or a woman. For the Capitalist state to ensure that that man or women fires the trigger on the workers they had to be frightened, isolated and alone. In those circumstances the army remains oppressing the working class. To change the political complexion of the army and the actions of its members needed an ideology and an organization.

It is an indictment of the precious isolation of much of the Marxist left that they feel this to be a useless occupation with regard to the community worker. The social workers themselves are too busy and preoccupied to develop on their own a Marxist theory and practice. When they have asked for assistance from the left they have either been met with hostility or by being told that social workers are agents of social control and all that they should do is be a member of a trades union. This obviously reflects the fact that the British left has never had to tell a tank commander to his face that he is an agent of social control as their sole political platform.

As a consequence the Left and Marxism as a theory has been greatly discredited amongst community workers. The impression is around that Marxism is a rather simplistic global theory concerned

Paul Corrigan

with large scale things; it has nothing to tell the community worker about their practice or the social worker about their theory. This approach is characterized in Cohen (1975). It is important to start to prove to the community workers that Marxism is a living theory which through theoretical and practical struggle can relate to their work; this has never been coherently attempted. Unfortunately all that can be laid out here is a beginning of one part of the necessary work. I will try to outline some of the day to day practice of communists and show the ways in which community workers can structure their own practice by learning from them.

The structural position of community work in late capitalism

Most community workers start off with an appreciation of the fact that their position is full of contradictions. The *experiences* of these contradictions are painful and continually provide a spur for the community worker to attempt to understand their *structural* position. This understanding is vital if we are to see the possibilities and difficulties of political struggle.

Why did the state start employing community workers? Why spend resources on it? The answers contained here are sketchy but such an outline is important.

Capitalism needs capital and it needs labour. In getting the necessary labour together in the 19th century the bourgeoisie had to bring together a large number of workers into an urban environment. That environment necessarily had very little capital 'wasted' on it, since capital expended on the workers' dwellings would not accumulate at the pace of that invested in the cotton industry, or elsewhere in the means of production. It is not only the material environment of these workers that was impoverished; they had also of necessity to be politically impoverished, subordinated to the political will of capital. The economic and political conditions of these cities have been brilliantly outlined by Engels (Engels 1844); the social formations that these conditions created have been studied by sociologists ever since. In embryo form it was the working class; though Steadman Jones (1971) has shown that it was not simply the organized might of the working class as a class that existed but a series of communities. He also shows how it was not simply the organized working class that constituted a threat to the smooth running of capitalism, but that these communities were a threat too.

The political, moral, and ideological state of these areas posed a real threat. They were full of disease, crime and sedition; that at least was clear. Yet how did this come about? Why were the god-fearing English bourgeoisie so cursed with these threats? *The Times* provides an outline brilliantly in an 1854 editorial which is full of fear.

'Meanwhile the character and the conduct of the people are constantly being formed under the influence of their surroundings. While we are disputing which ought to be considered the most beneficial system of education, we leave the great mass of the people to be influenced and formed by the very worst possible teachers. Certain teachers indeed, could be called instructors for evil . . . In the very heart of the apparently well ordered community, enough evil teaching was going on to startle, if not alarm, the most firm-minded . . . The middle classes who pass their lives in the steady and unrepining duties of life may find it hard to believe in such atrocities. Unfortunately, they know little of the working classes; only now and then when some startling fact is brought before us, do we entertain even the suspicion that there is a society close to our own of which we are completely ignorant as if it dwelt in another land, and spoke a different language, with which we never conversed, and in fact never saw.'

Here we see that the major form of fear was based around the complete invisibility of the social dynamics and relationships of these working class communities. Something was happening, and whatever it was had been directly created by the class relationships of the urban capitalist cities. Large numbers of workers and their families had begun living in close proximity to each other; each with the same troubles; each with the same interests. Not surprisingly they spoke to one another; shared their solutions to problems; acted together; created a culture based upon their material experience. At one and the same time the bourgeoisie had created its position of power and its own greatest problem. In this way the working class community in urban capitalism became of political importance; its destruction became of importance to the bourgeoisie and its state. Much of public health legislation enacted at the time can be seen as clear attempts to destroy these communities. The use of public health legislation to clear the dangerous classes from areas of London (Stedman-Jones 1971); the use of planning legislation to build trouble free areas (Ashworth 1968); the use of Nuisance Removal Acts to destroy what were seen as 'nuisances' to local bourgeois communities (Midwinter 1969); all these were accompanied by the attempted ideological destruction of these communities by the use of school (Hurt 1973).

Thus much of early public welfare legislation had a clear control function aimed at the destruction of these communities. They were further destroyed when it became economically necessary to do so. The increasing value of such land and the change in the prime locations of capital ensured that it was essential for whole communities to be uprooted and destroyed. In this way, working class communities, created by capitalism were destroyed by it.

However, 1834 is not 1974. The difference between the two is that now the working class is *created;* it is *there* as a politically active constituent within capitalism and has to be taken into account. Enclose the land in the 1830s to move labour to the towns where capital needs it, and you have a series of revolts. What would happen in the North-East today if troops just tried to move the population to the Midlands and break up those communities? The crudity of control by the state in the 19th century is no longer possible. New tactics are now necessary. They are also necessary to ensure the full involvement of all working class in bourgeois society and ideology. The Plowden report on primary education spotlighted the economic and control problems for the state which had failed to involve the working class population in their own 'education' and disciplining. Recent work on schooling has highlighted the problem of control in these schools themselves and has pointed out the importance of the working class community acting as a counter balance to the state instrusions (Corrigan 1975). Therefore, in the 19th and 20th century it has become imperative to break up the working class communities of urban capitalism.

However, they do have positive functions for the maintenance of control in the city. They do allow certain forms of discipline and assistance to the 'disadvantaged' within that community in its own way. Consequently its *complete* destruction is not necessarily a good thing for the State. The elements of it that are conducive to control need to be maintained; the elements which are dangerous to capitalism need to be destroyed by the State for its own safety and 'progress'. Community work has become a tactic within this complex State function; education in its many guises has become another; as has an increased intervention by planning authorities. Yet it is community work which interests us here.

This structural analysis of the rôle of community work for the State does provide the community worker with some strength. Such an analysis shows that he is fairly essential to the maintenance of stability and 'progress' at the present conjuncture. He is not simply a pretty addition to the social work teams that can be dispensed with whenever he 'goes to far'. On the contrary he is necessary, and any local authority which, politically bitten by its community workers in their activities, claims that it will never employ them again, very quickly finds it essential to employ them in another guise, that of 'Action social worker' or the like. Their structural rôle remains the same though; and will remain the same until the capitalist state rejects that strategy in favour of total repression—an unlikely event.

Why structures need coherent ideologies to work perfectly

If this is the structural position, how is it that there is any possibility of working *for* rather than *against* the working class? This possibility emerges from the failure of the State or any other institution to create a water-tight ideology which would enable community workers to carry out their work purely on the basis of the intentions of the State.

Within case work, a long period of time was spent, initially with the Charity Organization Society and later on with academic institutions, creating the ideology of social work. Even in this field there were a number of difficulties emerging, mainly from the persistant refusal of the reality of social work clients to live their lives within the ordered individualist framework of that ideology. For this is the difficulty of bourgeois ideologies when put into practice in trying to combat elements of working class life—they always fail to comprehend that culture. Bourgeois institutions of education, are now 'failing' because those institutions are being served by an ideology which treats working class culture as pathological. The people that live within that culture do not comprehend it that way; consequently there is a clash of ideologies which increasingly the intruding bourgeois teachers are losing.

It is difficult in case-work and in teaching, both State institutions which have been going for 100 years; consider the difficulties for community work. In 10 years it has been essential to create a methodology and an ideology which will assist in creating working class communities; yet crucially it will only assist in creating those aspects of the working class community which are not combative with the ruling class. Community work ideology has to allow the community worker to act as an intermediary between two very different cultures; and an intermediary which will assist the working class, a class which

61

has persisted in maintaining a 'simplistic' Them and Us view of outsiders.

From the way in which community work has functioned over the past ten years, it is possible to note the failures in the necessary creation of that ideology. One has only got to look through community work text books; or at the Association of Community work; or indeed at the State community experiments like the Community Development Projects to realise that a great deal of unrest exists within the profession. Many revolutionaries may feel that the State has had a number of success stories with community work, in that many struggles have been 'cooled out', and activities such as squatting may appear to have become regularized and disciplined as part of the local State apparatus. These may well be viewed as successful attempts to recreate the 'better' bourgeois elements of control within the communities. Yet for the most part nearly all community work is in a condition which runs from confusion to ferment. The ideology which would allow for the smooth functioning of the state apparatus of community work has not been successfully created by the ideological State factories—the universities and the polytechnics.

This very lack of ideology is important to this paper since it once more provides the background to the possibilities for working class politics within the structure. Given a well-worked out, practical bourgeois ideology of community work there would be few members of the profession searching among articles such as this; the struggle for any combative ideology would be infinitely more difficult.

Community Work: Who does it in 1975?

So far we have an analysis which sees the State as needing community work; an ideology which serves that function very badly. It is also important for us to talk about the nature of the background of the individuals who are carrying out the work. Many Marxists may dismiss this as irrelevant, and in many situations they would be correct, but given this ideological vacuum there is room for individual consciousness to play an important part. For if everyone who joined community work came from a *coherent* class background they would obviously effect the way in which the contradictions outlined above would work. For example if every community worker came from the second sons and daughters of the factory owning bourgeoisie, the opportunities for change would be lessened.

We know little about the background of community workers; and little about the background of social workers as a whole. However, three major sources of community workers would appear all to be areas under some form of extreme class pressure at the moment; these are social work; the church; and the working class itself. Within social work, the social case work theory of pathology is collapsing on all fronts. In many cases this has simplistically led people from working with individuals to groups and from groups to communities; in the hope of finding that all the more individual problems become small when analysed in the wider perspective. Group work, and community work have emerged from this movement. Yet the pathology ideology has been just as readily applied to individual, group and community work; and the social worker who rejects its use in the one sometimes finds its application in the wider field. Consequently, social work as a whole has been forced to reject the pathology model as inoperative. The individuals within social work who venture into community work tend to do so because they feel that there are a series of answers outside of the individual's direct situation which will assist intervention. However, such individuals who enter community work from this background, enter with a view of the world already radicalized, already in certain ways spoiling for a fight with the State; and already having seen through the pathology ideology.

The entrants from the Church come similarly disillusioned, though this time less with theology than with certain forms of institutions. Most of them are still Christians; joining community work in an attempt to take the meaning of Christianity to a modern situation not in a missionary sense but in trying personally to enact Christian principles. The debate about the relevance of Christianity to changing capitalism is one which has been taking place since the beginning of that social system. In this article what is important to us, is that a Christian background, combined with a perception of the failure of the orthodox church usually leads to a commitment to structural social change of some description.

Thus there are two major groups who are certainly dissaffected; who are wanting to express their attempts to 'help' people in a wider sense; and who have no ready-to-hand method or ideology to carry this out.

These are joined in community work by an increasing group, the local working class recruit. These are recruited because of the necessity to work with working class culture, and they have been employed to contact organically with that culture. Consequently they may become the sort of community worker that the State is looking for, capable of calming down and cooling out the worst elements of local political aggravation. However, at the same time they are on the knife edge of a contradiction, 'working' as they do in the community that they were brought up in. They are assailed all the time by actions, ideas and sentiments which they are now employed to transform. In many cases this proves impossible and they become part of the movement *against* the State. The working class, the ex-con, the black or whoever, are increasingly becoming sensitive to the dangers of co-option by the State and are using their position to work as much as possible for the community. Some of the tactics used in this struggle are brilliantly outlined by America's most worthwhile contribution to the community work literature, Tom Wolfe's *Mau-Mauing the Flak Catcher* (1969), a most practical guide to the working class community worker on the techniques of extracting funds from the State.

Yet the *individuals* who enter community work, are not intelligible purely in terms of their backgrounds; equally important is an analysis in terms of the ideologies surrounding them before their entry. The late 1960s and 1970s have seen a resurgence of a recognizable class struggle, which has reached the media in increasingly coherent accounts of events. Nowadays *The Times* also provides a simplified class analysis of events. More and more contemporary events are intelligible only through seeing the struggle between employed and employer, with the State's pluralist neutrality being once and for all disproved by interventions in Prices and Incomes. Where does this leave our prospective community worker? Thinking of entering an aspect of work which is about change; surrounded by a world which seems increasingly understandable in terms of class struggle leading to change. Any community worker who was working on change through the ballot box could not have failed to learn something from the Miners' methods of changing Government policy 1970-74.

Of less importance over this period has been the resurgence of Marxism. The politics of Marxism in this country is curious; it has in nearly all its manifestations failed to turn its attention to the sphere of non-industrial politics. Thus the community worker is affected by the *theory* that it is only the proletariat who can change the world;

but the *theory* and *practice* of British Marxism leads him or her immediately down to the factory gates, away from the community which they are working in. Therefore community work like many other professions sees an increasing number of Marxists entering its ranks; yet these Marxists are not assisted in their day to day praxis by their theory.

The prerequisites of an ideology that would challenge the structural position of community workers

Obviously the analysis of the position of community workers is a controversial one, but it does provide an explanation of one of the present day self-evident truths, i.e. that there are a large number of dissaffected left-inclined individuals straining against a structure of employment which is attempting all the time to force them into actions against their 'conscience'. The difficulties of this position spring from being unable to find a 'method' or a 'theory' which will allow them to stay without days of self-introspection. The rest of this paper will be suggesting alternative models from outside of the main stream of social work to assist these individuals and groups. Most leftists and all Marxists, at some time or another find their class analysis to be completely immobilizing in terms of political actions. Some Marxists never seem to get themselves out of this frozen political form; their analysis points to the incontrovertible fact that the ownership of the means of production is the crucial political factor in change; equally obviously the proletariat is the class that will change that ownership. The Marxist then feels that he as an individual (in many cases a bourgeois too) can either join a revolutionary party and act under the orders of the proletariat, or act spasmodically in relationship to the working class at the means of production. Many community workers feel this *immobilization through analysis* too; the little cannot be changed without the big and I cannot change the big.

This has led to the curious position of many community workers having a class analysis of society which is totally useless to them in terms of their day-to-day activities in the field. Here they turn to the tactics taught in community work education; non-intervention; crisis and conflict creation; policy change; group consciousness-raising. If however we look at a group of Marxists who have in the past managed to maintain their class analysis in terms of their day-to-day activities, we can perceive the ways in which such an analysis acts not as an immobilization but as a direct guide to such action.

The activities of the Communist at the grass-roots—community work at its very best

British Marxism has got Marxism a bad name with community activists. Stan Cohen's (1975) attack upon it represents a familiar reaction. Yet this reaction from social workers is to a theory which has *directly* informed some of the best political activists in history on a practical day to day basis. It is the activities of these individuals that I would like to use as a constructive guideline for the radical community worker's *day to day work*. If we look at the work of Communist activists in changing the world, they have had spectacular successes. The Communist parties that have been involved in successfully overthrowing State power are the obvious ones; but there is a great deal of activity that has taken place in the urban capitalist communities like the one that the community worker now works in. This day to day Communist politicization is only intelligible as part of a class analysis. It represents the *practice* that is part of every syllable of the best of Marxist literature and theory.

It is interesting then that activities of the community workers and the Marxist activist entering a new area are similar in a number of respects. They are both entering the area in order to intervene in structural change; they confront similar sorts of issues and confront similar problems of organization. Yet the one has several advantages over the other. The Marxist usually enters precisely in order to act *tactically* within a much wider *strategy* and theory, which in the end includes the overthrow of State power. Indeed he or she is usually part of a party dedicated to that historic task. However, contrary to Cohen's analysis his major weapon is his *living Marxist theory,* a theory which informs him of the day to day activities of capitalist society in a much clearer way than the morality of suffering, or rightness or wrongness.

The Marxist agitator is also capable of being disciplined for failure; a discipline which at the moment most community workers can only carry out ideologically, by themselves or with their fellow workers. It is the party or cadre which assists the Marxist to maintain his strategy in the face of a world trying to deviate him from it. It is interesting to note that many community workers are trying to set up forms of employment where this occurs now. Success in this task, in creating strategic discipline, will add greatly to their successful intervention.

Therefore there are two constructive things that this section could do; it can point out the efficacy of a dialectical class theory of the welfare state; and it can point out the practical lessons that community workers can learn from the literature of the agitator. In real terms the latter is the more useful in the space available, but everyone must be aware that these tactics are imbedded in a class analysis of society which is necessary to give them life and force. The similarities of the issues that confront the Marxist and the community worker are many; what is important is *the different way in which political decisions are made.* I will pick out two examples of this, but there are many.

(a) *Guilt and Intervention*

The debate within the left activists about the extent of intervention, necessary or correct, into working class political action does appear to mirror the discussion about intervention and non-intervention in community work. The difference is in the method by which a decision is made.

The Marxist debate between the Menshiviks and the Bolsheviks outlined in Lenin's 'What is to be done?' is about the extent of intervention necessary for the individual or the party committed to change.

> 'Class political consciousness can be brought to the workers *only from without*, that is from outside the economic struggle, from outside the sphere of relations between workers and employers. The sphere from which alone it is possible to obtain this knowledge is the sphere of the relationships of *all* classes and strata to the state and the government, the sphere of the interrelationships between *all* classes. For that reason, the reply to the question as to what must be done to bring political knowledge to the workers cannot merely be the answer with which in the majority of cases, the practical workers content themselves, namely; "To go amongst the workers".' (Lenin 1970: 182.)

This condemnation of non-intervention as a method of working commands the attention of community workers not because it is *correct or incorrect,* since such a judgment is fundamentally the sphere of political theory, but the criteria by which non-intervention is dismissed. Lenin does not say that it is *wrong or right* morally to intervene in workers' lives as most social literature does. He merely states what is necessary and correct from an analysis.

67

Within community work the debate around intervention or not, has been based upon the morality of it. Thus the old school of social work seemed to see their interventions as necessary in order to help, and in some cases save the working class. The new non-interventionalists react against this, feeling that it is arrogant and harmful. In many cases they may well be correct, but selecting methodology of political work by means of morality will not lead to a correct selection. It may well be wrong to intervene in the class struggle from outside (assuming that community workers are déclasse) but the ways in which we judge it wrong or right are based upon the moral judgments of the world around us, the bourgeoisie.

Lenin condemns the Social Democratic study circle which:

> 'has "contacts with the workers" and rests content with issuing leaflets in which abuses in the factories, the government's partiality towards capitalists, and the tyranny of the police are strongly condemned. At workers meetings the discussions never, or rarely ever, go beyond the limits of these subjects. In fact the ideal leader as the majority of the members of such circles picture him, is something far more in the nature of a trades union secretary than a socialist political leader . . . the ideal should be not a trades union secretary but the tribune of the people, who is able to react to every manifestation of tyranny or oppression, no matter where it appears, no matter what stratum or class of people it effects; who is able to generalise all these manifestations and produce a single picture of police violence and capitalist exploitation; who is able to take advantage of every event, however small, in order to set forth before *all* his socialist convictions and his democratic demands, in order to clarify to *all* and everyone the world historic significance of the struggle for the emancipation of the proletariat.' (Lenin 1970: 182-183.)

Once more the nature of the judgment about intervention can be of importance for community workers.

The problem of how far to intrude ones own consciousness into the situation; how far to uncover ones background takes up a great deal of community meetings. What Lenin is saying is that the intervention of consciousness of a socialist activist is not a matter of pure ideational honesty, rather it is important to take every opportunity to link up with the day-to-day experiences of oppression of the working class. These day-to-day experiences are the material base of class struggle, and in some ways they are understood better by working class people than by socialist activists or community workers. Therefore it is not a matter of either admitting a socialist background; or of not pushing the consciousness of those that you are working with. Rather it is a matter of all the time raising the large scale in their own day-to-day experiences—otherwise Lenin claims you are doing nothing.

For the Bolshevik activists took their class analysis seriously, they believed that the working class *of necessity* experienced the full oppression of capitalism and as such need no one to point out the nature of that *day to day* oppression. Community workers with a class analysis have no such confidence in it; consciousness-raising for them is still seen in terms of building bricks, leading the community to an ever increasing consciousness over a long period of time moving along a prescribed pattern. The pattern outlined by the Bolsheviks does not have this similarity to an 'O' and 'A' level curricula, rather it is a constant dialectic from the day to day to the wider analysis. Consciousness stems all the time from a relationship between a theory and a set of material experiences; that theory needs at least rudimentary outlining from the very beginning. There are still very many workers' families in community organizations that have a much clearer perception and analysis of Them and Us than do the socialist community workers painfully building up a class-consciousness amongst the people of their area.

Thus, in terms of whether to intervene, the new paradigm that I am trying to build up for social workers needs to be seen in terms of the materialist analysis behind it. The working class experience oppression every day, the community worker needs to recognize his interventions in the light of working with that experience *and* a theory which explains and transcends it *from the start*. Not to do this leads to the problem of creating a functioning organization which then he or she may want to 'take off' to a different level in terms of a wider perspective, only to find that all the experiences of that organization have been understood in the common sense terms that the community worker has been working with as his 'first stage of consciousness building'.

This is not to say that all community workers must go about mouthing the necessary Marxist rhetoric of many of our new socialist activists; rather they must *realise* the class nature of every aspect of the society that they, and the people they are working with, are living in and use every opportunity to make sense of the world in those terms.

Therefore there is an intervention, non-intervention debate within this paradigm but one that is treated as a *practical political problem* rather than as one of morality to be solved by the rightness or wrongness of intervention. The whole relationship between morality and politics is a broad one; here it is important to stress the way in which a Marxist's morality is at the *base* of his political principles rather than at the *forefront*. Social democrats and liberals always see this distinction as a simple means-end dichotomy which says that all the means justify the ends of revolution; such political thinking links directly in most western minds with the Gulag Achipeligo. In real political terms though the relationship between morality and politics is far from complex. For Communists the overall strategy and the day-to-day tactics *are* informed by a morality, but one that does not derive from the society around us and therefore *must* at times seem 'hard'. However, the morality stems from the overall necessity for increasing the likelihood of change; a change that *can* only be carried out by the mass of the people. Therefore directly a Marxist intervenes too much, his politics becomes ineffective because he becomes too much a leader; if he intervenes too little he is guilty of leaving the situation encapsulated, or shirking his rôle. Thus if he makes the wrong decision it is not morally wrong in its *context,* but politically ineffective in its context and therefore morally wrong *overall.*

An example of intervention in a tenants dispute will provide llumination. The tenants are meeting to discuss the lack of repairs in the 15 story block. They blame a particular council official who the activist *knows* is not to blame and that this line of reasoning will not solve the problem. At all levels the tenants in their meeting seem to refuse to be gently nudged to a wider analysis of the problem which might lead to some fruitful action. To intervene or not to intervene more fully might be a normal or a political question. If we follow the tactics of the Marxist activist who intervenes too strongly, we may well try leading the next meeting with a discussion of the councils overall housing policy and its position in the latest financial crisis. His words may well persuade a meeting which does not understand too clearly to take drastic action. However, he will discover fairly quickly, once that action took place, that he was on his own. Therefore the results of *this* intervention in *this* way is to fail not only to further an analysis of the group involved, but to fail also to effect the policy. One can judge these actions morally; (the worker was wrong to intervene too fully) or politically (he was ineffective). If we look at the latter, though, the ineffectiveness is due mainly to an analysis of the *politics* of an action which failed to appreciate the *total necessity* of engaging the people involved at all times. It is at this level that the *morality* of political intervention operates.

There are times when it is vital to intervene and attack a set of ideas; there are times when any form of intervention from outside would emasculate the action. For community work activities to date, the infusion of a day-to-day morality drawn from the society around us, has greatly weakened any possibilities of actions being taken on political grounds, and nowhere has this been clearer than on the issue of intervention.

(b) *Which problems?*

As has been said above, the Bolshevik knows that the working class experiences a series of class problems every day, all the time. A community worker whilst knowing that they should experience this all the time, is grossly perplexed by the fact that the working class does not seem to be loudly groaning under it yoke. It *seems* quite happy most of the time. This occasionally leads to outbursts of moralistic horror from community workers trying to get the workers to realise that they should be unhappy; such a set of actions usually creates a response of horror from the resident population. It is interesting to see how a Bolshevik acts when confronted with a seemingly complacent population.

'But we were not yet clear how to develop the people's struggles. Many of the people were friendly. But there was no 'issue'. Our canvassers would ask people, "Have you any problems?" and they would say "No". But there were problems—what were they? And why did people say that there were no problems, when the places that they were living in were so bad? Was it because they were so inured to these conditions? This indeed is one of the most serious features that one discovers when working in the movement. Was it because they were defeatist and felt it was a waste of time to do anything, and so passed these things off with a shrug of their shoulders? The main centre of our activities was Fieldgate Mansions—several blocks of some 270 flats. It occurred to me that if the people did not know or wouldn't talk of their problems, we ought to suggest them. But what to suggest?

One Sunday morning we were canvassing, and when we had finished I walked around the building looking for something, I walked around and up and down several flights of stairs, but I couldn't get a hint of a thing. I went home—it was very perplexing. In these days we were feeling our way, there was a difference between helping someone who approached you with a problem (as with an eviction fight) and trying to get people to begin in an elementary fashion to organize to improve their conditions for themselves. That same evening I decided to walk over to Fieldgate Mansions, only 100 yards away and look around a bit to see if I could get an idea. I saw a flame flickering on a landing and suddenly noticed something that I hadn't done all those weeks previously —namely that the stairs were lighted with open gas-jet flares. I knocked

71

on the first door introducing myself, I asked the woman who opened the door, whether or not these things were a danger, and immediately I had a torrent of information and cursing of the landlord . . . within ten minutes I was sitting around the table with half a dozen women drinking a cup of tea and listening to their stories about the gas lighting.' (Piratin: 36-38.)

Phil Piratin was a member of the Communist Party in the East End of London in the 1930s. His account of how the Party Members worked with tenants in the field of housing struggles is easily worth inclusion in the most orthodox of community work courses. He outlines several of the all-important rules; the relationship between public 'issues' many of which people may feel to be beyond their experience; and the ever present private troubles, which people learn to live with but hate. Piratin knows that these private experiences are inevitably there; that it is a matter of political technique to discover them, to allow people to express them. After months of searching he was never going to say that the working class of Stepney were content, but he was prepared to see the discovery of personal political issues as a *very long term process;* prepared to see them as part of the very process of political intervention, knowing that they will be there in the end.

Conclusions

How do these two examples assist the disaffected community worker? How do they add to his ability to combat his structural position and act for his 'clients'?

Firstly, they call upon a mass of experience which sees most interventions as unequivocally *political*. As such they represent the nature of community work a great deal clearer than any technique that neglects to see the work as primarily one of power.

Secondly, the morality of such action has been decided before any intervention is planned. If a community worker believes that it is wrong to intervene in working class life; if he or she has made this as a political judgment then it is very strange to be engaged in work which must of its very essence negate in some form of intervention at some time. The *moral* fears about when to intervene or not in a political position which *must* lead to intervention sooner or later, usually leads to the politically correct moments of intervention being lost in a welter of soul searching.

Thirdly, that the Bolshevik is an intervener in social situations who

72

acts upon an analysis which knows that there are inevitable forms of everyday oppression of the working class, and that these experiences lead themselves to actions. This knowledge means that one of the major parts of the process is working to find out these specific experiential problems rather than creating bourgeois 'issues'.

Fourthly, that in the process of consciousness raising there is a necessity to 'start as one means to continue' by relating as many of these experiential issues to the wider class analysis of the causes of oppression. To work on a stepping stone theory of consciousness change is to find oneself stuck in the middle of the river for so long that the final stones are rendered invisible to the 'community'. Consciousness does not move in a straight line across a political set of actions. Therefore, what I am suggesting is not that community workers should become Bolsheviks, for such a transformation is idealistic unless it takes place within an organized working class, rather I am suggesting that it is only by perceiving their structural situation and the opportunities of their work in a directly *political* way, that they will be able to work their way out of existential angst that all of us community activists from the outside, find ourselves in. Such a project must be carried out in a group fashion as all progressive politics must. Similarly, to neglect at every stage the possible links with the organized labour movement, even as present constituted, is to ensure that you end up in a blind alley.

References cited

Ashworth, W. (1968), 'History of Town Planning in England and Wales', Routledge and Kegan Paul.

Cohen, S. (1975), 'It's all Right for You to Talk' in *Radical Social Work*, Roy Bailey and Mike Brak (eds.), Edward Arnold.

Corrigan, P. D. (1975), 'The Smash Street Kids', Paladin.

Engels, F. (1844), 'The Condition of the English Working Class', Panther.

Hurt, J. (1973), 'Education and Evolution', Paladin.

Lenin (1970), 'What is to be Done' (first published 1901) in *Selected Works of Lenin*, Vol I, Progress Publishers.

Midwinter, E. (1969), 'Victorian Social Reform', Longmans.

Piratin, P. (1948), 'Our Flag Stays Red', Thames Publications.

Stedman-Jones, G. (1971), 'Outcast London', Oxford University Press.

Wolfe, T. (1969), 'Mau-Mauing the Flak Catcher', Sphere.

WHOSE GRASS ROOTS? CITIZENS, COUNCILLORS AND RESEARCHERS

Jon Davies

T he annals of 'Community Action' contain a number of stories in which the action takes place between:

(a) a group of local citizens concerned about some redevelopment scheme (or lack of one),

(b) the local Council responsible for such schemes, and

(c) the local University or Polytechnic, where *research* into such schemes is very often of direct and controversial use.

Very often the progress of this triadic inter-play is so painful and mutually embarrassing that all concerned agree, like good chaps, to say nothing. The Bristol Project is a case in point, where a book, 'Stress and Release in an Urban Estate' (Spencer 1964)—can be produced with scarcely any reference to the local Housing Authority or to the 'stress and release' implicit in the relationship between the researchers and the local Council. Other books—William Hampton's on Sheffield (Hampton 1970), my own on Newcastle (Davies 1972a) —are rather more forthcoming, albeit in a coy and oblique way. Both books contain accounts of what seems to be the natural progression from social research to social action, and of the demonstrable use of a University as a major local provider of scarce expertise and as a place relatively free from control or interference by a local Council. These inter-connections have of course been given official recognition in the Community Development Projects, although the very official nature of these Projects gives rise to a rather different set of problems to those encountered in more spontaneous and less lavish enterprises. I should like to look at some of these issues to see what they tell us both about inter-institutional and intra-institutional structures and processes, and about the whole nature of 'power' in our provincial Cities: and I will do so from two perspectives, that of a University-based researcher-activist (which I once was) and that of local Councillor (which I now am).

Jon Davies

1. *The Researcher-Activist Issue*

In order to illustrate some of the political and ethical problems engendered by this kind of action I will use Hampton's book on Sheffield. When I first read the book I assumed that the tacit 'apologies' and explicit protestations it contains indicated that its writing and publication took place in an atmosphere of conflict arising out of Sheffield Council's expressed displeasure. Professor Crick, then head of Sheffield's Department of Policies, assured me that this was not so and this, of course, makes the propitiatory protestations even more interesting!

The apologetics tell us a great deal about the political ethics of the readers to whom they are addressed i.e. about what the authors assume to be the opinions held by their audience—including Councillors, Vice-Chancellors and research funding bodies. In the Foreword to the book Professor Crick describes 'the particular tale (in the final chapter) of the . . . involvement of one of our research workers (strictly without my knowledge or permission!) in organizing a local residents association.' In the 'final chapter' referred to by Crick we have a footnote on this subject which refers to a Mr. Geoffrey Green, a young research student who in April, 1969, started the residents association (mentioned by Crick) by distributing leaflets in Walkely, the area concerned. (It is unclear in the text *why* Mr. Green did this.) The footnote by Hampton reads as follows: 'Mr. Green acted as my research assistant for one year, while the material for the present study was being collected. He had left the local research project before he commenced his political activities, and, naturally, none of the research material was used to assist his campaign.'

Further references to the text describe how Green came to stand in the local elections as an Independent candidate and how by so doing he made the Ward highly marginal—in a City where at the time one seat made all the difference to control of the Council. Hampton describes Mr. Green's election campaign: 'Mr. Green's election campaign was remarkable both for the enthusiasm of his supporters and for the responsible tone adopted. There was no demagogy and no easy promises. His election address consisted of a 2,000 word essay, complete with a map of the area, entitled "For more consultation between people and planners." His election meeting, attended by nearly 300 people, was addressed by an architect and by a town planner from the University.' Note the apologetic tone.

76

I quote at some length from Hampton's book because it raises some rather fundamental professional or ethical problems. Consider, for example, the claim, tacit at any rate, in Crick's 'strictly without my knowledge or permission!' Is the Professor, a liberal as far as I know, claiming that he has the right to order a research assistant to stop engaging in politics? Where, in a research assistant's terms of employment, is such a right vested in a professor? And even if it was, how would such a right look when set, for example, against the clear-cut rights of many trade unionists, rights specified in their conditions of employment, to participate in the work of 'public bodies', not to mention the rights 'conferred' by Section 5(c) of the (now dead) Industrial Relations Act, 'establishing' a right to join and to take part in trade union activities; or the convention, more honoured than not, that employers will not try to prevent or to penalise employees taking 'time off' to take part in, say, the work of local Council and its Committees—*and its elections*.

Readers of Crick's Foreword could be forgiven for assuming him to be saying (a) that Mr. Green was obliged to ask his permission to engage in local politics and (b) that he, the Professor, could if he so chose, legitimately refuse to give this permission. The corollary of this, if this is indeed what the Foreword implies, is that a University-based researcher who 'goes political' in spite of a contrary instruction by the Department Head or Professor can be punished in some way— the sack perhaps? There is no doubt in my mind that a sufficient number of senior staff would indeed subscribe to the thesis implicit in Crick's words: and, more worryingly, there are a large number of less senior staff who would also accept it. Universities are amongst the most archaic and autocratic of our institutions, with much too much power vested in Professors and Heads of Departments, with contracts of employment which are virtually meaningless, and with an almost total lack of the traditional Trade Union defence structures.

From Mr. Hampton there is a rather different statement, although equally there seems to be the view that 'politics' are legitimate for researchers *only* if they cease to be researchers. There is the claim made here that: 'naturally, none of the research material was used to assist his campaign.' Naturally? Let us picture what happened in the course of the research; it certainly happened to me. Mr. Green is carrying out his research, he discovers, while so engaged, that the people of Walkley Ward feel that they are getting a rough deal from

77

the Council. Mr. Green, whether, to use the immortal Rex/Moore phrase, as 'citizen and sociologist' or as sociologist or as citizen, feels that he wants to and that he is able to do something. So he does, he goes political.

There are two issues here: first the question; for whom is the research being done, either in the sense of contractual obligations giving certain parties legal rights to control the use and publication of data; and in the sense for whose *benefit*? Secondly, the distinction between neutrality and objectivity.

Let us take the first question. All research—contrary to Mannheim's views, takes place within a definite social context; there are no 'free floating' intellectuals. When research is carried out by local Universities into local planning or redevelopment problems, then this particular context produces a whole range of 'Significant Others' with particular inter-connections posing particular research problems.

The fact is, that in say, Sheffield or Newcastle, the University is about the only institution which can mobilise a range of resources and expertise capable of confronting the Civic Centre or Town Hall on anything like equal terms; this tends to upset the City Fathers, especially when the rival institution starts looking at 'their' patch, the City. As Crick puts it: 'The idea of an objective study of Sheffield politics was not one that we expected would be received with universal enthusiasm by local councillors. There is a natural suspicion of 'us up here' . . . indeed some political scientists can be a little optimistic to think that it can be readily accepted that we are 'just studying' local politics when we value our freedom of expression on matters of public policy quite as much as our reputation for being impartial and objective scholars.'

The Hampton study was financed by a grant from the SSRC. This makes the research—in its financial aspects—as independent as anything short of 'independent means'. Yet one assumes that in the course of interviewing all Sheffield's Councillors and Aldermen and in compiling various basic bits of information, which tend to be most easily available from local authorities, various 'tacit' bargains were done with the Town Hall, even if only to state (note, not necessarily to plead) the 'scientific' nature of the investigation and its eschewal of political partisanship. These bargains are most usually tacit and are kept that way by academics who too easily internalise a self imposed veto on any activities which might make the bargain explicit, i.e. by infringing it. Mr. Green's electioneering, one senses, transgressed the veto. Clearly Hampton felt obliged to proclaim the entirely separate nature of Mr. Green-as-researcher and Mr. Green-as-candidate. Yet why is this done so readily? Why do academics indulge in self-inflicted political castration? By what right do City Fathers assume, and Universities apparently support the idea that research and action based on it should not go hand in hand? If I'm doing research into, say the impact of a clearance scheme on Byker; I have an independent source of cash and no legally enforceable contractual obligations other than, say, the standard terms of appointment as a University lecturer; and in the course of my research I come to the conclusion that the scheme is hopelessly wrong. I get up and say so—and I know what I am talking about *because* of my research—and I say so, quite deliberately emphasizing that it is in the interests of the affected citizenry and NOT the sensibilities of the City Fathers that I take as my important reference—i.e. it is surely up to me to answer 'Research for whose benefit?' and to say that the City Fathers are already well looked after. (The City of Newcastle employs 12,000 people, including whole batteries of planners, lawyers, engineers, public health inspectors, treasurers etc.) Even if only in the interest of 'participatory democracy' never mind any left-wing urge I personally may feel, it is my choice, maybe even my duty to use skills and data, in the interests of, in this case, residents affected by redevelopment schemes.

The University, certainly in Newcastle, is the only institution with the necessary resources—lawyers, planners, architects, engineers, students, duplicating machines, financial independence—capable of handling the Civic Centre. In Newcastle, in the suburb of Jesmond, where a lot of University people live, changes were effected in a Civic Centre scheme on the strength, in part, of a highly technical job on shopping needs done by, inter alia, a lecturer in the Town and Country Planning Department. Unfortunately, in other parts of town these resources—except in the form of peripatetic sociologists—are absent.

It is arguable, of course, that the conscience-striken researcher would be discharging his obligations by making his findings public, i.e. by publishing them: attempts have, of course, been made to prevent publication. Publication seems to be the solution proposed by Crick and Green in a *New Society* article (Crick and Green 1968). There are snags here, not least the years that go between field research and publication.

A more serious problem, however, is the innate tendency of local government, officers and Councillors, to clam up and defend when criticised. I am a local Councillor, so I know why; there's a bloody sociologist sneaking round my ward causing trouble. The main diet of local councillors is power, the only Standing Order of any use is a majority. As Hampton delicately puts it 'The vigorous support given to the Walkley Action Group, as Mr. Green's supporters called themselves, caused both political parties to treat it seriously' (Hampton 1970:291). I bet they did, with one Ward in it between Labour and Conservative in Sheffield. Publications, dryly academic, go down the memory hole as far as local Councillors are concerned. Campaigns are of greater consequence, and here, surely the researcher is in a very good position. A better position, for example, than those insurance agents whose ubiquity in working class areas put such a squeeze on Lloyd George and caused him to make major modifications in the draft of the National Insurance Act, 1911.

Mr. Hampton is quite clear on this: while 'a local leadership quickly emerged' to run the Walkley Action Group, 'the original stimulus of someone versed in the techniques of social action was necessary' and, after discussing the possible uses of community workers employed by local authorities, Hampton concludes that 'no social worker could have acted with the political initiative shown by Mr. Green.'

This takes us on to the politics of community action: i.e. how independent is the University of local government? This really involves a study of the 'power elite' of the City in question. Suffice it to say that control based on the 'community of familiars' i.e. of Good Well Thinking Chaps Vice Chancellors, leaders of the Councils, local business and professional men—is a very definite possibility. For example, in Newcastle, a local Trust supports the Council of Social Service, which in turn has connections with the University, and the Trust also, it is rumoured supports the building of a Theatre: and the University would also like to keep it sweet in case research money is needed. On the other levels, the University people, especially at the *professorial* level, are part of the 'urban squirearchy' being J.P.s, members of hospital management boards active in local educational and cultural activities, etc. etc.

Let us ignore all this, and assume that those connections in no way inhibit the deep commitment of Vice Chancellors, Professors, etc. to 'academic freedom'. What *power* can local authorities exercise? How could they pressure an unwilling Vice Chancellor to 'control' a member of his staff. In comes the Town and Country Planning legislation. Universities need land, local authorities control the zoning of land. Universities need planning permission from local authorities. Even when the bulk of the University is built, the University needs local authorities to, for example close streets running through the campus, or to put meters on nearby parking areas—see Newcastle Council meeting for October, 1971. Universities need local authorities to compulsorily purchase land and buildings, to demolish those buildings, and then to convey the land to the University. The University is as dependent on the local authority, and vice versa, as is, for example the Scottish and Newcastle Breweries, St. James' Park Football Club, Reyrolle-Parsons, Marks and Spencer, etc.

When I was first standing for election to Newcastle Council, a research section of my department got involved, totally unknown to me, in a controversy in the local press about a 'slum' area known as Garth Heads. The press described the research section as intending to organize a demonstration about the squalid living conditions they had discovered. This caused certain City Fathers to complain about the University getting mixed up in politics; and the general effect was to portray me as using departmental research to further my election campaign. I was, in fact, totally innocent of the 'charge', but at the time, the Vice Chancellor was negotiating with the Town Hall for the sale of land for a new Psychology and Biochemistry building. These negotiations were, it seemed, being embarrassed by the undue publicity about Garth Heads. Telephones buzzed. Its an odd story, all done by telephones; the only written communication I received from the Vice Chancellor stressed the necessity to keep politics separate on the ground that mixing the two would either result in bias or give people the excuse or cause to make that accusation.

This, of course, raises the issue of objectivity, often confused with neutrality, and therefore often leading to a misleading comparison of the position of researchers with that of civil servants. Civil servants are required to be neutral 'outside working hours' as it were. Inside working hours, *like any professional*, they are obliged to be *objective*.

The 'neutral' stipulation is quasi-contractual in that it has to be accepted as part of the conditions of employment (I don't know

whether the *Esta Code* which contains the conditions is legally enforceable). In other words there is a clear and explicit instruction to
civil servants, from their employers, that they must be neutral, i.e.
eschew activities in political parties (God knows whether this includes joining Residents Associations!). The rationale for this injunc-
tion is that civil servants who are not neutral cannot give objective
advice to a Minister of another (or the same?) persuasion.

Yet surely our position as researchers is very different, unless like
civil servants we are (1) expressly forbidden in our conditions of
service to be 'political' and (2) we are expressly employed to report
to *one* audience with a view to formulating policy. There is nothing
in any University conditions of employment that I have seen insisting
that we be neutral; nor are we part of a closed system in which our
contribution may constitute the entire contribution; nor are we involved in making policy, with all the constraints involved in that
business. Indeed, our universe of discourse is totally public—hence
publications—and in theory anyway, partial statements are 100 per
cent. respectable, if only because there is the permanent check on them
of 'further research' and the possibility of ending up at best as negative data and at worst as totally irrelevant.

The arguably close connection therefore between neutrality and
objectivity does not apply to researchers. There is no *prima facie*
assumption that politics and objectivity are incompatible; each case
must be argued on its merits. The researcher says: there is my work.
Show me, if you can, where, when and how it is biased. Prove it,
don't just assume it. *The guarantee of objectivity lies in argument,
the incessant questioning and disputing which does and should go on.*
If my partisanship is reflected in what I write, then my peers will
very soon write me off.

British sociologists immobilized perhaps by the laws of libel, tend
to avoid analyses of the sociology of sociology, i.e of the particular
contexts within which research is carried out, and the effects of this
context on the finished product. Occasionally we get echoes of the
'stress and release' of research teams; but in the main verbal gossip is
the main vehicle of news in this field. In order to establish a proper
professional ethic we surely need empirical accounts of research
projects; and nowhere are these accounts more needed than for those
projects involving University and Town Hall, especially now that
Government money, under the Urban Aid Programme, has pre-

cipitated a strange alliance of those two peculiar institutions.

2. *The Councillor-Activist Issue.*

Most big cities have now had considerable experience of 'grass roots community action' whether of the official Community Development Project or of other less formalized and more independent bodies. The City of Newcastle upon Tyne has certainly played host (often unwillingly) to a range of 'participators' from left-wing tenants' associations to right-wing rate payers' organizations. Some of our City Fathers are not too keen on 'community action'. Consider this response to a Home Office 'offer' of a Community Development Project. 'A Government offer to help to pinpoint many of Newcastle's social problems has been turned down by the city finance committee. Members decided last night that they knew where the problems were, and didn't need anybody to remind them . . . Councillor Mrs. Collins (Labour) said, "I've seen some of these university wallahs with some of their expertise. We have even got members of the council who are in this on both sides—my God!" She felt sociologists were often removed from the true needs of the people . . . Council leader Alderman Arthur Grey (Conservative) said: "Why don't we tell the Home Office we know of people's problems, we know where they live and we do not want their help"' (The Journal, Newcastle, June 29, 1971).

The City Council later agreed to participate, but the initial distaste lingers on, and mine grows apace.

This section puts forward some reasons why the rôle constraints of local councillors, and not some inherent character defect make it more than probable that they will be at least wary of and more likely actively hostile towards community 'activists'.

Even grass roots activities as institutionalized and as tamed as CDP still merit a fair degree of 'watching'. Perceptive readers may note that my analysis is the ally of left-wing criticism of CDPs, viz that they are fink enterprizes and indeed represent, in the institutional sense, a clear acceptance of councillor power; trouble there may be, but more from hard-nosed individuals making martyrs of themselves than from any institutionalized conflict.

Professional Rivalry

Activists and councillors are in direct competition for the same resource, viz. the 'support' of the people living in a particular area.

Without this support, neither can survive; and both councillor and activist have to be able to say; 'I know more about this specific area than anyone else' and that 'I will actively promote the interests of the people living in the area.' This rôle constraint is heavier on Labour Party councillors than on Tories, because the social problems most likely to promote grass roots movements, or to attract CDP activists, occur in Labour areas. It is interesting to note that the first time (in Newcastle) that a major redevelopment scheme (a motorway) caused trouble in a Tory area, the Ward councillors showed themselves unable to respond and they all lost their seats to Independents.

For councillors, however, there is the vexation that other demands of their rôle make it unlikely that they can be as 'ward-specific' in their knowledge and responses as can an activist (see my article, 'The Local Councillors Dilemma' Davies 1972b). Most County Borough Councillors are members of political parties and very often the 'party line', the party record and party loyalties make it very costly and perhaps impossible to respond to Ward interests when those interests are in conflict with party policy.

To date at any rate Liberal candidates in local elections have been effectively free of party constraints and have been able, like activists, to put 'community politics' first; hence the resentment we 'party hacks' have for liberal candidates who seem to have the advantages of a party label without any of the disadvantages.

For party councillors times are particularly trying when one's party is in power for then, added to the constraint of the 'party line' (which puts a block on public criticism of the Council) there are the whole range of subtle (and not so subtle) pressures and invitations to act as the front-man for political colleagues and officials. The councillor who persistently acts as an ombudsman for his Ward very soon provokes irritation and is eventually simply frozen out of all the patterns of information-flow and the perpetual 'brokerage' that constitutes the political aspect of local government.

Meanwhile, back in the Ward, the full-time activist, perhaps employing social survey techniques and using official data, can very quickly achieve as compendious and as systematic a knowledge of the problems of a particular Ward as even the most conscientious Councillor can amass in many an evening of canvassing and case-handling. There are several cases of researchers responding to their findings by 'going political'. I have already discussed Hampton's book

84

on Sheffield where Geoffrey Green obtained over 700 votes in Walkley after, it seems, about one year's residence and research in the area.

Clearly local Councillors are well advised if not to try to block at least to try to influence and control the activities of the highly-motivated young people who tend to turn up as local activists; hence, in part, the CDPs over which a local Council Committee is given at least some measure of formal control. Formal control does not, however, mean that a Councillor for a Ward containing a CDP can rest easy, for the very logic of these projects means trouble.

The Inevitability of Negative Thinking

The American 'War on Poverty' from which our 'Community Development Projects' derive (it being standard British practice to copy failed American schemes) endeavoured in part to mobilize against the local Town Halls. Federal money was to finance this mobilization. I was in America when all this started and there was even then a clear career structure in the minds of the scarcely-employable sociology graduates of radical views, who joined 'the War'. They *expected* resistance from the local bosses, and had a 'scenario' in their minds of a year or so in a city getting to know all about it, Town Hall and all; a year or so activating local groups to 'demand' things from the Town Hall; a year or so of increasing Town Hall displeasure, culminating in a bust-up and then a year or so of writing up the history of yet another example of the obduracy, stupidity, parochialism, etc. of that eternal bumble, the City Councillor. From America, of course, have come precisely such documents, and here they have tended to become prescriptive scripts, departed from only when things like mortgage or marital commitments so decree. In a sense, our activists would be most disappointed if we Councillors turned out to be anything other than obdurate, stupid, etc. We would deprive them of a book and the career in lecturing, etc. that this provides.

Tied in with this is the fact that the very logic of CDPs has them situated in areas where things *are* wrong, where the Council, local industry, etc. is guilty of crimes of either omission or commission. How many community activists have gone into an area, looked around, counted heads, and then come to the conclusion that the local authority is one hundred per cent. benign and efficient, that the resource-input into the area is totally adequate, and that therefore the only

85

thing to do is to resign and join the dole queue?

So the activists are on a ride to ruction and we councillors are on a hiding to nothing. All we can do is to try to join and control the protest movements which will inevitably arise; but this, of course, is incompatible with the CDP ethic of spontaneous grass roots democracy, run by the grass roots for the grass roots. I have yet to come across a community worker who regards the local councillor as being a genuine part of the grass roots—the key criticism often being that we do not live in the Wards we represent. The criticism also, of course, reflects the fact that the other rôles we have to play as party members (see above) mean that we cannot 'take instructions' solely from residents in our Wards. At the same time, though, we have to secure the Ward in order to be able to operate at all at the other levels. Spontaneous grass-roots movements in effect create rivals for Ward Favour—a Chairman of a Residents' Association, a Committee of Tenants—and their rivalry is all the more threatening because of their total commitment to local or Ward interests.

Local councillors representing CDP type wards cannot sit back and comfortably observe the in-roads made by 'spontaneous' movements. It is of the essence of intra-Ward politics to be able to claim credit for everything and to permit no rivals for public esteem. (This even effects one's relationship with one's fellow ward Councillors. At elections for triple vacancies it is not unknown for one comrade to present himself as the only or the best Labour or Tory candidate in order to win the highest 'personal' vote, thereby establishing the longest term of office.) So the one thing elected representatives cannot permit (let alone encourage) are movements over which they have little or no influence.

It may well be that CDP operators, dedicated to a belief in self-sufficient grass roots community movements do indeed quite genuinely wish to take a back seat and to, ideally, make themselves redundant. But no Councillor can be expected to efface himself in this way, for the necessary precondition for the exercise of power is the possession of it.

And how genuine is the community worker's self-effacement? In a very real sense it is a form of denial of responsibility rather like that indulged in by local Council officials. Officials react to criticism or protest by saying, 'We don't make decisions, its the Council.' Activists react to Councillor's criticism of protest by saying, 'It's not us, its the people who are protesting and attacking you.' As an ex-activist, however, I know perfectly well how central is the guiding hand of the imported expert, grass roots or no grass roots; and the denial of responsibility can very often be simply a device to set Councillor and Citizen directly at each others throats while the activist sits with a 'told you so' smirk on his face.

Politics is Property: A note from Norman Mailer (1968:104)

What have you got that we need?

What have you got that you need to keep and that we can take away if you try to stop us getting what we need?

What have we got that you want?

What have we got that you need that we can stop you from getting if you refuse to give us what we want you not to have?

If we have nothing that you need, HOW CAN WE CONTROL YOU?

If you have nothing that we want, WHY DO WE NEED YOU?

The problem of corruption

Power we are told, tends to corrupt; but the one thing that corrupts more is the wanting but not having of it. In some ways, politics is a form of prostitution by instalments. In order to get onto this or that committee or in order to get a policy changed so as to benefit one's ward, we Councillors have perpetually to sacrifice a little bit of idealism or abandon yet another of one's friends. We have to accept the humiliation of voting—on the Whip's instructions—for a policy we may detest. At group meetings, we may have to suffer the indignity of having a cherished belief bashed down by the weight of the assorted Deadheads and Cynics—our future selves.

A far cry from the ideological luxury of 'grass roots community action'; and in a strange twist, the 'demands' with which grass-roots activists confront local authorities can only be responded to by the self-same set of machinating bumbles and callous bureaucrats who are the very object of grass roots suspicion and contempt! On the one hand, councillors—protagonists of Weber's 'Ethic of Ways and Means' (Gerth and Mills 1970:121). On the other, virginal activists, wearing the halo of the 'Ethic of Absolute Ends'—yet relying upon the Councillors to solve the problem of total ineffectiveness that this second ethic leads to. They have an easy moral victory at in a sense, our expense: and we pay them for it!

The Power Elite

Politics is as much concerned with maintaining secrecy as with gaining publicity. I personally find it difficult to understand precisely why local councillors are *so* keen on secrecy, but it is clear that whether for tactical reasons or simply to keep certain sordid or un-dignified dealings out of the public eye, politicians devote a deal of time ensuring (or trying to ensure) that the flow of information is limited to defined and un-hostile groups—a small caucus inside a political party, or a party inside a Civic Centre, or even both parties plus officials inside a City which maintain their boundaries not so much on the basis of mutual trust but more often because any sudden lifting of the stone would reveal us *all* in positions of varying degrees of indelicacy. (See the Watergate Caper, where the basic response of the accused to the squealer is 'You Too' rather than 'Not Me.')

The circles of people who-are-in-the-know-but-not-inclined-to-tell, extend beyond the actual Town Hall and into the other political administrative bureaucracies of the City—Magistrates Benches, Ad Hoc Authorities, Voluntary Bodies, Amenity Societies, Trade Unions, Association of Trade, Chambers of Commerce, Consulates, etc. all part of the 'Community of Familiars' all quietly and often un-questioningly sure of the propriety of the constructive whisper. To-gether they constitute 'the power structure'.

And into this come Community Activists and Researchers, dedi-cated (?) to analysing and revealing, even to making statements like this: 'Although the project is located within a small neighbourhood, it is clear that programmes and politics implemented there should be seen in a wider city and regional context.'

Of course—but suddenly we local political impresarios are the *subject* of research! We *are* (aren't we?) the power structure; and research both makes that *explicit* (and that's dangerous) and involves criticism. No one likes being the subject of research, least of all those who need secrecy in order to survive. To the subjects, research—even in so simple a form as a straightforward description—is highly threatening, especially as we lose control over what inferences are drawn from the initial description, by a whole series of 'others' who have to date not even been allowed to look upon the awful face of Councillor J. McTwit, Junior, Chairman of the Allotments Committee.

Research, therefore, is basically threatening. Councillors—whether consciously or not—accept with relief the definitions of the problem in magical-geographical terms; to define the problems of an area as being the product of that area (and this is the message implicit in, for example the title of the Newcastle activity as 'The *Benwell* CDP') is a political act easily subsumed by the status quo. Yet we also know that the problems of Benwell must be seen in a 'wider' context—City, Region, National. And this involves inter alia, looking at the local 'power structure' i.e. US. And there they are, ostensibly studying Benwell, in fact studying us!

And there is proof of this. A document dated 22 January, 1973, addressed as from the Home Office, appears to be setting the country's CDP onto the task of studying, not Benwell, but us! Those invited to the assembly at Kinsgate House were circulated with a document entitled 'Notes on suggested question on the Political Structures of the Local Authorities in CDP.' A copy of this document follows.

1. *Party Organization*
   (a) Which Party is in Power.
   (b) Size of Majority   (a) elected councillors
                                 (b) Aldermen
   (To London project—please indicate pre-Reorganization situation)
   (c) Summary of Trend since World War I—e.g. nearly all/all Labour since 1930's—Marginal over last 10 years.
   (d) Anticipate Trend after Reorganization—e.g. L/C/Lib. Marginal/can't tell at all.

2. *The Councillors*: N.B.—And is this typical also of leader and key Committee.
   Sex
   Age   20-29)
         30-39) Young
         40-49)
         50-59 Middle-aged
         Over 60 Elderly
   Place of birth* that local authority
                   elesewhere in UK
                   outside UK
*if known, otherwise estimate percentage of locals.

3. *House Tenure** of Councillors Percentage of owner/occupiers
council tenants
private tenants
other
*if known/ or estimate percentage of council tenants.

4. *Occupation*: None/retired
Housewife
Self employed
Professional
Exec. Admin.
Manual

5. *Local Government Experience*:
0-4
5-9
10 years or more (or estimate percentage there over ten years).

6. *Membership of other Organization*:
e.g. T.U.'s
T.A.'s
Other   (or estimate percentage Trade Unionists or other local
working class activist).

7. Percentage of Party Activists—and official by Class/ e.g. nearly all
working class, 75 per cent. professional/executive.

8. What do local political parties claim as their membership? Estimate
of attendance at Ward meetings?

9. What appear to be the key influences on the local parties? e.g. a
particular Trade Union—say Miners (NUM) or local Labour
party in a mining area.
Local employers—say car industry in Coventy, estate agents,
builder on a local Conservative party.

Degree and Strength of Existing Community Organization

1. *Political Parties*:   size   paid agents?
estimated active membership
Non-Parliamentary Left. estimated size.
Relevant *Pressure Groups*: e.g. CPAG, Case Con., LAG, etc.

2. *Trade Unions*:   (1) What are the most influential unions in the
Trades' Council?
(2) What, if any, shop stewards' organizations
are there?

(3) Are there local industries still largely un-
unionized e.g. sections of casual/or female
employment.

3. *Tenants' and Residents' Associations*—specify. Number
Size

Are these linked/ e.g. by Federations/Community Forums, Neighbourhood, Councils, etc., in any way.

4. *Cultural and other Recreational Clubs*
e.g. Working Men's Clubs Number
Sports Clubs
Ethnic minority social/cultural associations. Size

5. *Churches/Chapels/Mosques*
Number
Size
Other activities—e.g. Welfare work
cultural/recreational clubs.

6. Claimants' and Unemployed Workers' Unions.

7. P.T.A.s (and other Education groups, free schools, etc.),

8. Women's groups.

9. Other: please specify.

In each case, please specify if these exist within the CDP target area
or in the local authority at all (and if so, how accessible to the Project
Areas). London projects—please state nearest in GLC area.

Conclusions

The person who sent out the above papers claimed, when I put the
point to her, that it was a 'personal' and not an 'official' document:
yet it was sent out from official headquarters. The basic point, though,
is that whether we are looking at documents of this type or at books
such as those written by Hampton, then the *politics* of community
action can too easily spill over into the *literature* of community action:
and that such literature is too often characterized by shy hints, gentle-
manly prevarications and cautious omissions. It is time to 'tell it as it
is', and to take the political consequences of an honest and open
analysis, as otherwise no party to the game will find himself any
better off, in terms of comprehension of the problem, after going
through the often very disturbing experience of local power plays
than he was before. To date, and no doubt in future, it has been the
local Councillor who has been portrayed as the silly villain of the

business: but this article tries to show that the academic and the action-researchers are in need of a little salutary self-analysis, and that the mote in their eyes is at least as undesirable as the beam in the eyes of the politicians.

References cited

Davies, J. (1972a), 'The Evangelistic Bureaucrat: A Study of a Planning Exercise in Newcastle', Tavistock Press.

Davies, J. (1972b), 'The Local Councillors Dilemma', *Official Architecture and Planning*, 25 February.

Crick, B. and Green, G. (1968), 'People and Planning' *New Society*, 5th September.

Gerth, H. and Mills, C.W. (1970), 'From Max Weber', Routledge and Kegan Paul.

Hampton, W. (1970), 'Democracy and Community: A Study of Politics in Sheffield', Oxford University Press.

Mailer, N. (1968), 'Miami and the Seige of Chicago', Weidenfeld and Nicolson.

Spencer, J. (1964), 'Stress and Release in an Urban Estate', Tavistock Publications.

SOCIO-POLITICAL CORRELATES OF COMMUNITY ACTION: CONFLICT, POLITICAL INTEGRATION, AND CITIZEN INFLUENCE*

Neil Gilbert and Harry Specht

This paper is an analysis of the relationship between the degrees of conflict and political integration in communities and the degrees of citizen influence in community action. By using data from a nationwide study of the Model Cities Programme in the United States we will analyse how social conflict and political integration were related to the degree of citizen influence in the 148 cities that participated in the Model Cities Programme.[1] Following a discussion of the three major variables and a description of the methodology used in the study, we will present our findings. Our interpretation of the data will be presented in the concluding section.

Conflict and Political Integration

Generations of community workers, community organizers and social planners have debated about the means by which to generate and implement community change. In the community planning literature questions about social conflict, its uses and abuses, have been central to this debate (e.g., Rothman 1968; Brager and Specht 1973; Perlman and Gurin 1972; Kramer and Specht 1969; Gilbert and Specht 1974a; Gilbert 1970; Shaller 1966; Alinsky 1946). The meaning of social conflict and its merits and liabilities in community action has been one of the major conceptual and practice issues that distinguishes the different schools of thought in community action. Schaller (1966:80), in his review of community organization literature on conflict, notes that:

* This study is a follow-up and revision of summary findings initially reported in Neil Gilbert and Harry Specht, *The Model Cities Programme: A Comparative Analysis of Participating Cities: Process, Product, Performance and Prediction* (Washington, D.C.: U.S. Government Printing Office, 1973). Research for this study was supported in part by the Committee on Research, University of California, Berkeley. The authors would like to thank Charlane Brown for her diligent and helpful work as our research assistant.

'(T)here are those who argue that conflict is a beneficial element in the social process because conflict *almost invariably* results in a shift in the distribution of power. The advocates of this position contend that the redistribution of power not only offers the benefits of rejuvenating social institutions and providing seats for newcomers at the bargaining table, but also that it yields other more general salutory consequences and stimulates change in all facets of the social order.' (emphasis added)

The extreme position is best represented by Alinsky (1946:153):

'A people's organization is a conflict group. This must be openly and fully recognised. Its sole reason for coming into being is to wage war against all evils which cause suffering and unhappiness. A people's organization is the banding together of multitudes of men and women to fight for those rights which insure a decent way of life.'

From this perspective, the generation of social conflict is seen as a necessary ingredient for the success of any effort to achieve community change.

The polar view, articulated by the Biddles (1965), is based on the belief that the search for consensus and unity is a central objective of the community action enterprise; from this perspective the reconciliation of different interests in the community should be the major objective guiding practice in community organization and planning. Here emphasis is placed upon co-operation, altruism, and the 'common welfare' broadly defined rather than conflict, self-interest, and the 'common welfare' defined as a matter of opposing group preferences. As Barbara Wootton (1945: 140-141), a persuasive advocate of social planning, explains:

'To show that no plan or policy is likely to rebound to the personal advantage of every citizen is, however, in no way to prove either that no policies can commend themselves as desirable to those who do not personally stand to gain, and may actually lose by them, or that the only 'goods' in the world are those which can be literally bought or sold.'

The conceptual and practice issues on which this position turns are concerned with the meaning of political integration and its effects on community action. The meaning of political integration like that of social conflict, is actively debated: can it allow for 'citizen participation' or is it only 'citizen co-operation'; does it 'create community' or 'cool the mark out'; will it eventuate in community control or in a subtle means of controlling the community?

Of course, many writers have attempted to reconcile the strains and dilemmas that inhere in social conflict and political integration (e.g., Specht 1969; Walton 1969). Numerous additional variables have been introduced to clarify the relationship between conflict and integration. These include: the goals of community action, which is a useful concept for ordering practice in terms of whether an objective is viewed as an end or a means (Rothman 1969; Rein and Morris 1969); organizational context (Kramer 1969; Sundquist 1969); characteristics of participants (Gilbert and Eaton 1970; Gilbert 1970; Zurcher 1970); and characteristics of communities (Mogulof 1970). Rothman (1968:35), in discussing different models of community organization practice, says:

'By assessing when one or another mode of action is or is not appropriate, the practitioner takes an analytical, problem-solving stand and does not become the captive of a particular ideological or methodological approach to practice. Practitioners, consequently, should be attuned through training to the differential utility of each approach and should acquire the knowledge and skill which permit them to utilise each of the models as seems appropriate and necessary.'

'The community practitioner should also become sensitive to the mixed uses of these techniques within a single practice context; for problems require such blending, and organizational structures permit adaptations.'

Citizen influence

During the 1960s the most prominent policy issues in defining the action system for community planning concerned the appropriate rôles and relationships of local citizen organizations and community planning agencies.[2] Ideas about 'community control' and 'citizen participation' were hotly debated and poorly defined. Interpretations often varied according to personal inclinations and political perspectives. For example, two major critiques of the War on Poverty, one by Clark and Hopkins (1969) and the other by Moynihan (1969), expressed dissatisfaction with the implementation of citizen participation in the Economic Opportunity Programme. Clark and Hopkins said that there was too little participation and Moynihan that there was too much. Similarly, both the Democrats and the Republicans levelled charges of inadequate citizen participation and developed legislation to correct matters, each party carrying forward quite different objectives under the same populist banner.

'Citizen participation' and 'community control' are ideas that can be adapted to a wide range of programmatic and political objectives. Hardly anyone disagrees with the thought that citizens should participate and that communities should control, but collectivities of any size or class or colour can be called 'communities'. And as Arnestein (1969) and Kramer (1970:126-127) so clearly illustrate, 'participation' can take many forms ranging from passive observation to assertive direction. Thus, it is not surprising to find the Republicans' revenue-

95

sharing programme (which seeks to enhance the participation and control of mayors and governors) justified with the same rhetoric as the Economic Opportunity Programme (which seeks to increase the participation and control by the poor).

A large part of the research on citizen participation in community action is concerned with testing the proposition that the greater the degree of citizen influence in decision making in the planning process, the higher the level of performance in programme implementation. This proposition rest upon findings from small group research (Lippitt and White 1960; Leviane and Butler 1952) as well as community analyses of the kind reported above.

Yin, *et al.* (1973: 50-51) conclude that, from the few systematic efforts made to study the impact of citizen participation on programme effectiveness, more often than not citizen participation appears to have positive effects on programme effectiveness. However, the data presented to support this point are not unequivocal.

The case as it is generally made is that when people participate directly in determining policies that affect their lives, decisions arrived at are more likely to produce support and commitment for implementation than when policies are otherwise determined. In the context of the Model Cities Programme this would suggest that in communities where citizen influence was weak during the planning phase, local support and commitment required for programme implementation would be difficult to muster.

This proposition has special significance because citizen participation is not simply a neutral means to facilitate the desired outcome of programme implementation which, if it does not work, can be easily discarded in favour of other approaches. Rather, citizen participation is both a means and a valued end in its own right which can pose some perplexing choices for the planning enterprise as analysed by Gilbert and Specht (1974: 178-199). However, it should be emphasised that this is not a zero-sum proposition, but one that addresses the issue of the degrees of citizen participation associated with different levels of programme performance. We shall attempt to deal with this proposition in our analysis of findings.

The Model Cities Programme

In the 1960s the shape of community planning in the United States was transformed. Three main ingredients contributed to this transformation. First, there was the citizen participation movement with its roots in civil rights efforts, the planning programmes spawned by the President's Committee on Juvenile Delinquency and the Economic Opportunity Programme of 1964. Through the citizen participation movement, decision making for community planning was carried, sometimes unwillingly, from the back rooms of political clubs and the executive chambers of blue ribbon panels to the broader community where a more diverse group of actors could play the rôles of 'community spokesmen'. Second, the agenda for community planning was expanded to include not only the traditional focus on physical development but also concerns for social welfare planning which had been hitherto relegated primarily to the private/voluntary planning efforts of local health and welfare councils. Finally, procedures were introduced to expedite the co-ordination of national grant-in-aid programmes at the local level.

The transformation of community planning was, in large part, a response to a number of problems and concerns to which many federally initiated attempts to improve community well-being had been addressed. The federal initiatives culminated in the Model Cities Programme in 1966.

Of the many policies and programmes that contributed to this development, the Urban Renewal Programme and the Economic Opportunity Programme were foremost among the community planning efforts that paved the way to Model Cities. Experience with these programmes, both the set-backs and the achievements, influenced thinking about the Model Cities Programme.

The Demonstration Cities and Metropolitan Development Act of 1966, the legislation that established the Model Cities Programme, called for a comprehensive approach in combined physical and social planning to attack the problems of urban decay and human strife affecting large sections of cities throughout the nation. The act authorized the provision of financial and technical assistance to cities of all sizes 'to plan, develop, and carry out locally prepared comprehensive city demonstration programmes containing new and imaginative proposals to rebuild and revitalize large slum and blighted areas' (U.S. Congress 1966:1).

For the cities selected, participation in the programme was expected to last approximately six years. The first year was to be devoted to planning, the product of which was a document—the Comprehensive

Demonstration Plan (CDP). The CDP was to designate the specific content and objectives of programmes to be implemented in the following action year and to set the general framework for programmes over a continuing five-year period. The data used in our analysis covers approximately only the first two years, the planning period and the first programme year.[3]

The first major task in launching the Model Cities Programme was to select the cities that were to receive grants.[4] All cities were eligible to submit applications for grants. By the Spring of 1968, 75 cities were selected from an original 193 applicants for first-round funding. The cities and towns chosen had populations ranging in size from approximately 2,300 to 8,000,000. A similar process was used in the following year to select another 73 cities bringing the total to 148 cities given grants over the two-year period.

A City Demonstration Agency (CDA) was organized in each of the Model Cities to do the job of planning the programme. At the conclusion of the period of planning, which might have lasted anywhere from ten months to two years, the CDAs submitted their CDPs to the Department of Housing and Urban Development (HUD).[5] Much of the work of the CDA during this period had to do with the creation of the action system that produced the plan. By statute, that action system was required to be composed of residents of the Model Neighbourhood Area (MNA), political leaders, and the CDA staff. However, cities varied considerably in the ways these elements were combined. The arrangements varied in terms of the number and sizes of policy-making groups, authority structure, communications systems, decision making and allocating systems, and degree of inputs from citizens and experts.

At that particular moment in history there was no general consensus at any level of government as to where the balance of influence for decision making should lie. It seemed to us, then, an excellent opportunity to study some of the effects of the variations of this important feature of action systems.

Methodology

This report is part of a larger study which examines many variables in the Model Cities Programme in the period of time between the initial selection of applicants in 1967-1968 to the Spring of 1971. The variables of major concern in this paper are the degree of citizen influence and the socio-political characteristics of conflict and political integration.

Measuring Citizen Influence—To obtain measures of citizen influence in the planning process, structured interviews were conducted with eleven HUD officials (known as 'deskmen') in Washington D.C., each of whom had direct responsibility for Model Cities Programmes in from twelve-to-thirty cities within their designated regions. These officials had covered all of the first- and second-round programmes over the planning period and through the first action year. The HUD officials were asked to rate each of the programmes under their jurisdiction along a five-point continuum of citizen influence on decision making as it appeared during the last quarter of the planning period. The extremes and mid-point of this continuum were defined as follows:

> *Weak citizen participation* (staff influence is the major determinant in decision making)—MNA residents functioned primarily to 'legitimise' the planning processes and products originated by the CDA staff. At this end of the continuum residents play a residual rôle in decisions and generally rubber stamp the decisions of CDA staff.
> *Moderate citizen participation* (parity relationships between resident groups and CDA staff)—MNA residents and CDA staff shared responsibility for key planning decisions. At this mid-point on the continuum, residents and staff could be characterised as 'equal partners' in the planning enterprise.
> *Strong citizen participation* (resident influence is the major determinant in decision making)—MNA residents exerted preponderant influence in the planning process. At this end of the continuum, residents could be characterised as directors of the planning process.

The last quarter of the planning period was selected as the time to judge degree of citizen influence because it was during this quarter that decision making in the CDAs focused on the actual programme proposals for the first programme year that were included in the CDP. Also, focusing on the last quarter allowed for the fact that citizen participation often varied over the planning period and accurate generalizations about the entire period would be more difficult to make than generalizations about a strategic quarter.

Even so, the interviews were conducted in August 1971. Therefore, the respondents were being asked about events that had transpired two-to-three years before and the accuracy of recall was a matter of concern in analysis of responses. For this reason, a second set of measures of the degree of citizen influence was obtained through content analysis of documents. That is, in order to develop some external check on the deskmen's perceptions, additional data were obtained from narrative documents written on each programme about the events under consideration at the time the events took place. These narrative reports, known as 'briefing memos', were prepared by HUD regional staff (known as 'leadmen') at the end of the planning period. The briefing memos evaluated each programme's experience in terms of progress made, obstacles to planning encountered, and general programme strengths and weaknesses; one of the main headings around which most of these reports were organized referred to citizen participation. Using these documents, three judges rated each programme on a three-point continuum using the aforementioned criteria. The two sets of ratings (interviews with HUD officials and a composite measure of the three judges' content analyses) were correlated and demonstrated a high degree of association (gamma .667). The interview ratings were then collapsed into a three point continuum (1, 2=weak, 3=moderate, 4, 5=strong) and a very strong degree of association (gamma .769) between the two sets of judgements emerged. The collapsed interview ratings were selected as our indicator of citizen influence in the planning process primarily because, of the two measures, it contained the least missing data.

It should be noted that this indicator represents a 'federal perspective' on what happened in the Model Cities Programme. In many respects this perspective probably allows for as clear a view of the Model Cities Programme nationwide as could be hoped for. The informants were close enough to a number of programmes for a long enough period of time to be able to make informed comparative judgements. Yet they were removed enough from each individual city to make judgements with a reasonable degree of objectivity (as compared to, for example, local CDA staff or citizen participants whose strong investments in their own programmes might be expected to colour their views).

It should be noted too, that the two sets of judgements used for developing the measure of citizen influence are, strictly speaking, not totally independent. That is, originally, the briefing memos were reports prepared by the regional HUD leadmen for consumption by the deskmen in Washington D.C. Hence, the views of the Washington officials who were interviewed were formed partly out of the information they received in these reports as well as through their direct contacts with the programmes. It was anticipated that if the deskmen's recall was reasonably accurate, the two sets of judgements would show a high degree of consistency, which they did.

MNA conflict—The HUD officials interviewed were asked to rate the cities under their jurisdiction in terms of the degree of conflict that accompanied the development of the MNA citizen participation structure. *A low degree of conflict* was described as involving virtually no contest for leadership and jurisdiction among residents in the development of the MNA citizen participation structure. *Moderate conflict* involved genuine contests for leadership among individuals and groups in the MNA; elections held in these situations were lively, but did not provoke intense feelings. *High conflict* situations were characterized as those in which the struggle for leadership was heated and intense.

Sufficient information on this variable was not found in the briefing memos to allow comparative ratings to be made through the content analysis. Therefore the indicators of MNA conflict in the development of citizen participation structures were based exclusively on the interview ratings. However, we did have an indicator of community turbulence/conflict during the planning years (1967-1968) that was based on data from a nationwide survey conducted by the Lemburg Centre for the Study of Violence, Brandeis University. This second set of data was somewhat different from our indicator of MNA conflict. These data focused on reported incidents of disorder for entire cities rather than MNAs and the disorders reported were more extreme forms of social conflict than were usually manifest in struggles for MNA leadership. Though the indicators of MNA conflict and community turbulence/conflict were not entirely comparable, it was expected that there would be a measure of correspondence between the degree of turbulence/conflict in the larger community and that which emerged in the Model Cities target neighbourhood. Correlation between these two indicators showed a strong degree of association (gamma .618) and in the absence of more comparable data against which to match the subjective interview ratings, this relationship gives us some confidence in the accuracy of the MNA conflict indicator.

Political Integration of MNA Leaders—For this indicator HUD officials were asked to rate each city under their jurisdiction in regard to the extent to which the leadership of MNA citizen participation structures were integrated into the administrative and political apparatus of city government. Raters made their judgement according to degree of political integration as reflected in the following descriptions:

> *Low degree of political integration*—MNA citizen participation leadership is not fully accepted and engaged by city government.
> *Moderate degree of political integration*—MNA citizen participation leadership is accepted by city government and engaged on an informal ad hoc basis when support and co-operation on specific projects are sought.
> *High degree of political integration*—MNA citizen participation leadership is engaged in formal on-going communications and co-operation with city government.

Findings

Conflict—The requirements for citizen participation held forth the opportunity for individuals and groups within the MNAs to achieve positions of relative influence and to reap some of the benefits that typically accrue to such positions. All MNA residents and groups obviously could not share equally in these benefits, and competition to control the resident organization in the MNA developed to varying degrees in different Model Cities as the organizational structure for citizen participation took shape. In approximately half of the Model Cities there was a low degree of conflict, with little competition for leadership in the development of the MNA citizen participation structure. The remaining cities were split almost evenly between those in which there was a moderate degree of conflict, with lively elections and real contests for leadership, and those in which there was a high degree of conflict, with pronounced struggles for leadership clearly visible and felt in the development of the citizen participation structure.

As indicated in Table 1, there is a strong relationship (gamma .664) between the degree of conflict within the MNA and the pattern of influence that emerged. In other words, the higher the degree of conflict in the development of citizen organizations, the greater the likelihood that citizen influence would be strong.

There are two ways in which this relationship may come about. On the one hand, in programmes where it appeared that residents were going to have major decision-making powers, the incentive to compete for leadership positions would be greater than in programmes where staff control of decision making was established at the outset. On the other hand, in cities in which there are high degrees of conflict in the MNA, resident organizations are more likely to be militant and assertive than in cities where little conflict accompanied the

Socio-Political Correlates of Community Action

TABLE 1

Model Neighbourhood Area (MNA) Conflict and Pattern of Influence

Pattern of Influence	Degree of MNA Conflict		
	Low	Medium	High
Staff Dominant	73%	57%	21%
Parity	24%	27%	32%
Resident Dominant	3%	17%	47%
Total	100% (n=66)	101%* (n=30)	100% (n=34)

* Due to rounding
(gamma .644)

development of the citizen participation structure. Moreover the types of resident organizations that were forged through conflict would have the ability and the inclination to struggle with CDA staff for an influential rôle in Model Cities' decision making. The nature of our data does not allow us to distinguish clearly which of these possibilities describes the process that actually occurred. Moreover, it is possible that one or the other process occurred in some cities, and both together in other cities.

Political Integration—While conflict in the MNA reflects the quality of turbulence and instability in the environment, political integration reflects elements of stability in the informal linkages, established lines of communication, and working relationships existing between the MNA and the formal political apparatus of the city. As illustrated in Table 2 there is a moderate correlation (gamma .426) between political integration and patterns of influence.

But an examination of these data reveals that this relationship differs from the relationship between conflict and patterns of influence in an important way. Whereas a high degree of conflict was most likely to occur along with a resident-dominant pattern of influence, high political integration occurred most frequently when decision making influence was shared between CDA staff and residents in a parity-type arrangement.

Conflict and Political Integration Combined—Having examined conflict and political integration separately, we see that each relates directly, but in a somewhat different manner to patterns of influence.

Neil Gilbert and Harry Specht

TABLE 2

Political Integration of Model Neighbourhood Area (MNA) Leadership
and Pattern of Influence

Pattern of Influence				Political Integration of MNA Leadership		
				Low	Medium	High
Staff Dominant	...	...	...	73%	56%	21%
Parity	...	...	...	12%	23%	62%
Resident Dominant		...	...	15%	21%	17%
			Total	100% (n=59)	100% (n=43)	100% (n=29)

(gamma .426)

By combining these two characteristics it is possible to analyse the extent to which there are distinctive socio-political environments associated with the emergence of different patterns of influence. The results of this analysis, shown in Table 3, reveals that, indeed, three fairly well-bounded socio-political environments can be identified in which each pattern of influence occurs with the greatest frequency. Thus, at one end of the citizen influence continuum, *the cities in which there are staff-dominant patterns of influence are most likely to have socio-political environments characterized by low degrees of political integration and low degrees of conflict*. Forty-four per cent. of all staff-dominant cities are in this category and another 41 per cent. are in neighbouring categories, as noted in Table 3A. At the other extreme, *socio-political environments in the cities with resident-dominant patterns of influence are most likely to be characterized by high degrees of conflict and low-to-moderate degrees of political integration*. Sixty-two per cent. of all resident-dominant cities are in this category and another fifteen per cent. are in neighbouring categories, as noted in Table 3C. And finally, *parity-type patterns are found most frequently in cities with socio-political environments characterized by high degrees of political integration and low-to-medium degrees of conflict*. Twenty-seven per cent. of all cities with parity-type patterns of influence fall into this category, with an additional thirty-three per cent. found in neighbouring cells, as noted in Table 3C.

TABLE 3

Patterns of Influence and the Socio-Political Environment

Degree of Conflict	A. Cities with Staff-Dominant Patterns of Influence			B. Cities with Parity Patterns of Influence			C. Cities with Resident-Dominant Patterns of Influence		
	Degree of Political Integration			Degree of Political Integration			Degree of Political Integration		
	Low	Medium	High	Low	Medium	High	Low	Medium	High
Low	44%	15%	8%	9%	12%	27%	5%	5%	0%
Medium	9%	17%	0%	3%	9%	12%	10%	5%	5%
High	3%	3%	2%	9%	9%	12%	29%	33%	10%
Total	101%*			102%*			102%*		
	(n=66)			(n=34)			(n=21)		

* due to rounding.

Analysis

These findings have implications for community action from two different viewpoints. First we shall discuss how they illuminate the relationships among conflict, political integration and citizen influence. Second, we will consider some of the implications of these relationships for social-policy planning.

Conflict, Political Integration and the Political System—A theoretical explanation of our findings suggests that where there were low degrees of conflict in the development of the citizen participation structure, two possible conditions might have existed within the MNA. First, is the case where residents and resident groups were unassertive, poorly organized, and politically inactive. Here there was little conflict because the initial organizational structures to serve as a vehicle for the expression of competing interests did not exist and the political ambition and skills to create such a vehicle were neither available in the necessary mass nor cultivated through technical assistance. In this case we would anticipate low degrees of political integration merely because there is no viable local structure with which the city's political apparatus can be linked. These circumstances describe a socio-political environment that is highly conducive to the development of staff-dominant patterns of influence, as reflected in the findings in Table 3A.

The second case for limited conflict involves MNAs in which strong, well recognized citizen organizations were in existence prior to the onset of Model Cities. Here internal conflicts had already been resolved or at least mitigated and MNA leaders were able to keep constituents under control. In this case we would anticipate moderate-to-high degrees of political integration because once a stable citizens' organization has been built, its leaders often may seek to enhance their legitimacy and power by establishing formal relationships with city hall. Moreover, efforts by the city's political apparatus to co-opt such citizen organizations are frequent and represent a good deal of what urban politics is all about. This socio-political environment provides fertile ground for the development of parity-type patterns of influence, as reflected in the findings in Table 3B.

According to this interpretation of the findings the one socio-political environment that we would have expected to find least of all is one in which *both* conflict and political integration are high. The reason for this, in line with the explanation of the above cases, is that MNA leaders and organizations achieve integration into the city's political apparatus, at least in part, by exhibiting their capacity to maintain a degree of control and insure some stability over the organizational activities within the MNA. At the same time, political intergration tends to reinforce stabilization within the MNA by enhancing the legitimacy of these leaders and organizations and making the formal political system readily available to them for mediating differences and dissatisfactions that might arise in the MNA. Hence, the prospects for intense conflict to be found in environments with high degrees of political integration would seem quite limited. As indicated in Table 3, in all, there were only seven cities that fell into this category.

Policy Implications—A planning process that included a strong element of citizen influences was the first link in a cumulative chain of Model Cities objectives. This chain of objectives consists of: (a) a planning process involving a strong element of citizen influence which leads to the development of; (b) a high quality Comprehensive Demonstration Plan containing clearly stated and innovative policies derived from rational analysis to guide; (c) a process of programme implementation involving a high degree of co-ordination of services and citizen particpation and leading to; (d) a high quality of performance in establishing programmes aimed to improve the quality of life in urban communities. This chain of objectives represents a theoretical model which assumes that each link is connected with the next in line. It is possible, of course, that none of these objectives are related or that some are inversely related, or that the 'chain' really involves some combination of only two or three of these objectives.

While there were different interpretations held by HUD staff concerning whether a 'strong element' meant that citizen groups were to have controlling influence or an equal share of decision making authority, staff-dominant patterns of influence clearly did not fit this initial objective. From a policy perspective there are two issues regarding this objective of citizen influence. First what characteristics are associated with the development of different kinds of citizen influence systems in community action? The preceding analysis suggests the ways that the socio-political environment is related to the emergence of different degrees of citizen influence. This analysis helps to explain the conditions under which the first link in the chain of Model Cities objectives was forged. Socio-political environments are composed, in part, of community workers, planners, citizen groups, and politicians. It is unclear as to how much influence each of these sets of actors can exercise in shaping a particular socio-political environment at a given point in time, regardless of the school of thought concerning the use of conflict and political integration to which they might subscribe. What the analysis does indicate, however, is the direction efforts to shape the socio-political environment would take in order to develop different types of citizen influence systems, in circumstances where the opportunity and power to affect the socio-political environments exists. Because of the uncertainty about the degrees of citizen influence that was desirable to achieve the first Model Cities objective, our analysis suggests two possible and somewhat contradictory directions: movement toward a high degree of political integration and low to moderate degrees of conflict (conditions for parity) or toward a low degree of political integration and high degree of conflict (conditions for citizen dominance).

The second policy issue concerns how the degree to which achievement of the initial citizen participation objective relates to the achievement of other Model Cities objectives—links 'b', 'c', and 'd' in the model. Analysis on this issue is useful to provide some insight into the relative desirability of parity versus citizen dominant patterns of influence, hence, reducing the uncertainty around achievement of the initial Model Cities objective.

To explore this issue we measured the programmatic outcome of Model Cities in a variety of ways including the following: quality of the CDP; quality, speed and efficiency of programme implementation; and degree of co-ordination with other agencies in planning and programme implementation. Our findings, reported in a previous publication (Gilbert and Specht 1973), are that cities that achieved a parity-type system of influence do better on *all* measures of outcome than others. Cities with a resident-dominant pattern of influence do worst on almost all measures of outcome. And cities that develop a staff-dominant pattern of influence fall in between the other two types on almost all outcome measures.

Thus in terms of ultimate social planning objectives, it appears that socio-political environments characterized by high degrees of conflict and low degrees of political integration do not lead to productive outcomes; neither do environments in which conflict and political integration are both low. High degrees of political integration, in combination with low-to-moderate degrees of conflict seem to be the conditions under which community action efforts are most likely to yield programmatic results.

That is not to say that conflict is, necessarily, dysfunctional. We have looked at cities at a fixed point in time and we have not studied the process of community action over time. The latter approach might very likely reveal that there is a dynamic relationship between conflict and political integration over time. It is not unlikely that, in the process of community change, an intensification of conflict precedes an increase in political integration; that is, in socio-political environments in which there is low political integration, social conflict may be a necessary ingredient to create a new socio-political environment. However, in the Model Cities, conflict by itself was insufficient to achieve desirable programmatic outcomes. Political integration was the other necessary ingredient.

Notes

[1] More details of the methodology and findings from the larger study are reported in Gilbert and Specht 1973; 1974b. In these publications we have analysed the relationship of conflict and integration to other variables such as programme outcomes, and chief executive behaviour. In addition, we have discussed the relationship of factors such as community size, proportion of racial minorities and methods of selecting communities for participation in the programme to the degree of citizen influence that is achieved in the programme.

[2] For a representative sampling of the vast literature in this area see Kramer (1969), Rossi and Dentler (1961), Gilbert (1970), Rose (1972), Warren (1969), Hyman and Katz (1970), Moynihan (1969), Clark and Hopkins (1969), and Austin (1972).

[3] In some cases our data does not cover the entire period of planning and first year programme, because at the time data were gathered (Spring 1971) only 117 of the cities had completed six months of the first year of programme and only 65 had completed twelve months of the first year programme.

[4] This process is described in detail in Gilbert and Specht (1974b).

[5] For further details on the Model Cities Programme legislation, guidelines and operational procedures see U.S. Department of Housing and Urban Development (1966; 1970) and Marshall Kaplan (1971).

References Cited

Alinsky, S. (1946), *Reveille for Radicals*, University of Chicago Press, Chicago.

Arnstein, S. (1969), 'A Ladder of Citizen Participation', *Journal of the American Institute of Planners*, 35:4 July.

Austin, D. M. (1972), 'Resident Participation: Political Mobilization or Organizational Co-optation?', *Public Administration Review*, 32 September.

Biddle, W. and Biddle, L. J. (1965), *The Community Development Process*, Holt, Rinehart and Winston, New York.

Brager, G. and Specht, H. (1973), *Community Organizing*, Columbia University Press, New York.

Clark, K. B. and Hopkins, J. (1969), *A Relevant War Against Poverty: A Study of Community Action Programmes and Observable Social Change*, Harper and Row, New York.

Gilbert, N. (1970), *Clients or Constituents*, Jossey-Bass, San Francisco.

Gilbert, N. and Eaton, J. (1970), 'Who Speaks for the Poor? Research Report', *Journal of the American Institute of Planners*, 36:4 November.

Gilbert, N. and Specht, H. (1973), *The Model Cities Programme: A Comparative Analysis of Participating Cities—Process, Product, Performance and Predictions*, U.S. Printing Office, Washington D.C.

Gilbert, N. and Specht, H. (1974a), *Dimensions of Social Welfare Policy*, Prentice Hall, Englewood Cliffs.

Gilbert, N. and Specht, H. (1974b), 'Picking Winners: Federal Discretion and Local Experience as Bases for Planning Grant Allocations', *Public Administration Review* 34:4 November/December.

Hyman, H. and Katz, E. M. (1970), *Urban Planning for Social Welfare: A Model Cities Approach*, Praeger, New York.

Kaplan, M. (1971), 'Model Cities and National Urban Policy', *American Society and Planning Officials*, Chicago, Illinois.

Kramer, R. (1969), *Participation of the Poor*, Prentice Hall, Englewood Cliffs.

Kramer, R. (1970), *Community Development in Israel and the Netherlands*, University of California, Institute of International Studies, Berkeley.

Kramer, R. and Specht, H. (1969), *Readings in Community Organization Practice*, Prentice Hall, Englewood Cliffs.

Levine, J. and Butler, J. (1952), 'Lecture versus Group Decision in Changing Behaviour', *Journal of Applied Psychology*, 36 February.

Lippitt, R. and White, R. (1960), 'Leader Behaviour and Member Reaction in Three Social Climates', pp. 585-611 in Dorwin Cartwright and Alvin Zander (eds.), *Group Dynamics Research and Theory*, Harper and Row, New York.

Mogulof, M. (1970), 'Black Community Development in Five Western Cities', *Social Work*, 15:1 January.

Moynihan, D. P. (1969), *Maximum Feasible Misunderstanding*, Free Press, New York.

Perlman, R. and Gurin, A. (1972), *Community Organization and Social Planning*, Wiley, New York.

Rein, M. and Morris, R. (1969), 'Goals, Structures and Strategies for Community Change', pp. 188-200 in Ralph Kramer and Harry Specht (eds.), *Readings in Community Organization Practice*, Prentice Hall, Englewood Cliffs.

Socio-Political Correlates of Community Action

Rose, S. (1972), The Betrayal of the Poor: The Transformation of Community Action, Schenkman Publishing Co., Cambridge.

Rothman, J. (1968), 'Three Models of Community Organization Practice', Social Work Practice, Columbia University Press, New York.

Rothman, J. (1969), 'An Analysis of Goals and Roles in Community Organization Practice', pp. 260-268 in Ralph Kramer and Harry Specht (eds.), Readings in Community Organization Practice, Prentice Hall, Englewood Cliffs.

Rossi, P. and Dentler, R. (1961), The Politics of Urban Renewal, Free Press, New York.

Schaller, L. S. (1966), Community Organization, Conflict and Reconciliation, Abingdon Press, Nashville.

Specht, H. (1969), 'Disruptive Tactics', Social Work, 14:2 April.

Sundquist, J. (1969), Making Federalism Work, The Brookings Institution, Washington D.C.

U.S. Congress (1966), Demonstration Cities and Metropolitan Development Act 1966, Public Law 89-754, 89th Congress.

U.S. Department of Housing and Urban Development (1966), Improving the Quality of Urban Life: A Programme Guide to Model Neighbourhoods in Demonstration Cities, U.S. Printing Office, Washington D.C.

U.S. Department of Housing and Urban Development (1970), The Model Cities Programme, U.S. Printing Office, Washington D.C.

Walton, R. (1969), 'Two Strategies of Social Change and Their Dilemmas', pp. 337-345 in Ralph Kramer and Harry Specht (eds.), Readings in Community Organization Practice, Prentice Hall, Englewood Cliffs.

Warren, R. (1969), 'Model Cities First Round: Politics, Planning, and Participation', Journal of the American Institute of Planners, 35:4, July.

Wootton, B. (1945), Freedom under Planning, University of North Carolina Press, Chapel Hill.

Yin, R. K., et al. (1973), Citizen Organization: Increasing Client Control Over Services, Rand Corporation, Santa Monica, CA.

Zurcher, L. B. (1970), The Poverty Warriors, University of Texas Press, Austin, Texas.

BREAD AND JUSTICE: THE NATIONAL WELFARE RIGHTS ORGANISATION

Hilary Rose

This account of the National Welfare Rights Organisation (NWRO) is one of a series of studies in community action, in which a key objective is to explore and account for the differences in perspectives and achievements between the welfare rights movements which developed during the mid 1960s first in the United States and then in Britain. Although the major preoccupation of the paper is with NWRO as indisputably the major and most durable manifestation of the American welfare rights movement, in order for us to be able to consider important comparative questions, such as why in Britain we have both the Claimant Unions (CUs) and the Child Poverty Action Group (CPAG), we have to begin by examining, however briefly, the external history of the social forces and events which surrounded the birth of the movement. As the paper will suggest, these differences and similarities between the welfare rights movement (the UK organisations having both consciously and unconsciously been influenced by the US experience) stem not only from economic considerations, but also from significant political and cultural differences between the two societies. These differences are played out within the internal history in terms of the people, the ideas, the structures and struggles of the movements themselves. It is then, a brief outline of the particular domestic problems facing America in the 1960s with which I will begin.

The Crisis of the Cities and the Great Society

The crisis in the Northern cities of the United States during the

Acknowledgements

I would like to thank the many members of NWRO who generously gave me their time; Frances Piven, Richard Cloward, Mike Miller for helpful discussions; the members of my research advisory committee Mary Mackintosh, Norman Dennis, Peter Townsend, John Spencer & Richard Mills for their encouragement and guidance, and the Gulbenkian Foundation for financial support.

1960s and the political response of the Great Society programme, was the culmination of a long and complex process, beginning with the modernisation of the agrarian economy of the South, and the subsequent mass expulsion of surplus labour from the land. Steadily during the twentieth century, and rapidly from the 1940s onward, the black rural worker, unable to sustain himself and his family, migrated to the Southern cities and, in even greater numbers, to those of the North in search of employment. Not only were employment prospects better in the North but relief levels were higher and administered in a less grossly discriminatory way. The administration, or rather non administration of welfare, together with the change in the economic base, was able, despite the rising tide of the civil rights movement and increasing voting participation by Southern blacks from the mid-fifties onwards, to maintain white hegemony. Thus, as Piven and Cloward (1971:223) emphasise, the process of migration facilitated the emergence of a white majority able to control the South by voting where it hitherto had as a minority dominated by straightforwardly repressive means.[1]

While the black rural worker had fled from the effects of the modernisation of agriculture, his skills were modest in contrast to the skilled labour required by the highly technologically advanced North. Periods of recession exacerbated the problem and Northern employers were not free of the discriminatory attitudes of the South. Despite the vagaries in the overall unemployment level, blacks generally experienced twice the unemployment of whites. The ex-rural worker became the man on *Tally's Corner*,[2] unemployed, casually employed or underemployed. Thus through his own work he was unable to sustain a family and instead 'family' increasingly became the woman and her children, the instability of the man's position as a worker undermining the stability of the man's rôle as husband and father. Nor did the administrative rules of welfare do anything to help the family as a whole unit; 'the man in the house' rule was deployed against him if he needed welfare aid for his family; to secure that aid he had to leave home.

As in the South the economic structures and the welfare arrangements combined to sharpen the situation of the blacks. Nor with the breakdown in the old political alliances, itself to no small extent a result of the mass migration of population, was it clear to where the blacks could turn politically. As the major Northern cities became increasingly inhabited by poor blacks and the whites retreated to the suburbs, the crisis in city financing and the failure to create social services on a nationwide basis magnified the problem.

Economic distress and social dislocation, particularly of the black urban family, produced a crisis of social order. Riots were common and increasingly political in orientation, in that the people engaged in rioting and the objectives they sought to destroy were rationally intelligible. Thus, as the Kerner Commission (1968) was to point out, rioters were not the hoodlum of the white suburban stereotype but were often the educated black who might appear to have a stake in the future. Because disorder means that men and women can no longer take the ordering and routine of their lives for granted, even though that disorder arises from their all consuming social distress, they also begin to question the inevitability of particular social arrangements. Thus with the American experience the questioning of society by the urbanised blacks questioned the legitimacy of white hegemony. Despite the heterogeneity of the questioning—from the rioters, Rosa Parkes, Martin Luther King, George Wiley (Director of NWRO), Stokely Carmichael, George Jackson to Angela Davies—sociologically all contributed to the questioning of the social order. In that many of these—and most dramatically King in that his was a pacifist militancy—linked the cause of the black in America directly with the prosecution of the war in Vietnam, the movement of the American black was linked with a great wave of social unrest which swept almost the entire world in the sixties. In so far that every social movement draws on the zeitgeist of the time, it is important to note, even if impossible to explore this macro-social context.

However, for American presidents, first Kennedy then Johnson, the crisis in American society which manifested itself in the city was seen as a crisis in liberal democracy. The objectives of the Great Society programme, and the War on Poverty were to tackle the problem of the socially dangerous exclusion of the urban blacks. Excluded from both the economic and the political structure, their lack of social affiliation made them a continous risk to the stability of the cities.

The poverty programme with its emphasis on Federal support for local initiatives for the poor—and even by the poor—if necessary taking on local States, reflects the recognition that the programme was to be a means of incorporating the urban poor, and thereby take the heat out of the dangerous protest of ethnic and minority groups. This essentially political objective of the poverty programme has often been misinterpreted by social observers, particularly those pre-occupied by social policy and issues of poverty and welfare. Because the statistical fact is that numerically more whites than blacks are poor (although blacks are proportionally over-represented) the black emphasis within the Great Society programmes was felt to be a puzzling mistake possibly precipitated by the bad conscience of the white liberal.

The possibility that the blacks represented a political threat and therefore their problems required a political response was largely ignored. Poverty was seen as a technical issue requiring measurement, legislative and administrative action. At best the awareness that the politics of poverty mattered, tended to be limited to expressions such as the 'rediscovery of poverty'. In this explanatory model social policy analysts note the significance of books, such as Michael Harrington's *The Other America,* for changing the construction of social reality within the dominant culture. While the construction of social reality is a constant arena of debate and important in its own right, few asked the sociologically—and socially—important question of why did this new perception of the social world emerge at this particular time?

It is also a curious fact that while social policy commentators will explain the defeat of the war on poverty by the war in Vietnam, thus accepting a structural explanation of failure, they tend to look to individuals as innovators rather than to the structural needs of society which disposes government at particular times to listen to social policy reformers. Some observers, notably D. P. Moynihan (1969:127) and to a lesser extent P. Marris and M. Rein (1967:21) have interpreted this combination of strategies as the result of the key personnel near to Presidents Kennedy and Johnson. Donovan (1967:32) too makes a similar type of analysis, quoting for example Smith's work on the key role of Richard Boone in drafting the community action aspect of the OEO programme (Office of Economic Opportunity). And, as for Walter Heller (1967) Johnson's top economic adviser, it would appear that the whole cornucopia of concensus politics and the great society flowed from his personal biro. A kind of 'great man' theory of social reform lives on serving to explain social changes, while elsewhere it receives scant credence amongst sociologists and historians. While it would be naïve to ignore the contributions of particular individuals in formulating the US government's strategies of reform, they must be set against the needs of government to look for that advice in the first place.

Federal government, particularly under Johnson, was faced in practical terms with the problem E. B. McPherson (1973:77) had formulated as the central dilemma of liberal democratic theory, namely how to balance a committment to an egalitarian ideology in the context of a capitalist economy which is markedy inegalitarian in its effect. The *Dilemma of Social Reform*, Marris and Rein title their study of the workings out of the poverty programme, is precisely the dilemma of contemporary liberal democracy. In city after city, despite the energy of the Federal government's actions, the social system has a remarkable capacity to resist those changes which it both seeks politically and yet which also run in contradiction to the requirements of the economic order.

Thus the contradictions embedded within the vision of the Great Society are embedded in a variety of other social reform organisations, not least within NWRO. The war on poverty was to be seen as an attempt to overcome these contradictions, and to bring a critical dimension of citizenship to an excluded group within society. This dimension was what T. H. Marshall in a prescient essay, (1965) has termed the third aspect of citizenship, the area of social and welfare rights which, in addition to the historically primary requirements of voting rights and legal rights, was needed for the fulfilment of liberal democracy. It was the pursuit of these welfare rights which Federal government—and NWRO with distinctly fewer reservations —were to seek in the 1960s. NWROs main organising slogan was appropriately enough 'Bread and Justice!'.

The Birth of a Movement

NWRO was thus very much the child of the civil rights movement and the poverty programme. Like the civil rights movement itself NWRO is a radical phenomenon without being part of the radical movement, its history deeply involved with the struggle for civil rights both in thinking and in terms of the common background of leading members. In 1954, perhaps not insignificantly the year of the Supreme Court decision on desegregation, Jacobus Ten Broek (1954:239), the distinguished political scientist, published an article on public assistance in UCLA Law Review, which raised the question of the citizenship loss of the welfare recipient. He wrote: 'the individual soon loses control of his daily activities and his whole course and direction of his life, the capacity for self-direction presently atrophies and drops away. It is the welfare agency rather than the individual which decides which wants should be taken into account, the social worker exercised control . . . leads to an excessive intimacy which invites the arbitrary and whimsical uses of power.' Subsequently Charles Reich's (1963) legal consideration of the midnight searches used by the welfare investigators to harrass unsupported mothers raised the issue of the civil liberties status of welfare recipients. He argued that these women were effectively being denied their citizenship, guaranteed to them under the Constitution, by the activities of the welfare department. By stressing the citizenship deprivation of welfare recipients these early papers were able to mobilize American Civil Liberties Union on the side of the recipients. Reich's other, and legally revolutionary idea, was to argue that welfare benefits were new forms of property (1964). This notion, while it received a good deal of attention and was compatible with the arguments developed by Marshall in his discussion of citizenship, never gained clear acceptance in the courts.

At this stage, during the mid-sixties, the welfare recipients' lawyers, such at Ed Sparer, the founder of the Columbia Centre of Social Welfare Policy and Law, saw themselves as 'not merely as a technician whose function was to help the welfare system conform to what the elected representatives of the majority had agreed it should be. His mission was to utilise the legal process to help change the very nature of the welfare system, and, thereby, to change the ground rules of American society. No mere legal technician, he was a grand strategist. No mere advocate of other people's yearnings, he yearned for the change with his clients' (Sparer 1965: 363).

While disenchantment was to grow among the most committed lawyers, partly because of the changes in the Supreme Court and partly because of the way which poverty law became the new careerism, so that as Sparer observed 'the profession as a trade does more to support the lawyer than it does for his impoverished client', none the less throughout the sixties lawyers were to serve the welfare rights movement as they had served civil rights the previous decade.

Linking this legal suit with the mass mobilisation of community action, on a nationwide, not merely community basis, was to become the distinctive characteristic of the NWRO. In this way the welfare rights movement hoped to overcome the geographic specificity of community action which isolated can serve to preclude the kind of social change required in a large and complex society. Local actions, however militantly conducted, in for example the style of Saul Alinsky, the highly influential Chicagoan community organiser, can by their nature be isolated and contained. Thus community organising can, if only locally orientated, become like a case work procedure writ large, as an expressive—and maybe cheaper—way of adjusting people to accept a social and physical environment determined by others. In the new model one risk is that cooling people in, becomes a community rather than an individual activity.[3]

The contribution of first the civil rights movement and subsequently the welfare rights movement was to take community action, that is collective action based on the place of living as against that of working, and link it to a nationwide conception of change.

The sequence of events which led to the development of NWRO began in the internal criticism which civil rights organisations underwent during the early sixties. Up to that point most of them had contained both black and white members, from thence onwards most, particularly the most militant, were to continue as black separatist groups.[4] The Congress for Racial Equality was one such group, where the director James Farmer and his assistant George Wiley were, while black, unwilling to adopt the new separatist black power politics. Wiley who was eventually to become NWRO's first director, as a result of this internal struggle within CORE returned to the University of Syracuse where he had a teaching post in chemistry.

Consequently he was ready to listen to the suggestion made to him by S. M. Miller, a sociologist and welfare expert serving on CORE's research advisory group, where a welfare rights campaign had been discussed, that he, Wiley, join Citizens Crusade against Poverty. Instigated by Richard Boone (the Executive's chief draftsman for the community action aspects of the OEO programme) the Citizens Crusade—backed by such notables as: Walter Reuther, head of the Automobile Workers (UAW), Roy Wilkins of the National Association for the Advancement of Coloured Peoples, Dr. Eugene Carson Blake of the World Council of Churches, and Bayard Rustin—as the conscience of the OEO programme, holding a watching brief as it were for the poor. The opening public meeting of the Citizens Crusade was however a debacle. Foreshadowing events which were to

become routinised as part of the politics of poverty, the poor themselves attended and ruptured the polite concern of the meeting with
their demands. While the Crusade had invited the head of OEO
Sargent Shriver, to speak, it was Unity Blackwell's intervention, a
welfare recipient from Mississippi, which was to indicate the significance of 'Maximum feasible participation', 'help us', she said, 'catch
up—if you don't we'll run off and leave you' (Donovan 1967).

While Reuther was affronted by the presumptions of a welfare
recipient daring to speak about poverty at a meeting of experts (he
withdrew his promise of UAW money of $1 million), and Shriver
appeared to be hurt by the ingratitude of the poor, Wiley was better
equipped to recognise the embryo of a new political constituency and
its potential. Leaving the Crusade, Wiley became increasingly involved
with other academics and intellectuals such as Richard Cloward,
Richard Elman and Frances Fox Piven; gradually the idea of the
Poverty Rights Action Centre emerged, and within the year was
established in Washington as a reality.

A meeting in Syracuse, ostensibly to criticise the university for
closing down an OEO community organisers programme directed by
Warren Hagstrom,[5] played a similar catalytic rôle. While the manifest
agenda was how to shame the university into backing down (the
community organisers fieldwork directed by Warren Hagstrom had
been working against bad landlords—unfortunately one of the worst
was the university itself) the latent agenda was to discuss ways of
organising against poverty. It was an important meeting, not only
attended by the experts in poverty and the community organisers such
as Cloward, Piven and Miller, but also by the recognised leadership
of the oppressed minorities such as Cesar Chavez the grape pickers'
organiser, Martin Luther King of the Southern Christian Leadership
Conference and Jesse James, a Chicago priest and organiser. Chavez
particularly spoke eloquently of the potentiality of uniting all poor
people, but it was Richard Cloward who was to set out the programme
for (1) fund raising (2) setting up a poverty rights action group and
(3) linking up the various poverty groups into a nationwide movement.

For Cloward the idea of a poverty rights action centre stemmed
logically out of his earlier theoretical and practical work. As a crimin-
ologist (author with Ohlin of *Delinquency and Opportunity*) together
with James McCarthy as the administrative director and George

Braeger as the programme director, he had become a research director involved in the 1962 Mobilisation for Youth Project (MFY). This pioneering anti-delinquency project backed by the National Institute for Mental Health, the Ford Foundation and New York City, formed a pilot project to both the ideas and schemes which were to be worked out both as part of the War on Poverty and also as NWRO's strategy (Marris and Rein 1967: 19).

One of the key organising tools had been 'the neighbourhood store front' as a legal advice and community work base. The pioneer was the Stanton Street storefront in New York's Harlem, which rapidly became occupied with landlord/tenant issues and the stubborn facts of poverty. A theory of advocacy was developed out of the practice of the storefront together with a growing commitment to organising both on poverty and tenant issues. A theoretical justification for the militancy of the organising strategies was provided by George Braeger (1969) who argued that extremely poor people required targets and militant tactics to be moved from the profound inertia of long standing poverty (Braeger along with Hagstrom thus provided the community work justification for a militant style of work for very oppressed groups as against, for example, the enabling strategies suitable for use with locally influential people in community development).

Initially Stanton Street had been staffed by rights minded social workers; gradually they were stiffened by four lawyers to back them up. By 1965 the welfare families, organised by Ezra Birnbaum, the Stanton Street organiser, were well enough together to go for a winter grants campaign and also secure a meeting with the New York Commissioner of Welfare. A meeting which, because it yielded more money for recipients, helped foster a growing militancy and a rapidly growing membership.

The Crisis Theory of Welfare

The lessons derived from the Stanton Street phase were codified in an important series of articles published by *The Nation* during the early months of 1966 written by Cloward, first with Richard Elman (1966) and then with Frances Fox Piven (1966). The articles defined the nature of the welfare state, they spoke of the need for an ombudsman, and the need to mobilise the poor and create non-professional advocates to work with lawyers. The aim was to break the existing mosaic of welfare provisions and bring about one nationwide and just system of welfare.

Cloward and Piven's strategy crystalised around two main themes: the first was passive—the weight of the poor; the second was active—the power of disruption. The theory behind the weight of the poor was that as poor people were excluded from the welfare rolls, either by administrative process or by people's fear of stigma, society never felt the full extent of the problem. A campaign of massive enrollment was to be opened so that the sheer numbers of the poor, massively and passively would break the existing welfare systems and compel far-reaching reform. The second theme was the active pursuit of disruption, arguing that with little or nothing to lose, disruption would expose the injustice and malfunctioning of the welfare system. Thus the core of their strategy was of a piece with the theory of the civil rights movement—substituting enrollment for voter registration and disruption of welfare centres for the freedom rides to the South. Overall the theory bore evidence of the common stock—and in the ex-CORE workers' case, and there were several in NWRO—common personnel; its updating and its claim as a crisis theory of welfare came from an infusion of Alinsky-style rough, tough politics into the common inheritance.

Gilbert Steiner (1971:283) in an account sympathetic both to NWRO and to George Wiley, argues—not unlike Braeger—that because of the 'nature of the constituency which would be disaffected by long time lag between planning and results, Wiley had to move to action rapidly if he was to attract followers'. In fact the activity which was to lead up to the successful launching of NWRO in June 1966 was to involve not only the whole of Wiley's considerable energies but those of many others pursuing similar ends. Using the Washington office as a base, Wiley was an indefatigable traveller, meeting small embryonic welfare rights groups, talking with church and community leaders to encourage the setting-up of others. Cloward and Piven wrote and distributed some 20,000 leaflets urging the welfare rights strategy.

Such is the nature of welfare and community organising that these spontaneous groups neither knew of each others' quite near existence, nor of a nationwide movement, until they were linked up by George Wiley or his two assistants; first Edwin Day then Timothy Sampson (both, like Wiley, ex-CORE workers). Like Alinsky's model they operated as organisers of organisations rather than as building a movement from scratch upwards, as for example the Claimants Unions were to do in Britain. Not for nothing was the link of a chain chosen as NWRO's symbol.

The Ohio Example

The opportunity for action was presented by the high level of organisation already achieved by Ohio. In terms of practical action, the Ohioans would probably argue that they were ahead even of New York. The Rev. Paul Younger (there is a Paul Younger medal for the best organiser each year at NWRO) together with Edith Doering, had planned a march from Cleveland to the capital Columbus to lobby the Governor on the issue of inadequate welfare provision—which was then under 70 per cent. of the federal benefit levels. When the small group of forty marchers reached Columbus after a 115 mile walk they found not only that 2,000 recipients and friends were there to meet them, but also that joint actions had been triggered off, through NWRO's prompting, from Boston to Los Angeles, San Francisco to New York and Chicago. All in all NWRO was able to claim that over 6,000 recipients had demonstrated for their rights.

This series of demonstrations opened the way to the successful inauguration of NWRO in the month following. After a further 8 months of fairly continuous, if small, actions, it was possible to convene a nationwide meeting of welfare rights groups. Immensely varied in name and constituency, from West Side Mothers from Detroit to Kentucky's Committee to Save Unemployed Fathers—a group of white unemployed miners—NWRO enrolled them to act together. Gradually, despite the diversity of names, the main constituency and most of the leadership emerged as black women in their mid-thirties. While American Indians, Chicanos, Puerto Ricans and poor whites were members, the black AFDC (Aid to Families with Dependent Children) mothers were pre-eminent. At times the togetherness rhetoric of NWRO bound the separatist tendencies of the diverse ethnic communities.

Some of the earliest women leaders to emerge at this stage became the present leadership of NWRO, like Johnnie Tillmon (a pioneer welfare rights organiser in Watts, Los Angeles, with five children, so that in early political meetings she always took the baby) who became and held for five years the Chairmanship of the organisation, stepping down in 1971 to join the Washington staff.

Problems of Organising

One basic dilemma of building an organisation of the dispossessed is that as people are organised they gain in confidence and can either be co-opted or creamed off into the work situation. As indigenous leaders emerge they are either able to find jobs through their new skills or, particularly in the context of a poverty programme, they become hired as 'participators', as professional poor people. On the fairly standard $10,000 a year, perhaps, nearly three times what a woman with three children would get on welfare, the ex-AFDC mother is supposed to represent, even while she is herself changing and with new possibilities opening for her children, the people she has left behind. Another interpretation of maximum feasible participation might well be maximum feasible co-option. Certainly more than one observer long experienced in community politics, has observed that the OEO budgets paying salaries, baby sitters, travel expenses, although it mobilised the poor, also bought them.

NWRO, like other poverty agencies, took leaders who ran two or three blocks, a task which in the context of the physically and psychologically raw life of the ghetto is no small achievement, and, through linking up the little groups, made local leaders into players on a national pitch, sometimes even international as both Johnnie Tillmon, when chairman, went to a Helsinki social welfare meeting, and the present chairman, Beulah Sanders, has been to Paris to the Stockholm Peace Conference. Yet because the constitution was brought ready made by Sampson and Wiley to the groups in the process of linking them, the structure was not permitted to grow from the needs of the groups but was imposed on them externally. The constitution is a parliamentary model whereby local groups elect members to higher organisations, at city, state and eventually national levels, however, its weakness is that its apparent democratic form became easily manipulable, both by the political leadership and also by the civil service (the staff) who ostensibly neutrally serve it. There is an insufficient thrust from the grass roots (and the scale of American society exacerbates rather than eases the problem) to control the leadership, and maintain its accountability to the membership. Thus one of the first acts of the National Executive Committee was to examine the constitution and double the period of time that members were allowed to serve on the National Committee.

The everyday reality of being a member recipient as against being a leader recipient forms too sharp a contrast for the leadership to be renewed easily, and most of the original leadership located by Wiley are still around. The hierarchical structure helps the leaders stay leaders, and despite some power struggles within the elite, which have changed the order of dominance within it and have excluded a few, broadly speaking it appears to facilitate the fulfilment of Michels' iron law of oligarchy. Even within the constitution some anomolies continued to exist, in that it was not the chairman of a state or city group who represented the area but a 'representative' whose authenticity as a local activist working in a local group might be seriously at question—a problem clearly left over from the period when the original link up phase was taking place. The dilemma is that despite both leaders and the staff being conscious of this particular issue, resolving it would have required existing leadership to have voted themselves out of office.

These problems of developing the right structure for the organisation and the renewal of the leadership were not problems which troubled NWRO in its growth phase. Once NWRO had reached its fifth and sixth year (1971-72) and could no longer take for granted massive involvement, problems of organisation began to be extensively debated. The owl of Minerva flew as usual, only at the dusk.

In the early phase it seemed that all forms of social action were equal. There was room for the militant street shouter and for the soft spoken lobbyist: the confidence of the movement knew no bounds. One year after the Ohio march NWRO was able to mobilise marches in 50 cities. Few were large yet NWRO was able to report in its newsletter *The Welfare Fighter* that 5,000 recipients had taken part. *The Welfare Fighter* was launched early on in the life of the organisation and acted as an effective means of keeping the movement in touch. The simple technique of reproducing press articles about local actions fostered confidence and emulative actions. Its coverage was of current issues both within the movement and within the welfare field, so that it stood—in Gilbert Steiner's expression—to poverty what *Variety* is to the stage—'indispensable' (Steiner 1971:286). With these means the NWRO was able to congratulate itself at its first national annual convention that the number of active welfare rights groups had doubled, with 161 locals from 37 states as against 67 locals from 19 states. Membership too had doubled, so that individual paid-up membership was around 5,000, and through families some 30,000 people were involved.

Recipients were mobilised chiefly around the prospect of getting special grants, much as they had in the Stanton Street Storefront. It was a new experience to recipients to learn that they had 'rights' to a washing machine, a telephone, furniture or clothing. Several blocks would be leafleted with checklists of rights, and residents were invited to complete the checklist and visit the welfare rights group for help. In New York the Republican Commissioner, J. R. Goldberg, (subsequently he resigned to become Director of the Association of Social Workers) attempted to defend the Republican administration by agreeing that of course it wanted people to get their rights and attempted to blame the Democrat administration of the previous 16 years for the deprivation. This sort of liberal attitude, particularly in New York with a Harlem steadily near the boil, aided the kinds of weapons of popular advocacy, lawyers and militant demonstrations which NWRO was able to mount. (*Christian Science Monitor*, 17 August 1968.) Where most advocates of community power and people's organisation stress the gains of the rehumanisation of down-trodden people, of togetherness of struggling for power, NWRO was able to point to its work with the pleasure of a very satisfactory cost benefit analysis, or of a very militant trade union in a thriving expanding business. When the drive for special grants was begun in 1967 total payments on these were running at $3 million a month; after one year total payments were running at $13 million a month, with individual households having received as much as $1,000.

Thus very early on NWRO was able to establish collective bargaining. 'We don't believe in this one to one business. The time it takes to get rights for one can be better spent in getting rights for seven, or eight or fifteen.' Whereas in the U.K. context Claimants' Unions, despite their collective rhetoric, are in fact only able to fight on one case at a time—though the one may involve a family or a single person—neither they nor CPAG can fight or negotiate on behalf of a group let alone a whole class of persons. Partly this reflects their ideology in that unions dislike labelling people as 'handicapped' or 'unsupported mother' and instead talk about the interests of all claimants, and partly the structure of the law and that of social security preclude it. Even CPAG, which attempts to raise the arguments for a particular category of claimant is handicapped by the intense individualism of a highly discretionary system.

The sheer weight of numbers of US inner city dwellers, primarily blacks, who were coming onto welfare, rapidly enrolled more welfare fighters formally or informally. Recipients, sometimes organised by churches, or with minority group leadership, but not infrequently acting quite spontaneously, went down to the welfare centre demanding their rights and better treatment.

The feeling of the new power of the combined poor at the grass roots was a source of satisfaction. Passive recipients had become active welfare fighters: 'People call me and say they've been down there— the social services department—so many times and there'd always be some reason why they couldn't get on welfare. Then I and some of the ladies[6] would go with them and they'd always get on. Sometimes we didn't need even say anything, just went along and they'd help.' (*The Welfare Fighter*: 1972.)

More academically a research report carried out for the Department of Health and Welfare suggested that although by and large only a very small percentage (4 per cent.) of recipients were organised, in cities where they were organised, non-organised AFDC mothers felt more confident.

The fast growing local organisations were able to consolidate and routinise the gains from the important court findings. Kelly v. Goldberg (1969) gave recipients the right not to be cut off without a hearing, a finding of considerable significance for the movement as it enabled activists to act without the threat of termination of benefit. The movement was sustained by the injection of poverty lawyers supported by OEO. Piven and Cloward for example suggest that in 1968 as many as 1,800 lawyers were active in neighbourhood services (Piven & Cloward 1971:306). In one city, Philadelphia, OEO even in 1972 supported 35 lawyers in central and neighbourhood store-fronts. While it is estimated that only 3.0 per cent. of the cases the OEO lawyers dealt with related to poverty issues, the impact was considerable because (1) American courts can take 'class' actions and because (2) many of the lawyers tried to work with the organised welfare rights group, and the effect therefore was much greater than individual case work could possibly be.

Another significant achievement of the lawyers was to overturn residence requirements, which were defined as unconstitutional. This helped NWRO in a very practical way; meeting in a city out of their normal state, the ladies would often go and claim welfare to help them stay in the city for the duration of the conference or demonstration. But in addition to the attack of specific unconstitutional aspects of welfare law, the lawyers conducted a sustained campaign on process. The contribution of 'discretion' so carefully delineated in the pioneering work of Ten Broek as degrading the poor, was systematically attacked by the lawyers supported by the welfare rights groups.

Similar battles to those which CPAG and the Claimants' Unions fought for the recipient to bring a 'friend', whether lawyer or NWRO representative, with him to discuss his case were fought and won.

Lobby Politics

In NWRO where a practice had developed of regarding all forms of social action as equally useful, lobby politics existed from the very inception. Thus as early as 1967 *The Welfare Fighter* was reporting NWRO mothers, at a hearing of the Finance Committee chaired by Senator Russell Long, concerning the 1967 amendments to the Social Security Acts—The Work Incentive Programme (WIN) which threatened the AFDC mothers with a choice between taking job training or losing benefit. Long refused to hear NWRO; angered, the leadership turned its attentions to HEW which they alleged had been very weak in opposition to the bill. But the sophistication behind these political objectives indicated a lobby orientation which sat oddly with the grass roots nature of the leadership. What the ladies brought to lobby politics was an existentialist testimony as to what the experience of poverty meant. Within one year of its inception the combination of shrewd lobby politics on highly specific social security objectives together with a populist thump became the distinctive hallmark of NWRO political style.

Indeed insofar that the original Poverty Rights Action Centre, before the link up was achieved, was located in Washington, the lobby and Capitol Hill orientation was built in from the beginning. In parenthesis Macklin Street as the location of CPAG, conveniently between Fleet Street and the House of Commons is equally eloquent of its goals, whereas Claimants' Unions have no central office, spend less effort on cultivating the conventional media and apart from one early abortive essay when they visited R. H. S. Crossman, then Secretary of State at the D.H.S.S., they have totally eschewed lobby politics (Rose 1973).

This combination of grass roots activism, legal suit and lobbying was almost certainly Wiley's goal for welfare rights directly reflecting his, but not the leaderships' background in the civil rights movement. Although he has argued that initially the hope of the Poverty Rights Action Group was merely to act as a link, from early on Wiley saw that 'Welfare' was a unique system operated jointly by Federal, local and state governments. By involving people at the local level, eventually they would see the importance of change at the national level. Their involvement would likely be a continuing process of education. For a welfare recipient, for example, getting involved with his local welfare department would eventually lead him to see why it is important for him to get Congress to change (NWRO Journal, 1970).

Lobbying reflected not only Wiley's experience in CORE but also the interests of a substantial section of the rapidly growing staff at the Washington office. At the height of NWRO's strength in 1968/69 there were no less than fifty paid staff, mainly based in Washington but also employed as community organisers out in the cities. The political significance of the community organiser was instantly recognised by the leadership in a particular area and was echoed in the constant struggles between the ladies and the community organisers, which not infrequently concluded with the organiser being sacked from a given city but relocated by Washington in another. Particular organisers like Bill Pastereich in Boston or Bruce Thomas in Chicago, who were widely regarded as outstanding, were nonetheless regarded with distinct ambivalence by the ladies (Baillis 1972:188). Volunteer workers, such as those from the Vista programme, and social work students carrying out field placements were more successfully kept as subordinate to local leadership. Their tasks were more administrative than overtly political than those of the community organiser, who was not infrequently felt to be organising the local leadership. None the less there is little evidence to suggest a similar political perception of the power wielded by the Washington office in determining the strategies of NWRO. The rather formal hierarchical structure of the tiered democracy of the organisation and the immense geographical distances between cities meant that the concerns of the whole organisation, and thereby the movement, only with difficulty became the active collective concern of the leadership, which of necessity was preoccupied with maintaining its own power base within city and regional levels of the organisation. The parliamentary model led to certain problems well recognised in British political life, of powerful civil servants having a considerable influence over policy. Even linguistically Wiley for example was almost interchangeably defined as the *Director* of NWRO and the *Leader* of NWRO. It is a curious conception of a parliamentary model which appoints its chief civil servant as prime minister.

Thus the crisis theory of welfare with its single minded pursuit of the enrollment of all the poor on the welfare lists, as developed by Cloward and Piven, was transformed partly by Wiley's own conception of lobby politics linked to community action clout and partly by the inflexible organisational structure which facilitated the process. Wiley was clearly right when he argued that the original conception had ignored the need for poor people to receive constant successes in their struggles, because otherwise they disappeared into the apathy generated by chronic poverty, and also that organising people over a sustained period of time was more difficult than mobilizing them for a sharp short struggle. In either event within one year of the original discussions of the Poverty Action Centre, Cloward and Piven's strategy had been replaced by that of Wiley. British observers failed by and large to see this, impressed by the community action side and the mass activity, they tended to miss the lobby politicking and the WIN programme in 1967. So that in 1972 we have Robert Holman (1972: 548) writing in *New Society* of 'Changes in Welfare Rights', discussing what he saw as a shift towards lobby politics, when what had actually happened was that the steam had gone out of NWRO's community action wing, leaving the lobby politics uncomfortably exposed. Over the years between the inception of the movement and now there have been three major challenges to NWRO: the Civil Rights movement, internal issues and most seriously Nixon's welfare reforms. First we discuss the challenge from civil rights.

A Civil Rights Rival?

Given that Wiley's strategy was modelled on the civil rights movement when Martin Luther King and the Southern Christian Leadership Conference moved in onto the issue of poverty with the Poor People's Campaign, NWRO felt itself to be threatened. The charismatic quality and the all embracing rhetoric of the religious leaders, not least Martin Luther King, threatened to move the growing NWRO from the centre of the stage to the wings. Wiley criticised King for launching his campaign without taking into account all the grass roots welfare rights groups and, therefore, without taking into account NWRO, but by February 1968 Wiley had achieved recognition from King and NWRO was assured a place in the campaign.

In April of 1968 Martin Luther King was assassinated and riots broke out in many cities. The newsletter (*The Welfare Fighter*: 1968 II, 6) carried a plain cover with black printing quoting Joe Hill the framed IWW martyr 'Don't mourn, organise'. Inside it reported the arrest of 37 NWRO leaders who had gone to Capitol Hill to hold a night long vigil. Later, on the eve of the Poor People's Campaign Wiley and the leadership together with Coretta King, Luther King's widow, marched through the burnt-out riot areas in Washington. There were several arrests ensuing from the march, which SCLC appeared to use as a reason for leaving the militant NWRO to one side in the ensuing campaign.

While the SCLC pledged that Resurrection City would remain until the system changed, it tamely agreed to close the city once the police threatened to arrest everyone. Their rhetoric was much tougher than their actions and there can be little doubt that the financial and psychological costs of the Poor People's Campaign were borne by the poor themselves and not by the state, city hall or even the middle classes. Although it is difficult to criticise King, who is regarded with respect by most blacks, his political style had certain long term weaknesses. He and his aides would select an issue, move in on it, mobilise an action, declare a victory and move off. In the issue however King could be a very tough politician; unfortunately his heirs on this occasion, perhaps shaken through his loss, were not, and the Poor People's Campaign and Resurrection City were by and large disastrous. What the poor needed was organising patiently over a period of years; three month or even six month campaigns were not enough.

After the setbacks of the Poor People's Campaign, which in the event NWRO might well have been glad not to have been massively involved in, the organisation went back to basic organising around trade union bread and butter issues. Warming up with a school clothing campaign the November *Welfare Fighter* (1968, II, 6) declared a special Winter Action Campaign; briskly rejecting traditional charitable relief they came out with a new slogan of 'Bread and Justice'. Their message was 'No thanks but no thanks America for your Thanksgiving baskets of beans and used clothing ... Salvation Army Xmas stockings

. . . soup line dinners . . . second hand toys'. Recipients could and did respond to these concrete and gettable goals and sit-ins and demonstrations proliferated. The newsletter, basically a collage of news clippings, reported actions in 19 cities. Chiefly by collating newsclippings but also with articles and news about poverty figures, whether leaders in the movement or one of the enemy, *The Welfare Fighter* played and continued to play a crucial informing and linking rôle in the movement. Always important in keeping people together, a movement's newspaper is doubly important in the context of an immensely large —numerically and geographically—society.

A Separatist Challenge?

Crisis is endemic in community organising but only one major crisis within NWRO has emerged into public. In 1969 when the Panthers and Black Power were becoming increasingly evident and therefore black consciousness was generally much higher, John Lewis, a black in charge of publications at the Washington head office, criticised the central office for having 'paternalistic, frequently racist attitudes about the policy decisions the recipients themselves should have made'. (*Washington Afro-American* 1969.)

Wiley handled the crisis with the aid of Hulbert James, also black, who after two years' effective organising in New York City had gone to the national office. With James' aid Wiley was able to fight off the challenge. Almost certainly a major reason for Wiley's success was that, although it was and remains true that there is racism within the organisation, insofar that mass organisations tend, unless there is an immense advance in consciousness, to carry over many of the attributes of the society they oppose, there is a deep and possibly deeper division between the professionals, that is the paid staff, and the AFDC leadership. The recipients were not ready to drop one tried black professional—Wiley, for another untried black professional— Lewis. A real challenge would be constituted by a recipient bid for the Directorship. Wiley was extremely gifted; he was also one of the few men in a predominantly women's world. This gave him a rôle which very few could play but which if they can, provides a curious security.

A great deal of Wiley's skill lay in his considerable ability to make good rhetoric and to act pragmatically. Thus while the first lobby campaign in 1967 was to denounce the work incentive amendments to the social security act—the WIN programme—Wiley backed by the Washington office, in fact accepted a $400,000 contract from the Department of Labour in 1968 as part of WIN programme. Resented fairly widely by the ladies as savouring of a sell out, only Philadelphia WRO went public in their denunciation. Steering between sell out and survival is an every day dilemma and while Wiley and the staff were able to convince the leadership that it was a rip off to help NWRO train more advocates and organisers, the problem until NWRO is self-funding continues. What perhaps is even more significant is that AFDC women perceived taking the contract as a political set back, the organisational requirements such as the several thousands of dollars needed to convene a meeting of the National Executive drawn from all over the States, or to maintain the office itself, compelled a compromise. Where the Lewis/Wiley struggle had been between more or less radical ideologies held by two professionals, it had not seemed an important issue to the AFDC leadership. The WIN contract was however their issue, but the organisational requirements ensured that they lost it.

Nixon's Challenge to NWRO

The major external challenge to NWRO was posed by Nixon's structural reforms to welfare—the Family Assistance Programme (initially set out in his welfare speech in August 1969). It was not easy for NWRO, or its allies the special policy analysts, to classify it immediately as success or defeat, which was clearly, as Marmor and Rein (1972) have pointed out, its intention. FAP represented the major nationwide reform which NWRO had campaigned for, yet one in which the levels were pitched so low as to be under those of all but eight poor Southern States. Finally after Cloward, Piven, Sparer, most of the key poverty analysts working closely with NWRO had argued it through, Wiley and NWRO decided to come out strongly against FAP. To have done otherwise would have meant welcoming lower rates—a certain route of alienating the membership—in pursuit of uniformity.

Deeper than ever into lobby politics, NWRO had to attack FAP on the grounds of its illiberality and at the same time expose those not inconsiderable numbers of congressmen, who were anti-FAP not as reformers but because however little the individual household received the national bill was 'crippling'. FAP was defeated at its first reading in the summer of 1970 and for those sections of NWRO staff most Capitol Hill oriented, it was seen as a great victory. Because the FAP story reflects the phase when NWRO appeared to be solely preoccupied with lobby politicking, some of the labyrinthine activity is reported below so that the organisational effort required from NWRO is recognised.

In the following June Nixon and the chairman of the Ways and Means Committee, Wilbur Mills, managed to persuade the House to pass a revised version. Written in closed committee, little was known about the revised bill (HRI) except insofar as it had been foreshadowed in Reagan's California system, until it was presented on May 26 1971. Immediately social policy experts, social workers' associations, concerned groups such as churches and welfare rights groups began to analyse and comment on it. The Detroit local chapter of the Association of Social Workers circulated a document both explaining and analysing the bill. They described HRI as 'in general, the aged and disabled come off well in the overall picture and the impact on families is mixed according to their location and categories within the group. Certainly the traditional concepts of a universal state-wide system of public welfare system that has prevailed since 1935 is totally rejected.' They went on to cite the black caucus in Congress who regarded the bill as 'institutionalised racism', in that the target in the bill was the AFDC mothers and their children. 'White congressmen have stated on the floor that the problem is black women and their illegitimate children' (Detroit A. S. W. July 27 1971).

In a similar vein, Senator Russell Long's address to the key Finance Committee, of which he is chairman, where hearings were to take place, was published as *The Welfare Mess—a Scandal of Illegitimacy and Desertion* (U.S. Government: 1971). Long was able to find poverty experts on his side and cited approvingly an article by D. P. Moynihan, the chief architect of the original FAP scheme, published in 1968 (The Welfare Crisis). In this Moynihan attacks the 'freedom' of the poor, 'to abandon their children in the certain knowledge that society will care for them' . . . he goes on to recall some idyllic past where if a man did abandon his family either they would starve or he would be brought back and horse whipped. Moynihan finished with a hymn of praise to the responsible middle-class-alimony-paying husband (omitting any mention of any possible tax allowance and therefore state subsidy).

As the organisation of the AFCD mother, NWRO was compelled to enter the lists. Alternative reforms were suggested; for example NWRO was initially interested in Senator Ribicoff's Amendment, until it became clear that this was only going to be very marginally better than the HRI Bill already passed in the House. In cash terms Ribicoff's Amendment meant $3,000 for a family of four whereas HRI meant $2,400 per annum. Fred Harris, a liberal Senator friendly to NWRO, had put in a rival scheme which would have yielded $4,000 per annum—the official federal poverty line. The most generous scheme was proposed by Senator McGovern, a presidential candidate and therefore presumably interested both in welfare reform for its own sake and as a means of securing the black vote; his proposals bore the mark of NWRO's involvement. The budget for a family of four was $6,500, and was to be adjusted both to local variations in the cost of living and also to the median family income in the USA in the years ahead. To all intents and purposes this was NWRO's bill, which when its financial implications were costed during McGovern's election campaign, he withdrew from in some embarrassment. To be fair, all the proposals, other than HRI, contained some measures of defence against inflation.

On civil liberties issues HRI was the most oppressive, even seeking to deny benefit to recipients (and therefore the children of recipients) where the recipient was incapacitated through drug or alcohol abuse and was unwilling to accept treatment. No other proposal suggested this. However while both Ribicoff's Amendment and HRI were pre-occupied with the question of the deserting parent crossing the state line, i.e. the black AFDC father could be fined $4,000 or sent to prison for a year or both, neither the Harris nor McGovern versions proposed this. HRI showed that it had no affection for representatives for recipients, proposing to limit them to persons 'of good character' and 'able to render claimants invaluable service' and 'otherwise competent'.

Thus FAP, now HRI, despite its apparent reformist elements, represented a formidable reversion to poor law legislation. Most of NWRO's national effort has therefore been devoted, particularly from the summer of 1971, towards working against the measure and against the three demonstration projects which New York, Illinois and California had sought permission to implement as pilot projects prior to the passing of the bill. However, because of Nixon's 'New Economic Programme', the administration subsequently announced its intention to postpone completing the bill for a year. In any event the opposition from the right as well as from the liberal wing of the House, left its political viability in doubt.

The elaborate exercise which NWRO had to pursue in response to FAP focused most of its time and talent towards Capitol Hill. While the AFDC leadership became well aware of the precise implications of the proposal, educating the membership proved to be an intractable task. During the autumn and winter of 1971 NWRO attempted to mobilise against the demonstration projects. Elizabeth Wickenden, in a commentary on the projects noted that the area selected in New York is 50:50 Puerto Rican and Black, and suggested that at least 24,000 people would be affected, drawn from some 7,000 families. Their grants could be cut from between 36 per cent. to as much as 50 per cent., but could be earned back by 'good behaviour' on the part of the recipients and their children. 'Good behaviour' is to be determined by the social worker and the school teacher.

Despite Wiley's own involvement in New York City the community remained inactive. Despite intense organisational effort the period of the massive street demonstrations, where the New York NWRO members tore a Welfare Centre apart, or the screaming of the ladies in Boston when the police attacked them which produced a three day and night city riot, was over. Nixon had not only snarled up NWRO with FAP, but had also changed the nature of the Indo-China war. His policy of Vietnamisation and escalation of the air war, meant that while the domestic war economy would continue with its profitability for the defence industry but its general inflationary effects, he had changed the colour of the corpses. For American blacks in particular, for who going to the war, being poor and being black were tied in one bag, Nixon had cut the string. Thus if it is possible to cite one factor which has reduced the pressure on the cities, from near breaking point back to chronic strain, this, the changing nature of the war would be the one. FAP demonstration projects, despite a major organisation effort failed. Lacking a ground swell, and unable to create one through organisational activity, NWRO turned by the winter of 1971 to find strength from new alliances with other movements. Eminent figures such as Gloria Steinem from the women's movement, or Dr. Spock from the Anti-War movement appeared on NWRO platforms. During the following spring the NWRO strategists attempted to shift the image of the movement away from the AFDC

mothers to their children, implicitly shifting the ideological justification of the movement from justice to compassion. The Children's
March for Survival took place at Easter (1972) but failed to secure
the media coverage and support which would have given encouragement for further actions (*Welfare Fighter*: 1972). The following year
George Wiley resigned and was not long after drowned in a boating
accident. Even though no longer active within NWRO, the loss was a
further blow. 'Sometimes we don't even have to have our leadership
assassinated.'[7]

Presently NWRO continues, a social form but an almost spent
force, finding it difficult to secure financial aid from churches, founda-
tions or government programmes, in a context where the deepening
economic crisis brings in its train other priorities than the situation of
poor black Americans. In addition apart from the aid of SDS students
in the earliest phase of establishing the grass roots organisation,
NWRO was for the most part left alone by political groups. Since
1971 however, the National Caucus of Labour Committees has inter-
vened in the organisation, claiming that the declining movement could
be rebuilt and new alliances created with workers and students. A few
of the leadership, particularly from New York and Philadelphia,
joined NCLC in a Committee to rebuild the NWRO. The majority
remained loyal. Thus in addition to the struggles within the leadership
primarily concerning the relative power of particular cities within the
National Committee, which had been a continuous feature of organisational life, a new kind of problem was introduced by the vociferous
presence of NCLC.

Achievements and Lessons

Looking back over the history of NWRO, and trying to make some
assessment of the welfare rights movement, we have to begin by
recognising its significance to those tens of thousands of recipients
who, whether they were formally members or not, felt themselves to
be part of the movement. Thus before we ask whether its decline in
the seventies was an inexorable aspect of the natural history of a social
movement, or whether different objectives and organisational forms
would have achieved more, we have to begin by acknowledging the
solid material gains and growth of self confidence among people
previously crushed by not only the oppression of poverty but for
many, also by the oppression of racism. To meet NWRO in action

was to meet a collectivity, whose self confidence and even gaiety continuously broke through a hard and at times physically dangerous struggle.

Poverty is an intensely isolating experience in advanced capitalist society, where rarely are people living and working together so generating the *gemeinschaft* which made for example the poverty undergone by the mining village in a depression endurable. What NWRO did was to take the isolated and private problem of poverty and transform it within the consciousness of those experiencing the situation into a public and social problem. The central principle of the welfare system, discretion, which served to isolate recipient from recipient, was seized by the movement, used as a key organising tool and turned back on the system itself.

None the less even from the all too brief account of the welfare rights movement presented here, it is evident that from the first year of NWRO's history there were two distinct innovative social forms balanced uneasily within the organisation. During the growth phase the incompatibility of these two, the pressure group focused on the Washington office and the local community action, was not seen as important. The high level of activity and exhilaration of the movement hindered the development of understanding of the contradictions embedded in the two social forms. Only when the level of mass involvement began to decline was it unambiguously plain that the rôle of the membership had been to legitimise and reinforce the activities of the pressure group.

Thus while the pressure group was able to mobilise the mass movement to block particular unfavourable developments like the Nixon bill, the very specificity of objectives and the rigidity of the ready made constitution inhibited the development of policy and new organisational forms through the thinking of the membership itself. Strategically, given that NWRO was operating in a large society where a nationwide meeting required considerable resources, the specificity of pressure group's objectives as against the unstructured and unopened character of a mass movement, the former was clearly an easier and in a sense more defensible choice. However, the corollary was that the movement was guided politically rather than served by its own experts—despite- or perhaps because of- the parliamentary model.

For that matter even the crisis theory of welfare which initially inspired the movement, failed to account for the relationship between the organised and the objectives of the movement. It was rather a theory of mobilisation to break the welfare system than one of organisation. Thus despite the crisis theory's dual strategy of enrolment plus disruption, it remains—despite Piven and Cloward's manifest enthusiasm for the activities of the movement—that the theory is one of passive materialism; that is, it does not articulate any organisational ways which the dialectical relationship between the subjective consciousness of the movement and the goals of the movement can be developed. Put another way the crisis theory was unable to receive the knowledge input derived from the experience of people themselves. Thus, at a strategic level, despite the immense innovatory strength of NWRO, in both the crisis model and the pressure model, the members of NWRO were footsoldiers led by professional generals.

In practical terms this meant that the development of alliances at a grass roots level with sections of the working class, the black or the women's movements was never fostered within either strategy. Only in decline did NWRO seek such alliances through the symbolic appearance on its platforms of elite members from other movements. Consequently where in the past the poor had been individually alone, they were in NWRO collectively alone. A theory of community action, that is action based on the problems of making a home rather than making a living, has—even though there are profound difficulties of so doing—to be related to a general theory of class, race and sex antagonisms within society. Thus the hardest lesson from the experience of the US welfare rights movement is the theoretical necessity to locate community action in a context larger than the welfare system, is that otherwise the state—central or local—can isolate and manipulate the action, resolving its own internal contradictions by renewing the social system through the innovations secured by the movement.

Footnotes

[1] A similar example of welfare policies exacerbating economic problems for a subordinate group is that of the Catholics in Northern Ireland. Discrimination in housing and employment has acted as a multiplier of generally high unemployment levels, and encouraged Catholic migration. The differential birth rate between Catholics and Protestants, without this 'encouraged' migration, would in certain evenly distributed areas, such as Derry, have generated a Catholic majority.

² Depite Eliott Liebow's (1967), classic study *Tally's Corner* (itself possibly one of the last occasions for the foreseeable future when a white sociologist will be accepted into black society), this dislocation of the black urban family through the employment situation exacerbated by welfare was not widely recognised. White society preferred to blame the victim. D. P. Moynihan's (1965) influential report blamed the welfare situation on the failure of the Negro famly.

³ Exemplified by the Nottingdale Project reported by Ditton and Morrison (1972: 171).

⁴ A similar development was to occur in Britain with the internal criticism and disintegration of the Campaign Against Racial Discrimination and the emergence of black groups.

⁵ Hagstrom was trained by Alinsky, but in addition to these 'rough tough' techniques had a theory of the key rôle of the poor bringing about social change. Nearer to Martin Luther King's conception of the moral and therefore political significance of the black, than Marcuse's conception of the catalytic potential of the disposed, Hagstrom's theory nonetheless had the merit of bringing the dimension of powerlessness into a model of change through organising (Hagstrom 1964).

⁶ The 'ladies' now seems an odd word to describe the women's leadership of NWRO. Anachronistic because of the growth of the women's movement, 'lady' was originally insisted on to make sure that NWRO members were treated with respect. Now it is used half seriously and half self-mockingly: both attitudes speaking for the complexity of their situation.

⁷ Personal letter from a NWRO member, 1973.

References

L. Baillis (1972), *Bread or Justice: Grass Roots Organising in the Welfare Rights Movement*, Ph.D. Thesis, Harvard, unpublished.

G. Braeger (1969), 'Organising the Unaffiliated in Low-Income Areas', in A. Etzioni (ed.): *A Sociological Reader in Complex Organisations*, Holt, Reinhart and Winston.

R. A. Cloward and R. M. Elman (1966), 'Poverty and the Welfare State: Part I: An Ombudsman for the Poor', *Nation*, February 28, pp. 230-235.

R. A. Cloward and F. F. Piven (1966), 'Poverty, Injustice and the Welfare State: Part 2: How Can Rights be Secured?' *Nation*, March 7, pp. 264-268.

R. A. Cloward and F. F. Piven (1966), 'The Weight of the Poor', *Nation*, May 2, pp. 510-517.

R. Ditton and E. Morrison (1972), *A Community Project in Nottingdale,* Allen Lane.

J. C. Donovan (1967), *The Politics of Poverty*, Pegasus.

W. Hagstrom (1964), 'The Power of the Poor' in F. Reismann, J. Cohen and A. Read (eds.): *The Mental Health of the Poor*, Free Press, pp. 205-226.

W. Heller (1967), *New Dimensions of Political Economy*, Harvard University Press.

Bread and Justice: The National Welfare Rights Organisation

R. Holman (1972), 'Changes in American Welfare Rights', *New Society*, September 21, pp. 548-550.

Kerner Commission (1968), *Report of the National Advisory Commission on Civil Disorders*, U.S. Government, p. 252.

J. Lewis (1969), 'Black Voices' in *Washington Afro-American*, August 19, cited by G. Steiner.

E. Liebow (1967), *Tally's Corner, Washington D.C.: A Study of Street Corner Men*, Routledge and Kegan Paul.

E. B. McPherson (1973), *Democratic Theory: Essays in Retrieval*, Oxford University Press.

T. Marmor and M. Rein (1972), 'Helping America's Poor', *New Society*, May 11, pp. 286-289.

P. Marris and M. Rein (1967), *The Dilemma of Social Reform*, Routledge and Kegan Paul.

The Moynihan Report (1965), *The Negro Family: The Case for National Action*, Office of Policy Planning and Research, U.S. Department of Labor, also in L. Rainwater and W. Yancey (eds.): *The Moynihan Report and the Politics of Controversy*, M.I.T..

D. P. Moynihan (1968), *The Welfare Crisis*.

D. P. Moynihan (1969), *Maximum Feasible Misunderstanding; Community Action in the War on Poverty*, New York.

National Welfare Rights Journal (1970), November: December.

F. F. Piven and R. Cloward (1971), *Regulating the Poor: The Social Functions of Welfare*, Pantheon.

C. Reich (1963), 'Midnight Welfare Searches and the Social Security Act', *Yale Law Journal*, Vol. 72, pp. 1347-1360.

C. Reich (1964), 'The New Property', *Yale Law Journal*, Vol. 73, pp. 733-787.

Russell Long Committee (1971), *The Welfare Mess: A Scandal of Illegitimacy and Desertion*, U.S. Government, December 14.

E. Sparer (1965), 'The Rôle of the Welfare Clients' Lawyer', *UCLA Law Review*, 12, pp. 361-380.

G. Steiner (1971), *The State of Welfare*, Brookings Institution.

J. Ten Broeck (1954), 'Public Assistance: A Normative Evaluation', *UCLA Law Review*, pp. 237-264.

The Welfare Fighter (1967), I, 19.

The Welfare Fighter (1968), II, 6.

The Welfare Fighter (1968), II, 14.

COMMUNITY ACTION, QUASI-COMMUNITY ACTION AND ANTI-COMMUNITY ACTION

Norman Dennis

The empirical study of Booth Street's and Hume Street's nine new cottages is a very small and simple example of the typical civic experience of a community of stable, respectable working-class families—Millfield, Sunderland. The context within which I use the term 'typical' is the period of Millfield's community action from 1967 to May 1971 when I was active in its residents' association, and 1971-74 when I was also Labour councillor for the ward. In May 1972 I was joined as councillor by Bob Hudson whose views I shared. Widespread local support for the Millfield residents' association and the election to the council of two community activists indicated that in so far as Millfield's experience was defined as unfavourable, similar causes of disquiet had effected the area prior to 1967. I use the term 'typical' with particular confidence (i) in relation to housing and town planning and (ii) during and immediately after my term as councillor. As a councillor I was able to examine these problems from the inside. I was a party to the on-going decision-process itself. Under standing orders I was entitled to inspect any document which had been considered by the council or by one of its committees, so long as it was in connection with my duties as a councillor.

The whole range of decisions and performances in Millfield 1971-74 reproduces in larger, more complicated and therefore more inaccessible and incomprehensible form the elements of the issue to be analyzed here. These larger and more complex issues will be dealt with elsewhere: the Well Street road; the Ailesbury Street road; Ailesbury Street's 'lifing'; the Holly Terrace site; the Washington Street clearances; the Neville Road Triangle; Duke Street;[1] and Booth Street case in full,[2] and other issues. In Millfield I generalize from the total population of decisions, not a sample. My population of decisions is composed of all those made, or operative in the ward, during my three years as a councillor, and running on to the time of writing (mid-September 1974). For the town as a whole, other decision-complexes have been studied, some of which are significant from the viewpoint of community action. In these cases the study has not been of either a population or a sample of decisions. I have studied those which have happened to come before me and in which I have take a particular interest because of their relevance for my Millfield work. Examples of these are the judgmental model for housing, the general information system for planning (GISP), and the DOE-sponsored (and H.M.S.O.-published) urban guidelines project.[3]

In the study of Booth Street's nine new bungalows, the reader might quickly conclude that the full and simple explanation of the events described is my behaviour and Bob Hudson's. I find that implausible or at best very partial. First, the sort of problem-for-Millfield posed by civic intervention in its life preceded our interest and participation. It could not therefore have been created by it. Secondly, the same type of story could be told about other areas when studied in similar detail. In order to illustrate this I deal, also elsewhere, with what I call 'The Millburn Street Maze'. Thirdly, in connection with the general town-wide issues, it would be attributing to us an extraordinary high political status—for which there would be no other evidence—to explain their course in terms of the civic centre's reaction to our presence somewhere on the scene or in the wings. Sunderland borough's 'headquarters' staff, the bureaucracy proper (APT and C Grades), numbered over 1,300 in 1973. Out of the dozens dealing with Millfield, not to speak of the others, very few would have heard of us, or would have been able to name any councillor outside a handful of prominent politicians. Fourthly, the notion that our behaviour and the civic centre's reaction to it (which would then have to be seen as retaliation against innocent parties) takes us very far in understanding the issues, implies that had we acted differently, decisions would have been wiser, their implementation more efficient, and so forth. For example, it might be suggested that we ought to have endeavoured to make ourselves more influential in the Labour group of councillors. I ought to have aimed for high office and a key decision-taking position, as a chairman or at least a member of the executive committee. I should then have been at a point on the lever arm where committees and departments would have responded to a light touch, and moved in the required direction. If I had tried to reach such positions, whether I would have succeeded is an important but unanswerable question. Alternatively (people might say) we should have used to the full our professional status or reputation if any (which would have been news to most people with whom Millfield had to deal at the civic centre), and worked with officers in a spirit of equality and give-and-take. Again, if I had tried, whether I would have succeeded in establishing such a relationship is a moot point. But let us say I could have been in 'the smoke-filled room' or could have abided by the dictum 'professional shall speak unto professional', instead of acting almost exclusively as a ward councillor. I had lived in Millfield since the early 1960s and during the whole of my term as Millfield's ward councillor I was committed to the notion that nothing should be done to Millfielders that was not done with them. As an officer of the residents' association and as ward councillor, what I might achieve should be capable of being achieved, in principle, by any Millfielder of average intelligence and alertness, cognizant of those facts and procedures within the purview of a working-class layman, by using the channels supposedly available to him.

I cannot say for certain that if I had taken a place in the smoke-filled room or the air-conditioned office, more would not have been achieved practically to relieve Millfield's burdens. I know, on the contrary, that Jon Davies, my colleague in the Department of Social Studies and a Newcastle-upon-Tyne councillor, has indeed achieved a great deal by combining a community-action rôle with that of the *effective* politician in the local party as he finds it.[4] That demands tremendous stamina, skill and principle.

But I should like to make two comments. If one is not otherwise powerful, one's presence in the smoke-filled room or in the air-conditioned office is tolerated only for so long as one is congenial company. One soon ceases to be congenial company if one's insistent contribution to the proceedings is, howsoever delicately and diplomatically, to unite the same old bundle of stinking rags and say, 'I want something doing about these'. The men in the smoke-filled room and the air-conditioned office have higher and more important things to think about than that, or so they believe. My experience in Sunderland has been that wheeling and dealing within the party (with one of two exceptions) and negotiations with officialdom have resulted in the 'recognition' that there are bigger and more worthwhile things to worry about than the ward. Little or nothing in the way of benefits for Millfield or places like it to have been achieved by people who have followed this strategy. Community action in Millfield, on the other hand, can claim many victories, hard-won and qualified, but victories nevertheless. Even in Booth Street, where the final result is not yet known, the residents' experience has been preferred to what had otherwise been in store for them, conventional slum-clearance. The bad things that have happened would have happened anyway, and worse.

My second comment is that one of my own 'oughts' is that concrete achievements are important but, as I suggested above, the processes by which they are brought about are also important. They should be obtained in such a way as to strengthen those processes which will make similar achievements for the same people easier in the future. In that connection I have taken the view, together with my fellow-councillor for Millfield, Bob Hudson,[5] that temporary or iso-lated concessions might be obtained, or secured more quickly, by the fluke presence of exceptional people taking a place among an élite of influence, but that permanent and solid improvements in the quality of civic activity, as it impinges on people like the Millfielders, can come about only by their greater knowledge, and greater self-confidence in their ability to control their own destiny through machinery and measures *regularly* available to *them*. It has been increasingly borne in on me—and I believe my case studies amply illustrate and confirm this—that a very high proportion of the 'techni-cal' and 'political' facts and factors which are 'beyond the grasp' of Millfielders, are in reality perfectly comprehensible to any Millfield ten-year-old not in the bottom quarter of the intelligence distribution. Let me put this in a more extreme form. A very high proportion of what passes for 'civic expertise' in a place like Millfield is pretty plain nonsense to any intelligent ten-year-old *who has confidence in the validity of his own perceptions;* but his confidence and his per-ceptions are systematically and powerfully under attack by opponents (many or most no doubt well-meaning) decked in all the paraphernalia of prestige and scientific professionalism. The growth of the civic bureaucracy, far from making community action redundant or im-possible, calls it forth and makes it indispensible.

I should now like to concede every point a self-interested critic or friendly commentator might want to make against all the fore-going. Let me readily admit, for purposes of argument, that technocracy will and should be the pattern of the future. Let me readily concede that someone better-informed than me, someone politically more adept, someone socially more sophisticated, someone more flexible, someone with a wider sweep, someone more objective, etc. (or less), could have played a more effective part in tackling Millfield's problems, in this case an aspect of Booth Street's problems. Nevertheless, it seems to me to be sociologically interesting to analyze carefully what *did* happen and what processes *were* set in train when a distinctive stance, a community-action stance—or quasi-community-action stance if purists are offended—elegant or clumsy, efficacious or useless, *was* adopted by Bob Hudson and me, *vis-à-vis* our electorate, our party comrades, our political opponents and the civic-centre bureaucracy, in the pusuit of a specified, concrete, clear set of objectives set out by the local community itself.

I shall deal mainly with the issue of the nine new bungalows in the Booth Street area as the issue developed from November 1972 to the beginning of demolition in September 1974. The background, briefly, was this. The Booth Street area, two-and-a-half terraces of single-storey brick houses ('Sunderland cottages'), had been voted into the clearance programme in 1965 on the grounds that, in 1965, all the cottages (with at most one or two unlikely exceptions) were unfit for human habitation. Subsequently there were plans for a road directly across the area, which would have decimated it. There was another plan for straightening another road to the south of the area, which would have cost sixteen cottages. What part these road plans played in the origin of the clearance proposal is not known. Such a *wider* public interest *might* have justified demolition. When asked to present themselves for close inspection, both the plans rapidly disappeared from sight in the fog of the future. Without explanation, and just *prior* to council-initiated participation, clearance was postponed from 1968 to 1972, but fixed for 1972.

In 1971 inspections were carried out for the representation of the area to the health committee and then to the council for the formal decision on its clearance-area status. Eighty-one of the ninety-eight cottages (not all of them, as in 1965) were classified by the public health inspector as unfit. Cottage by cottage, the 1971 findings bore no relation at all to the 'facts' displayed in the 'participation exercise' of 1969, which had been presented as the results of a council survey superior in quality to any hitherto undertaken in this country.

In the case of most of the cottages, the 1971 unfitness findings were contrary to the inhabitants' ideas of what was reasonably suitable for accommodation, as they were to mine. In no sense were Booth Streeters 'slummy' families. No one has ever tried to suggest in any way that they were. Their standards of reasonable suitability, that is, were those of moderately prosperous working-class people who, as wage-earners or pensioners, in common-sense terms were good managers of their private and family affairs, good neighbours and good citizens. (I shall not attempt to define 'good' as a term of common sense beyond the minimum notion of 'not troublesome to themselves or others.')

They fought the clearance-area designation and the compulsory purchase order. Both were revoked in June 1972. It had been a remarkable victory for community action, for it included having the compulsory purchase order recalled from Whitehall, to which safe-haven it had been hurriedly shipped by the civic-centre bureaucracy, when the prospect of Booth Street's victory locally looked a definite possibility.

June 1972 was the end of a long period of blight, stretching at least as far back at 1952, and by that time about one-third of the families wanted to be rehoused by the council. Some of these were newcomers who had taken tenancies with the hope and intention of being rehoused in the slum-clearance programme. They saw this as the best and quickest way to a council house. Others were established families who had become sickened by the circumstances of uncertainty, corporation neglect of the environment, and the slow decline of the habitations due to lack of maintenance and improvement. Maintenance and improvement attracted no government grants, and in any case was discouraging in the light of 'imminent'—but always postponed—clearance. Others were families wishing to move for all sorts of normal reasons. They had accumulated in the area over the years due to (i) unwillingness of the housing department to consider tenants from a clearance area until clearance took place; (ii) the difficulty of owner-occupiers to find buyers for their 'about to be cleared' cottages, and of buyers to obtain mortgages from a building society. Many of the one-third who wished to move, therefore, occupied houses which in their view, and the view of potential buyers— working-class owner-occupiers—made good homes, if freed from the clearance, and especially if made eligible for repair and modernization subsidies.

The consensus of local opinion, thrashed out since 1967, was that perhaps as many as ten, or even fifteen (but certainly not more) cottages would fail to find owner-occupier buyers on the private market. Depending on their location and condition, they ought to be revitalized (which by-and-large would be the sensible thing to do) or, exceptionally, demolished.

Locally it was established that, at the *upper* limit, thirty families would want to be rehoused. Those who wanted to stay supported the families who wanted to leave. Those who wanted to leave supported those who wanted to stay, in saying that rehousing should be voluntary, not compulsorily imposed on everyone in the area.

Without realizing it, the civic centre set up an experimental situation to test their predictions and policy and the Booth Streeters'. They influenced, interpreted and applied policy in 'their' way in the Hume Street and Booth Street part of the area. But in the Pickard Street part of the area 'our' policy was in effect applied. The Pickard Street site is not a perfect rectangle, and was adjudged too awkward a shape to be dealt with. The civic centre therefore left individual houses alone, and made no special efforts to persuade owners to sell. Once the right to improvement grants had been established and the threat of clearance indubitably lifted, Pickard Street realized our most *optimistic* predictions. The only cottage to be sold to the council was No. 1, Wilson the dairyman's. This was one of the best cottages in the area. A price of £2,250 was negotiated for it (before the steep rise in house prices) and the Wilsons were given the tenancy of a brand-new council house of their choice. By mid-September 1974 the only problems in Pickard Street were Mrs. Bell, the tenant of No. 7 (the council had not been able to make an offer of accommodation acceptable to her, even though she was one of the original would-be 'leavers' and inhabited a poor cottage) and—the wreckage of No. 1.

That is the background. I now turn to the detail of the nine new bungalows the only contribution that the civic centre even attempted to present as a seriously pursued constructive effort towards fulfilling the policies which had constituted in 1972 the victory settlement of five years of community action. (The revitalization of the corporation-owned property in the area was a topic which was persistently avoided and belittled by the civic centre.)

After the revocation of the compulsory purchase order, five months passed before the civic centre produced proposals for Hume Street and Booth Street, to be considered by the housing working group. It was possible to interpret them, not so much from what the borough architect said, as from the official minutes of what he produced and was supposed to have stated, as a plan for slum-clearance in slow motion. I attempted and failed to bring the record of the meeting into correspondence with what had actually happened at the meeting. I therefore had to secure afresh support for resolutions of the council which would deal with the main dangers to the community-action consensus which had already been incorporated as council policy in June. In January 1973, as a result of emergency measures, which certainly involved on this occasion and issue a degree of political élitism, the civic centre's successful use of the authoritative record was counteracted. The 'proposals', said to have been agreed in November and December 1972, were downgraded to 'illustrative principles'.

But in meetings the civic centre stressed and continued to stress and support proposals for demolition, rehousing and rebuilding in Booth Street and Hume Street. Demolition followed from the intractable 'technical facts of the case', which in turn brought the area under the unavoidable 'demands of the law'. (By the civic centre I mean the most influential case to emanate from the civic bureaucracy, to be advocated in committee and working group and, so far as possible, entered in the record as the committee's proceedings and decisions. Whether the particular officer who advocated the case or drafted the minutes was more aware or less aware of his brief and of the meaning and history of what he was putting forward or recording, is a separate matter altogether.)

In June 1973, a year less a few days since the day of Booth Street's jubilant celebrations, the housing working group was informed that, if one or more property could be obtained by the council, a complete block of houses would be available for redevelopment.[6]

During May-August 1973, attempts were made to persuade the council to comply with its own public and publicized devotion to participation in the abstract and communication in the abstract.[7] Booth Streeters and their councillors wanted to know, and could not discover, what council policy formally was *in the understanding of the civic centre* (the administrators of 'civic centre' policy). How far had it been implemented (rather, as nothing practically had been done in

Booth Street, how far had the preparations for implementation proceeded)? After a lengthy period and much effort, the town clerk was
induced to supply his list of council resolutions governing council
activity in Booth Street. His list included the approved proposals of
the civic centre's November 1972 plans for demolition and rebuilding.
It omitted the resolution which had cancelled the approval and made
them only illustrative principles—the cancellation which ensured that
other principles could be applied, especially revitalization.[8] His list
also omitted the housing committee's resolution giving the area a
residual life of at least fifteen years for improvement-grant purposes.
What were his reasons for regarding the approved resolutions of
January 15th 1973, which had restored the 'community-action' position
as 'invalid, null-and-void or otherwise irrelevant to council policy'?[9]
By the middle of 1973 an outsider objectively pursuing the record
might well conclude that, as Millfield had been sufficiently misguided
to oppose legal clearance which followed normally unchallenged
public procedures, and the council had been doubly misguided to let
them have their own way, then what was technically demanded
would need to be accomplished by such methods as would bring
about the correct result.

A few days later, on July 31st 1973, a meeting of the housing working group was held, and Booth Street was on the agenda. But it was
to be, characteristically, a matter of report, which meant probably
only a verbal report by 'the appropriate officers' at the meeting. No
papers were supplied with the agenda. Plans were displayed and
explained. Once again they were for demolition and new cottages.
There was nothing about the revitalization of the cottages the corporation was seeking and buying in the area. The plans of July 1973
appeared in the minutes as an 'interim stage' of the 'redevelopment'
of Booth Street on 'a progressive infill basis'. They provided for the
demolition of nearly all the properties the corporation had brought
into its possession over the previous thirteen months. (Forty cottages
were owned by the council by this time or were the subject of
negotiations for corporation ownership. Thirty-three would be demolished.) Apparently the cottage sought in June had been successfully purchased. The civic centre wanted permission to urgently
approach another three owners yet again for their cottages.[10] (The
eventual result from one of the owners was an angry demand that the
civic centre cease their 'harassment'.)[11]

In October no start had been made on new cottages. None had been made on the revitalization of corporation-owned properties. The housing committee was informed that only one cottage stood between the civic centre and a 'workable layout'. If acquisition failed, a modified, 'less satisfactory' solution would have to be found, and this would be presented to the November meeting of the housing committee.

The housing working group had been told early in June 1973 that the council's proposals had been submitted to the department of the environment. Five months later, and sixteen months after the rescinding of the clearance-area declaration, a meeting of the housing working group was held at which I moved that all practical steps to implement council policy on (i) the revitalization of corporation properties in Booth Street and (ii) the erection of new bungalows, should be taken immediately. The results were to be reported to the November meeting of the housing committee. I was assured that this was quite unnecessary. Permission had at last been obtained from the department of the environment. The report I wanted would be before the housing committee, without my needing to ask for it. The minutes did not record this unequivocal message of approval by the department of the environment in an equally unequivocal manner. The minutes recorded that the chairman had stated that 'following protracted discussions' with the DOE about the council's proposals for 'the rehabilitation of the Booth Street area' (another ambiguous expression: I had asked about the rehabilitation of individual corporation-owned cottages), 'a workable layout' had now been 'established'.[12] (All the phrases in quotation marks are equivocations.) I did not, however, plumb them all at the time. That was the last housing working group I was entitled to attend. Without documents being distributed beforehand on the subject, the housing committee of November 5th was presented with proposals for eleven bungalows. This time the euphemism for 'slum-clearance in slow motion' was that they were a 'first-phase solution' for the 'rehabilitation of a substantial part of the area'. One item on a long agenda of important items, the proposals were approved by the housing committee.

I let the housing committee know, however, that I had written a letter to the department of the environment about its part in holding up developments in Booth Street. I was complaining, I said, because a year before to the day, I had let the minister know that delays in

Booth Street already *to that time* (November 1972), threw a glaring light on the problems of a community as it had confronted or tried to co-operate with the local authority. The quality of the data the local authority discovers and creates, I had written, the paid officer with his claims to competence, the elected member with his claims to control—all could be 'richly explored' in Booth Street.[13] In June 1973 we had been assured that the department of the environment had received the proposals. In September 1973 the department of the environment had as firmly assured me that they would deal with the proposals quickly when they did reecive them.[14] It had now been made clear to the housing committee that the delays in implementation *did* lie with the dilitariness of the department of the environment. Thankfully the protracted discussions had reached a favourable conclusion. But the department of the environment's part in the affair, I told the housing committee, would not go by unremarked.

The minutes of the meeting of the housing committee of November 1973 stated the decision of the committee was that notwithstanding the provisions of standing orders *'and subject to the approval of the department of the environment'* the council should negotiate a price for the eleven new dwellings with its own public works department. What had been approved by the department, then, and what still had to be approved by the department, was in retrospect completely obscure. That was the last housing committee meeting I was permitted to attend, and I would not have been able to challenge the record if I had been dissatisfied with it. I confess, however, that I was satisfied at the time that all necessary appovals had been obtained, with the exception of a pure formality: DOE approval for the *relaxation of standing orders* to allow the public works department to carry out the work. This is what the wording and punctuation of the minutes actually stated.[15]

The DOE let me know that they would bring up the question of their responsibility for delays in Booth Street soon. They were holding a meeting with a deputation from Sunderland's housing committee later in November.[16] To all appearances, if anything at all was said, it would be a matter of criticism, chastisement, excuses, explanation and recrimination by one or both sides about past behaviour. The matter itself was settled.

This brings us to 1974. Papers supplied with the agenda of the housing committee of January 1974 confirmed that the paralysis was over. A joint report from the borough architect, the planning officer, the borough engineer, the housing manager and the programme planning manager—every authoritative official in sight—included Booth Street's eleven new houses among schemes which had been or would be allocated, the building of the houses to commence in May 1974 and to be completed by December.[17] This news reassured some Booth Streeters. It calmed the fears of others who sensed that the area was being run down, and who suspected that before long the council could step in and say that there was no further point in preserving the area. A compulsory purchase order would be made on the remainder of the 'stayers' to free the whole site for a redevelopment scheme which made planning, architectural, economic and engineering sense. But it did not calm the fears of everybody, and more and more residents were deciding that as they would have to go shortly anyway, there was no point in remaining in the area in its increasingly vandalized and dangerous state.

Fred Bews had lived in Booth Street for thirty-eight years. But he was finding that the state of the surrounding corporation-owned properties was passing the limits of what he could tolerate. He wrote to the town clerk and chief executive officer in March, as spokesman for the 'stayers'. He told the town clerk that he welcomed the prospect of the eleven new dwellings. But he and his neighbours wanted information about the revitalization of the many corporation-owned dwellings which were not affected by the rebuilding plan. When would anything be done about them?[18]

In his answer the town clerk dealt with the important point, revitalization, hardly at all. But in going into unnecessary detail about the new cottages—the 'settled' question—the town clerk once more threw Fred Bews and the other Booth Streetes into a state of confusion and consternation. For he remarked, in passing, that the council had now submitted its plans for the new houses to the department of the environment, and the department's decision was *'now awaited'*. As soon as the ruling on the proposals had been given, the council would take steps either to revitalize or to redevelop, whichever was appropriate.[19]

Almost two years had gone by since the years of frustration and worry had ended in victory. That is what Booth Streeters had believed in June 1972. According to the public legitimation of local democracy, Booth Street had won everything they needed to win. It had won, in particular, according to this rule; that binding decisions are taken by the council and its committees. This is one of the basic, or constitutive, rules of the game, a rule the player must follow if he is to be seen to be playing that particular game at all. There are different ways of playing a given game—the preferred rules. If these are broken the player may bring upon himself defeat or, if victory, disapprobation. But if a participant in a game breaks a constitutive rule he produces only senselessness.

For my part, I was increasingly aware of taking part senselessly in the game of 'local democracy' with players who were engaged in a different game altogether. Booth Streeters waited until March 1974 before this incident had a similar effect on them. Booth Streeters who even then still wanted to stay, or felt aggrieved that they were being forced out by local circumstances which had changed dramatically for the worse, due to the abandoned and dilapidated corporation-owned cottages, were informed of the town clerk's reply to their enquiries. That the proposals still waited to be approved, after they had been 'approved' so many times already, 'blew their minds'. What Garfinkel calls the particular, located 'organizations' of artful practices' by which social activities, procedures and results are acquired and assured[20] no longer succeeded in making sense to them. The moral bounds of description, inference and argument had been transgressed too far and once too often.

A few days later, in answering the televised complaints of Booth Street about the failure to revitalize corporation-owned cottages (which included straight accusations of 'corporation winkling') the chairman of the housing committee said in an interview that 'the plan' had been submitted to the department of the environment. The department had 'agreed in principle'. 'At the same time', he said', 'we have to go through the cost analysis.'[21]

The programme agreed by the borough engineer, the planning officer, the borough architect, the programme planning manager etc., to start building new houses in May, was not adhered to. In June 1974, the report of the director of architecture included the information that among work at the pre-contract stage was the erection of nine dwellings in the Booth Street area, programmed to commence in July-August 1974.[22]

In July 1974, as required by the new Local Government Act, the public was admitted to the monthly meeting of the housing committee.

Booth Street did not appear on the agenda (which members of the public saw). It was unexpectedly dealt with under the agenda item, 'report of the director of architecture' (which members of the public did not see). As previsaged in June, the number of new houses had been reduced from eleven to nine. The report neither explained nor drew attention to this reduction. The report dealt with the price negotiated with the director of works to carry out the contract. Seven cottages were to be revitalized. The chairman of the housing committee said that the department of the environment had 'indicated their reluctant consent'. When the negotiated price was approved by the committee and the council, he said, it would need to be submitted to the department of the environment—for its approval.

The average cost of each of the nine three-person bungalows and its site works was over £12,000. In addition to that, nearly £500 was added for each dwelling in respect of the salaries of the directors of engineering and architecture. Loan charges for each bungalow would amount to over £78,000. Not mentioned was the cost of acquiring the cottages which would be demolished. Some of these had originally been 'fit' even according to the civic centre's own classification. The housing committee's recommendation to accept the negotiated price came before the council. Apart from the chairman of the housing committee, Bob Hudson was the only councillor to speak. He did not analyze the figures which, unanalyzed, councillors had before them. He merely hinted that the financial burden the council was laying upon itself and upon the general community for sixty years ahead was due to its failure to secure the implementation of its own policies. Booth Street was to have been saved, and now it was all-but destroyed. He could not argue for the policy in terms of economic criteria—only out of 'what was due to justice'. The housing committee's recommendation to build nine bungalows and revitalize seven corporation-owned cottages was approved without dissent.[23]

On July 31st a Booth Streeter asked the chairman of the housing committee when work would start in the area (she, too, was mainly concerned about the revitalization of corporation-owned cottages, rather than the relatively clear-cut and certain demolition and new building). She was told it could be the next day or the next week. She was somewhat surprised to see several days later, therefore, a public notice in the *Echo* about the nine new houses. Representations could be lodged with the secretary of state for the environment by

August 28th.[24] Though there might be a start on the revitalization of corporation-owned cottages sooner, there could be no start on building new bungalows until the end of August.

She wrote to the secretary of state. She asked him to relax the building regulation in question, not in spite of possible health or safety risks, 'but in order to bring the existing health and safety risks to an end forthwith'. She submitted the following representations, she said, on behalf of herself and her neighbours. Well over two years before, the borough council had conclusively determined that the streets had been *wrongly* defined as a clearance area. For a year-and-a-half past, the area had been definitely classed as one with a life of at least another fifteen years for improvement-grant purposes. Many residents had obtained grants and spent money. But what was more important than the money, she wrote, was the work and the 'spirit' expended in improving their homes 'after years of blight'. She and her neighbours invited the secretary of state to walk round their streets.

> 'You shall see the mixed dust of everything that can crumble in drought, and the mildew of everything that can rust or rot. Rags and ashes. Rotten timber with torn-out nails. Old bricks and cement. Cinders, bones and ordure.
> 'This is what we now have to suffer from an authority which proclaims its concern for public health.'

She objected to the fact that officials seemed to have neglected to familiarize themselves with council policy. Constantly, both in home visits and in answering queries at the civic centre, they had 'asserted that the whole area is still due for clearance'. To their unbelieving eyes, she wrote, she and her neighbours had seen an official letter in which the director of housing had described it, *as recently as July 1974* as the Booth Street *clearance* area. She and her neighbours had been improving their properties, while the properties acquired by the corporation had been allowed to fall into 'complete ruin'.

A community of friends and neighbours had been destroyed. All that remained were isolated families. Rows of clean and neat cottages had been reduced to rubble and dirt. Danger threatened from fires and collapsing masonry. 'We live in fear of our lives, especially at night.' In the very direct interests of health and public safety, the permitted grounds for representations to the secretary of state, she asked that he grant permission, and do it quickly.[25]

On August 22nd, with no sign either of revitalization or of the demolition of corporation-owned properties variously gutted with fire, internally collapsed, leaking gas and giving access to the street to rats from the sewers, Booth Streeters were in touch with the press and local radio station. At a meeting held in one of the cottages, Grace Conaboy said that what Aldolf Hitler had failed to do, and the Kaiser before him (Pickard Street had been bombed in the first world war), the corporation had managed to bring about.[26] Later in the day the chairman of the housing committee used the local radio to reply to the criticisms. He said that the corporation had been waiting for necessary approvals from the department of the environment. This had now been given. Only the paper work remained to be completed he said, before the corporation started on the site.[27]

On September 11th 1974 angry Booth Streeters again contacted the press and radio. The deputy director of architecture told the *Echo* that the council would be starting on the site 'in the near future'.[28] Two days later two men appeared in Hume Street, taking a professional-looking interest in the properties. When questioned, they said they were from the civic centre—and work would be starting on September 16th. Work did not begin on the 16th. But late on the afternoon of the 17th men spent half-an-hour stripping the slates from an empty house.

On the 18th they returned to continue what was now known to be systematic demolition. It was work which *in no way depended upon permission from the department of the environment.* The houses had been empty for more than a year, and were already owned by the corporation. Indeed, it appears that when the officials said work was to begin on September 16th, the secretary of state's written ruling on the building regulations had not reached the civic centre. (Booth Streeters received a reply to their August representations on September 16th, which said that the civic centre was being sent permission by the same post.)[29] The start of demolition itself, of course, gave Booth Streeters no reassurance that their own homes were safe; quite the contrary.

Perhaps out of goodwill and adherence to the principles enunciated in its own publicity; perhaps because Booth Streeters were now notorious for appealing to the public with the facts as they saw them, they received an official letter letting them know that the council would provide 'normal' rights of 'support' to separating walls.[30] The letter also stated that demolition was the prelude to rebuilding.[31]

It may well be that the officer who drafted the letter thought it was helpful. But it was crucially unhelpful, for it mentioned nothing about the revitalization of corporation-owned property.

'Obviously' the lady writing for Booth Street and Hume Street said, 'demolition and rebuilding in some instances are now, unavoidably, welcome.' Booth Streeters who were still inclined to remain if things did not get much worse, however, were bound to be 'deeply unhappy' so long as the likelihood of the preservation of existing buildings and the retention of the remnants of the population of the area was not indicated by the *revitalization* of some corporation-owned property. There had been an accelerating outflow of families from the rapidly worsening physical environment. If, to two years of exaggerated uncertainty and vandalism, was added months on a building site without guarantees that some of the existing cottages would be still occupied at the end of the period, the 'predictable result' could be a 'final push' to the last of the Booth Streeters. 'When will *your* revitalization start—and why has it not started already?'[32]

For when demolition began, out of Hume Street's thirty-five families only five were still quite firm in their intention to withstand the tensions to which they had been subjected: the Heptons, John Walker, the Conaboys, the Hendersons and the Wilsons. As Grace Conaboy said in a radio interview, circumstances were getting her down—but she would not move. 'I'd stay if I was the only one in the street. Because I feel very deeply about this.'[33] Fifteen other cottages were still occupied by families who were wavering or who had definitely decided to leave. Fifteen of the cottages were empty. In Booth Street twenty-five cottages were vacant and wrecked. Eight families were uncertain, or making arrangements to leave. Only six families were foolhardy or foolish enough to be sticking it out, either 'on principle', or out of some residual belief in the corporation's good faith.

As to the attraction of a corporation tenancy, as distinct from the repulsion from Booth Street and its cottages, the council had planned to rehouse all the families in the 1969-73 clearance programme in seven months. Experience showed that in Millfield, even under threat of compulsion and with the knowledge that they would have no option but to leave before long, cleared families resisted many of the offers of alternative accommodation on the grounds that they were inferior to what was being taken from them to be destroyed. (For many years Millfield's cleared sites remained undeveloped.) The revised slum-clearance programme of 1971 recognized this fact. Though it was again, characteristically, called the 'accelerated' programme, Booth Street's rehousing was scheduled to take eleven months instead of seven. Deprived of the ability to exercise state coercion, but still able to inject a tremendous 'push' by passively allowing vandals to physically disintegrate the fabric of the cottages and to terminate the area's history of civic safety, the council had been able to offer acceptable tenancies to *under one half* of Hume Street's families in a period of twenty-two months—from June 1972 to September 1974—and in a period of sixteen months since the first families had actually moved out.

The 'constructive results' consisted of (i) whichever families felt or were better off in their council homes—results which could have been fully obtained by other methods; (ii) the fair prospect of two new bungalows in Hume Street and five in Booth Street—on sites where almost certainly seven families had been better off originally where they were; (iii) the much more dubious prospect of three revitalized corporation cottages in Hume Street and four in Booth Street—without any doubt more than seven very good cottages had been bought and allowed to be destroyed.

Had I been still on the council in July 1974, I am not at all sure that I could have supported my friend Bob Hudson in his stand, *ex debito justiciae*. I fear I would have stated publicly that, after all, community action had lost and anti-community action had won. No 'rational' (*Zweckrational*) person could agree that the expenditures involved could not be put to use on projects of higher social priority. No such rational person could confidently predict that the revitalization of the seven corporation cottages would ever need to be started. It had been 'proved' that the compulsory purchase order should never have been interfered with. Failure to accept the original 'facts' and to abide by the original 'professional advice' had resulted in terrifying absurdity. There could never be another Booth Street. Any community action of the same kind in the future would be spiked by the mere mention of the name. From that point of view, the expenditures would be worth it. Bob Hudson's value-rationality (*Wertrationalität*) *and the civic centre's goal-rationality* (*Zweckrationalität*) converged in the use of the same means.

The club of the Royal and Ancient Order of Buffaloes overlooks the Booth Street area. An influential Labour councillor was over-heard murmuring, as he stared out of the window at the devastation wrought by two years—or, if you like, twenty years—of corporation activity and inactivity, 'We made a mistake in Booth Street.' He did not mean that the civic centre and the councillors had bungled or manipulated Millfield into every disaster its inhabitants had suffered, and that he stood transfixed with guilt and shame. He meant, 'We should have knocked it all down, after all.' Like a doctor's mis-takes, a corpse cannot complain: or as Aesculapius is supposed to have said about bleeding a patient—it doesn't do him any damn good, but it shows the rest of the world that the doctor is earning his keep.

References

[1] Brief accounts of aspects of Duke Street issue are to be found in Dennis, N. (1974), 'Half Beating City Hall', *New Society*, 26, October 4th, p. 574; Hudson, B. (1974), 'The Duke Street Inquiry', *Community Action*, 13, April/May; Hudson, B., Dee, J., and Dennis, N. (1974), 'And the Winner is the Mincing Machine', *Community Action*, 15, August/September (John Dee was a Duke Street resident).

[2] Brief accounts of other aspects of the Booth Street issue are to be found in, Hudson, B. (1972), 'Death of a Community', *Community Action*, 3, July/August; Hudson, B. (1972), 'Booth Street', ibid., 4, September/October; Dennis, N. (1973), 'Urban Renewal', in Dickinson, D. *Voluntary Action*, B.B.C. Publications, London.

[3] *The Sunderland Study: Tackling Urban Problems*, H.M.S.O. (1973), London; Hudson, B. (1974), 'Guidelines to nowhere', *Municipal Journal*, August 2nd.

[4] Davies, J. (1974), *The Evangelist Bureaucrat*, Tavistock Publications, London.

[5] Hudson, B. (1971), 'What determines party politics at the town hall?', *Municipal Review*, July; Hudson, B. (1972), 'Leaving Democracy to the Politicians', *Municipal Journal*, May 12th; Hudson, B. (1972), 'Rebels against the system', *Municipal Journal*, June 23rd; Hudson, B. (1973), 'The prob-lems of getting information: a councillor's view', *Community Action*, 6, January/February; 'EPAs Urban aid and CDPs, *Municipal Journal*, October, 1974 (2 issues).

[6] Minutes, housing working group, June 4th, 1973.

[7] For example, 1973, 'Planning for involvement' (Sunderland), *Municipal Review*, May, p. 521. For later publicity on the same subject, regard for community opinion, see Bloom, L. A. (1974), 'Making members effective in Sunderland', *Municipal Journal*, September, p. 537. I believe that writers generally have a feeling of sincerity when they report in this manner, but make no distinction between what ought to be happening and what is actually happening.

[8] Town clerk and chief executive officer to N.D., JMT/SH/14823, July 26th 1973

[9] N.D. to Town clerk, July 29th 1973.

Norman Dennis

[10] Minutes, housing working groups, July 31st 1973.

[11] Town clerk to Booth Street resident, JMT/SEY/14823/A, October 12th 1973. Booth Street resident to town clerk, October 19th 1973.

[12] Minutes, housing working group, October 27th 1973.

[13] N.D. to minister with special responsibility for Sunderland, DOE, November 5th 1972.

[14] Department of the Environment (northern regional office) to N.D., no reference, September 6th 1973.

[15] Minutes, housing committee, November 5th 1973, Minutes, council, November 21st 1973.

[16] Department of the environment to N.D., HO/PK/850, November 9th 1973. Because of 'local' government reorganization I was not a member of the housing committee after November 5th 1973, although I was still a councillor. I have received no further information on the meeting, nor does any seem to have been supplied anywhere through documentation before committees.

[17] Agenda, housing committee, January 15th 1974.

[18] Fred Bews to town clerk, no date (about March 19th 1974).

[19] Town clerk to Fred Bews, JMT/PE/14823/A, March 18th or 19th 1974.

[20] Garfinkel, H. (1964), *Studies in Ethnomethodology*, Prentice-Hall, Hall, Englewood Cliffs, New Jersey, p. 32.

[21] Tyne Tees Television, March 27th 1974, tape transcript.

[22] Agenda, housing committee, June 11th 1974.

[23] Agenda, housing committee, July 9th 1974. Minutes, council, July 24th 1974.

[24] *Echo*, August 5th 1974, p. 14.

[25] Booth Street resident to secretary of state for the environment, August 16th 1974.

[26] 'Quarter to one', B.B.C. Radio Newcastle, August 22nd 1974, tape transcript; *Echo, August* 22nd 1974; *Northern Echo and Journal* (Newcastle), August 23rd 1974.

[27] 'Quarter to one', B.B.C. Radio Newcastle, September 11th 1974, tape transcript—the announcer recalled what the chairman had said on August 22nd.

[28] *Echo*, September 12th 1974.

[29] Department of the environment to Booth Street resident, BRA/VA/1968, September 13th 1974.

[30] Did Booth Streeters not have *more* than the 'normal' right to 'support'? The housing working group had agreed at my instigation that if and where a wall of an occupied cottage was exposed by demolition of a neighbouring property in the area, such a wall should be treated as the end wall of Bell Street had been treated—with new bricks. This was minuted thus: 'That consideration be given, in appropriate cases, to the corporation undertaking

the treatment of gable ends to render the properties wind and water tight'. Minutes, housing committee, December 4th 1972. The minute was, of course, 'the decision'. As minuted, then did it merely state the corporation would do what it was in any case legally bound to do?

[31] Borough solicitor to Booth Street residents, JMT/PG/14823/A, September 19th 1974.

[32] Booth Street resident to borough solicitor, September 20th 1974.

[33] 'Quarter to one', B.B.C. Radio Newcastle, August 22nd 1974, tape transcript. A similar sentiment was expressed by Mary Hepton. She had decided to leave. 'And all of a sudden I flared, and I said "Well, why should I go? Why should I let them have their own way?".' (*'Are you saying then, that this is a plot by the council?'*) 'It's a plot! Definitely! By the council, by Sunderland council!' 'Quarter to one', B.B.C. Radio Newcastle, September 11th 1974, tape transcript.

COMMUNITY ACTION IN A GLASGOW CLEARANCE AREA: CONSENSUS OR CONFLICT ?

Sidney Jacobs

The Maryhill (Gairbraid Avenue) housing treatment area in the north-west of Glasgow was, under the Housing (Scotland) Act 1969, earmarked for demolition in October 1970. The area, typical of its kind in the city, consisted mainly of rooms and kitchens in four-storey Victorian tenements in which there were no baths and and where the w.c's, situated between the landings, were shared by the occupants of each floor. It was a small compact area comprising only two densely populated blocks. There were 399 dwellings in Gairbraid of which 352 were occupied when rehousing began in July 1971.

The authorities took no account of local opinion when they decided to demolish the property and residents were neither informed nor consulted about their futures. With outside community action support, the people of Gairbraid decided to organize to protect local interests during the rehousing process. At a mass public meeting, they formed themselves into the Gairbraid Housing Committee (GHC) which aimed to ensure that residents were rehoused quickly in accommodation and areas of their choice. During its campaign, the GHC engaged in a variety of activities ranging from petitions to demonstrations. The authorities, officials and councillors alike, would probably agree in a definition of the Gairbraid campaign as being one where residents with little cause deliberately sought conflict and confrontation. Local people would describe things differently, feeling that their actions were mostly defensive in situations where they were allowed very little choice of alternatives. This difference in perception of the same events is hardly surprising. Those who control power tend to view any challenge, real or imagined, to the status quo as pure troublemaking. Those who question the exercise of this power perceive their own actions as an assertion of rights denied them by an intransigent authority. Forced to occupy subordinate positions in society, working class communities, when they attempt to redress the existing balance of inequalities, feel that it is the power structure and not themselves who initiate conflict. In these terms, depending on whether perceived from the standpoint of the powerful or of the powerless, conflict is differently defined. The purpose here, in analysing the events which occurred in Gairbraid, is to define conflict from the perspective of the local community.

Theory poses consensus and conflict as alternative models of community organizing. It is argued, by using the example of Gairbraid, that this distinction does not correspond with reality. While academics may decide, one way or another, for either consensus or conflict, this is not a real choice available to local people who, anyway, would be unfamiliar with the terminology. Consensus is possible only where the community has attained, or at least appears to have attained, the power to negotiate. In Alinsky's (1972:119) phrase, 'to attempt to operate on a good-will rather than on a power basis would be to attempt something that the world has not yet experienced'. Communities use all available strategies but, ultimately, are forced into confrontation because a conflict of interests between them and the authorities, is inherent in their situation. 'As a general rule', Jim Radford (1972:42) declares, 'I believe in exploring what are called the proper channels before resorting to direct action.' Indeed, the starting point of a community action campaign is not whether consensus or conflict is the most appropriate strategy to adopt but rather, evolves from the issues at stake, the organizational strength of the community, the nature of the opposition, the degree of participation and the experience of the local leadership. The campaign is not mapped out in advance but is decided by the community during the course of action. The strategies adopted by the community are determined pragmatically on virtually day-to-day evaluations of events. Community groups normally use a variety of tactics and interchangeably adopt strategies of both consensus and conflict. As Holman (1972:5) sensibly comments, 'no organization (not even an army) relies exclusively on one approach to obtain its objectives.' Nevertheless, even given considerable overlap between the two approaches, community campaigns may overall be classified into distinctly consensus and conflict camps: Gairbraid is decidedly among the latter. Although community action embraces a wide range of activities and is not alone in the use of conflict, it is as Bryant (1972:207) argues, 'the recognition and purposive use of conflict which helps to distinguish community action from other approaches to community work'. Consensus is pursued whenever tactically advantageous but is not the model that dominates campaigns. Conflict is considered inevitable and community action theory holds that through experience of, and involvement in organizing, a local leadership will emerge who appreciate the inevitability of conflict and recognize that their interests can only be advanced thereby.

In focusing on the Gairbraid campaign, the purpose is to argue that consensus was not a reasonable alternative available to the people of the area. The evidence presented can of course only attempt to demonstrate what is true for that particular community. It is freely admitted that the administration and the conditions prevailing in Glasgow are perhaps extreme among our cities. Nevertheless, Glasgow has sufficient in common with other urban centres in this country for the Gairbraid experience to contain at least a degree of generalized validity. It is suggested that Gairbraid accurately reflects the type of situation depicted by Coates and Silburn (1970: 223-4) when they write:

> 'For let it be clearly understood that while progress through co-operation is always pleasant to contemplate, there are all too many situations where progress is manifestly only likely to be achieved through conflict.'

The initial issues in Gairbraid

Glasgow Corporation's refusal to provide information, together with gross official indifference, were the issues around which the GHC began to organize. The authorities, having decided to demolish the property in Gairbraid, apparently did not feel it necessary to inform the residents of this fact. The only official communication received by them were Control of Occupation Orders which prohibited the selling or letting of property in the area without the authority's prior permission. The orders gave no indication of what was intended in the area and merely served to limit the numbers for whom the local authority had responsibility for rehousing. These were received almost three months after the treatment area resolution was passed instead of within the statutory required twenty-eight days. It was written in incomprehensible legaleze and was anyway, the wrong form. Local people, having been provided with no information whatsoever, naturally enough assumed, as indeed did the local councillors, that

Sydney Jacobs

'housing treatment' meant improvement rather than the demolition that was intended. Further enquiries were not invited and channels of communication with the authorities were virtually non-existent. Local people were left in no doubt that their exclusion from decision-making was to be absolute. It was the manner in which working class Glaswegians had always been treated.

Glasgow is by no means unique in its failure to inform or consult residents in clearance areas. Glasgow's performance in Gairbraid, although perhaps an extreme example of local authority insensitivity, is similar to that practised in most of our cities and is even remark-ably like the slum clearance in the United States described by Gans (1972:188-216). The right to know what is going to happen, when it is going to happen and the provision of a reasonable choice of alternatives, so readily taken for granted in a middle class milieu, are in working class areas like Gairbraid, issues for struggle. Moving home is a vastly different experience in the private as compared to the public housing sector. The differences in the services available, be-tween someone buying their way into the suburbs and someone attempting to rent from a local authority, are largely unquestioned and are regarded as normal. It is as if the needs, anxieties, aspirations or whatever it is that people feel when they move house, are some-how changed and are greater with increased financial mobility. It has come to be expected that slum clearance will tend to be harsh. In Gairbraid, a local councillor accused the GHC of using the Housing Department as a scapegoat for 'all the anxieties and resentments which will inevitably accompany large-scale rehousing' (Cable 1972).

In the provision of housing, there is no doubt that double standards prevail in our society. When moving house, among other things, people want to know what choice in both house and district will be available to them and when approximately the move is likely to take place. The middle class house buyer would find it inconceivable that any of this information could be denied him; in his world, the right of choice and the maximum pre-warning are unquestioned pre-requisites, tempered only by ability to pay. In the public sector, access to such information too, is not a question of rights, but instead is thought of as an unreasonable demand generated, if not by trouble-makers, by an ungrateful mass. In the classical deserving poor tradi-tion, people who receive 'free' council houses must patiently wait while the local authority decides for them. Housing policy is mostly

168

a matter of extensive clearance and building programmes costing millions, of officials having somehow to equate the massive demand for decent accommodation with existing shortages and the inferior stock available for letting. Housing policy is primarily a numbers game where individual needs and preferences are mostly incidental. Hindess (1971 : 77) suggests that within the Labour Party, councillors are mainly interested in political aspects of housing rather than in personal matters.

Glasgow Corporation provided Gairbraid with a minimum of information, in a manner guaranteed to create a maximum of distress. It was not a situation that a middle class population would have gladly suffered. Yet, when the GHC protested it was accused of seeking confrontation. Resentment and anger were certainly justified in Gairbraid; the people instead reacted by sending a petition to the Housing Manager, politely requesting information and a public meeting with a Housing Department official. The Housing Manager's initial response to the petition was to ignore it. It was only at this stage, five months after the Control of Occupation Orders were received, that Gairbraid finally decided to organize. The GHC was goaded into existence by official indifference. The community although shamefully treated had attempted a conciliatory approach which the authorities rebuffed. Although it was some time before conflict became explicit in the Gairbraid campaign, the official attitude had ruled out the possibility of consensus right from the beginning.

The area only contained 352 families when rehousing began. As a measure of their anxiety well over a hundred people attended the meeting to form the GHC. Apathy was not a problem in organizing in Gairbraid. Far more important was the widely held belief that it was pointless opposing the Corporation. As one resident said of herself, 'what can an old woman of seventy-six do against the Corporation, what's my say against the Corporation?' Lack of opposition is often mistakenly interpreted as acceptance or apathy where more accurately, it is caused by feelings of powerlessness. People in Gairbraid were acutely aware of the injustice being done to them, the GHC did not have to convince them of this but rather, had to establish credibility as a viable organization by demonstrating that success was ultimately possible. People knew they had a right to protest, the GHC's rôle was to provide them with the confidence to do so.

Once the GHC was formed it attempted to obtain an estimated date when rehousing from the area was due to start, but the authorities steadfastly refused to provide this information. This meant that long-term planning became increasingly hazardous. Questions such as whether to cancel the summer holidays, the advisability of redecorating or improving the house, buying new furniture, the children's schooling and so forth, all became clouded in uncertainty. The Corporation's silence resulted in the sudden stagnation of the community. A precise date was not even required but merely an approximate period of when rehousing was likely. For instance, if it was only a matter of months, then redecorating was not worthwhile but if a longer period was involved, life could be made more bearable if damp-prone walls were repapered. In this way, the authorities bear considerable responsibility for the early onset of the blight in Gairbraid. Local authorities seldom feel it necessary to inform people when their homes are going to be pulled down. In Gairbraid, if the Corporation knew, they certainly were not telling and no amount of prodding by the GHC was able to produce any information about the intended timing of the treatment programme. It was only at the last minute, just before rehousing began, that residents were told, and then only indirectly, by the arrival of the housing visitors.

That residents were not given the maximum prewarning of their rehousing, it is suggested, indicates total official insensitivity and disregard for people's dignity and well-being and cannot be excused. The Corporation's behaviour in Gairbraid contrasts dramatically with official rhetoric. The Gairbraid affair coincided with the launching in the city, at considerable public expense, of 'The Glasgow 1980 Exhibition' calling for increased local participation in planning. Its theme was the Corporation's wish to encourage local involvement in decision-making. By implication, it suggested that all that was needed was a less apathetic population rather than a more enlightened administration. However, the Gairbraid experience completely refutes the argument that the city is willing to enter into any meaningful dialogue about either policy or practice. It is simply not true that, based on a consensus model, all will be well if only channels of communication can be established. The Housing Department chose to ignore every opportunity to establish communications that was offered by the GHC. The petition sent to the Housing Manager was a request for information: it attempted neither to question nor to challenge policy. However, the reply when it finally arrived made no attempt to remedy

the abysmal level of information so far provided and clearly the
authorities did not wish to avail themselves of the opportunity to
involve local people in the rehousing process. Further intervention
by the local councillors and another two written requests from the
GHC were also necessary before the Housing Department would
allow one of its officials to address a public meeting in the area.

In proper perspective, the GHC was given no option but to protest,
the alternative was not consensus but complete acceptance of official
policy. The terms were dictated by the authorities who thus made
collision unavoidable if the GHC was in any way to protect local
interests. Given an intransigent administration, the question of whether
or not the GHC should have entered into negotiations with the
Housing Department rather than adopt a strategy of conflict does not
meaningfully apply. It is impossible to negotiate with a power structure
which ignores communications and which refuses to recognize the
legitimacy of the local group's existence let alone its grievances. For
co-operation, the minimum requirement is that both sides admit that
there are issues which are negotiable. Even if the Corporation had
acknowledged the necessity for negotiations with the GHC of which
they never conceived, the denial of even the most elementary of rights
in Gairbraid meant that the residents, for their part, had no room for
concessions. The GHC, representing less than four hundred families,
was pitted against an all-powerful Corporation which insisted on
reserving for itself complete control of decision-making. Being forced
to protest, each time the GHC succeeded in extracting a concession,
Goliath called foul and accused the local group of seeking confrontation.

The power to negotiate

Throughout the life of the Gairbraid committee—effectively from
May 1971 to September 1972—numerous letters and telephone calls
were directed at the authorities but with only one exception and that
was a complaint, did the authorities ever initiate contact with the
committee. On two occasions, however, the GHC did achieve official
status and recognition. The Corporation's Housing Committee convened two special meetings at the City Chambers at which senior
councillors and officials were present to meet with a delegation sent
from Gairbraid. The first was preceded by a BBC Scotland 'Current
Account' programme which featured Gairbraid and was highly critical

of Glasgow's rehousing policy and practice. As a result, questions were raised in the Council and for a while, housing, particularly the Housing Visitor's report and the behaviour of the Housing Department's counter clerks, became a political issue in the city. The second was after the GHC had organized a demonstration at the Housing Department which was prominently reported, with photographs, in five of Glasgow's daily newspapers. In both instances, the publicity reflected adversely on the Housing Department; that Gairbraid achieved meetings with the authorities may not be wholly unconnected with its ability to mount demonstrations and gain sympathetic press and television coverage.

For the first meeting at the City Chambers, the authorities marshalled an impressive gallery of personnel. In addition to senior councillors and the Housing Manager, a representative from almost every department, even remotely connected with rehousing, was present. Gairbraid was being taken seriously and, by the hostile reception received, was obviously seen as a threat. The delegation included the professional community workers: this proved a grave tactical error. The authorities seized the opportunity to blame 'outside troublemakers' for Gairbraid's problems. A scapegoat was thus provided which allowed the authorities to avoid discussing the real issues. From the start, it was obvious that Gairbraid would not receive a fair hearing nor was any serious consideration going to be given to their demands. The authorities never had any real intention of negotiating. Had the GHC any power of sanction, such as a trade union would have in threatening a withdrawal of labour, the delegation would have walked out of the meeting. The GHC, however, had no option but to remain, attempting to negotiate from a position of weakness.

The local community requires to disturb the balance of power before it can hope to negotiate successfully and it is a truism to add that concessions are won only in relation to the power or threat of it, that is wielded. The GHC had no serious expectations of concessions being granted as a direct result of the meeting which was viewed more as an opportunity to express the community's determination to continue their campaign. It is possible that had marginal rather than fundamental changes been demanded, a more amicable atmosphere might have prevailed. Whether this would also have been more productive is, however, questionable and moreover, the GHC would have thereby ceased to represent the true interests of their community. Complaints in Gairbraid were anything but marginal and to reflect local opinion the GHC had no option but to question the entire rehousing process.

The problem for community groups is how to attain a position of power. The GHC concentrated on the threat that their campaign would spread from the treatment area to include other parts of the city. The choice posed to the Corporation was: either rehouse the Gairbraid residents quickly in accommodation of their choosing or face organized opposition on a city-wide scale. For a threat to have potency, it must appear to have a reasonable chance of being carried out. Dissatisfaction with rehousing is well-known and widespread throughout Glasgow. The possibility of organization developing clearly exists although it would require a great deal of time, effort and resources, probably then, even on a limited scale, beyond Gairbraid's capabilities. However, given time the GHC just might have been able to organize elsewhere but, as it was, the area was too rapidly cleared for the possibility to be tested. The threat itself was certainly activated sufficiently for it to appear real. For instance the committee distributed leaflets outside a public meeting organized by the Corporation for the residents of a newly declared treatment area. These drew attention to the existing inequities of housing policy, gave warnings of what was to be expected, advised on individual rights and, with promised GHC support, the community was urged to organize in opposition to the Corporation. To the chagrin of the councillors and officials present, the leaflet was continually referred to during the meeting which prevented it being the mere public relations exercise planned. Soon after, similar leaflets, one in particular drawing attention to the system used for grading tenants, were distributed at a protest outside the Housing Department. The demonstration was prominently reported with an accompanying photograph in 'The Glasgow Herald'. The committee had posed the threat of 'many Gairbraids' and during this period and later, there was a marked rapid depopulation of the area.

The success achieved, created tactical dilemmas for the GHC. The problem was that the committee had no accurate means of ascertaining the current intentions of the Housing Department. To some extent, this was a rôle that the local councillors might have but did not perform although their inside knowledge was probably too minimal anyway to have been of much use. The only means of gauging official thinking was by the number and quality of offers of alternative accommodation received by the community at any given time. It is at best an imperfect guide, as 'good' offers could either be interpreted as a sign that the authorities had decided to avoid confrontation in the area, or these could be seen as a mere coincidence, as no matter what, some people were bound anyway to be decently rehoused. Similarly, 'no' offers could either mean that the authorities were disregarding the GHC or simply, that none were then available. Thus, it was always difficult to decide if the Housing Department's current behaviour was due to the GHC's efforts or not. The dilemma was that while action by the committee could jeopardize 'goodwill' or gains already won, inactivity was open to the misinterpretation that the committee had ceased to function as a viable force.

Continual rehousing in the area also meant that the committee's constituency and thus its potential support and power, were always diminishing. Thereby, as time passed, its ability to mount direct action campaigns decreased. The threat that the local leadership would be rehoused was forever present and only overcome by the recruitment of new members and by others continuing to serve after being rehoused. Of the twenty people who at one time or other considered themselves and were considered by others to be members, less than half joined the committee at its inception. In a situation of satisfactory offers, the danger of inactivity is that once the population has declined to a point where the Corporation estimate that further local protest is no longer possible, the door will be slammed shut for those remaining. It was therefore crucial that the GHC achieve concessions, particularly for those most vulnerable in the community, while it still had the strength to do so. In retrospect, many of the local activists feel that more consistent pressure ought to have been applied and that on too many occasions the authorities were 'let off the hook'. Be this as it may, it is true to say that in general when there was a satisfactory flow of decent houses on offer, the GHC did not engage in militant protest but was most active when these were not forthcoming. From the situation described, it is worth noting that the GHC's tactics were essentially defensive, being mainly responses to official policy and practice, rather than the other way around. The choice was between defending or neglecting what they considered their legitimate rights and in spite of demonstrations, it was the local community and not the Housing Department that was under seige.

Community Action in a Glasgow Clearance Area

Access to authority

Once rehousing is underway, no meaningful pattern in the distribution of offers is discernable. Throughout in Gairbraid, for no apparent reason, some families received (and rejected) several offers while others had few or none at all. Offers did not seem to be related to social need. Priority was not necessarily given to the old-aged pensioner living alone, the infirm, the overcrowded, the unsupported mother, the family living under particularly unsafe or insanitary conditions or the family left until last in a building. In other words, no indication is given to those left waiting, of when an offer is likely to arrive: it could be the next day or as likely the next year. Under these conditions the local postman increasingly assumes importance as life comes to revolve around the hope that tomorrow's post will bring word from the Housing Department. Even then, people have little idea of the type of accommodation or area that they are likely to be offered. From when an area is earmarked for clearance, until the last family is rehoused, life is continual uncertainty. Where a local authority rehouses thousands each year and where much of it is in relet property whose availability is not always predictable, a certain degree of uncertainty is probably unavoidable. It is suggested, however, that total and absolute uncertainty, as created by Glasgow Corporation, is completely unnecessary, cruel and inexcusable. It is a situation that, quite rightly, would not be tolerated by the middle class. The attempt to alleviate this uncertainty, particularly in the rate of offers and in the choice of alternatives, was the core of the Gairbraid campaign. The Corporation seemed determined that they themselves should control all decision-making, that it was for them alone to decide when offers would be made and to whom these should go. The procedure was that people would have to wait, in rapidly deteriorating and intolerable conditions, until the Housing Department was ready to make an offer. The decision as to the suitability of house and district is taken by the officials and not the applicant. Housing Visitors did note area preference which in theory allows for individual choice but, in practice, is a sham, as the arbitrary and completely invalid grading system operated by Glasgow is the determining factor in house and area allocations. Area preference is only considered when it does not conflict with the grade allotted.

The GHC was determined that people would not be left to the whim of the Corporation, that residents would have some influence

175

and control over rehousing. Indeed, if the committee was to establish any credibility in the community it had to go some way towards achieving these objectives. Irrespective of how successful the GHC was on any other count, had it failed to influence the quality and flow of offers, it would have been regarded by the community as a failure. It was in these terms that local people understood the campaign and this was what the GHC was all about. In whatever sophisticated way politicians, academics, community workers and other outsiders, friend or foe may view community action, for the 'average' Gairbraid resident what really mattered was where, when and how he was rehoused.

A public meeting with an official of the Housing Department was the GHC's first objective. When finally held, the official who attended refused an invitation for a return visit to the area and instead dealt with grievances by proposing that residents write for appointments to see him at the Housing Department. Attempts to do so, however, proved singularly unsuccessful: letters invariably went unanswered and interviews were rarely granted. The chairman of the GHC even had a counter clerk deny the existence of this particular official. The GHC thus failed in its initial attempt to gain access to authority.

The beginning of rehousing from Gairbraid was immediately accompanied by a rapid decline in living conditions. Offers of alternative accommodation were uniformly poor and in many instances were considered as bad or even worse than the tenements people were being forced to leave in Gairbraid. The GHC encouraged residents to refuse unsatisfactory offers and struggled to ensure that conditions in the area, particularly the essential services, were properly maintained. Pressure was intensified and the GHC became a force to be reckoned with by councillors and Corporation Departments alike. The accumulative effect of the campaign was that offers improved, maintenance was undertaken and the Housing Department was forced to send its official to attend a second public meeting in Gairbraid. There he was forcibly reminded of his failure to fulfill his earlier promise of easy accessibility. Although he was subsequently no more available than before, through persistent effort, people did manage to see a relatively senior member of his staff. Gradually, increasingly more residents were granted interviews with him, and with this foot in the door, the GHC began to organize visits to the Housing Department.

Demanding interviews with the official, GHC members began to accompany groups of residents to the Housing Department. The procedure followed was that a committee member was present during individual interviews and interceded on the resident's behalf whenever necessary. As it developed, appointments were made to see the official, sometimes as often as every day during the week and the number of people seen at each session could be as high as twelve. The GHC had found a way of alleviating the uncertainty and anxiety inherent in the rehousing process. No longer did the individual have patiently to await word from the Housing Department he could instead take the initiative and bring his case to them. Hitherto, visits to the Housing Department were a frustrating and demoralizing experience. The working class often spend hours of their day waiting in endless queues in one austere public office after another. For them, bureaucracy does not begin on the other side of the Channel. The waiting room in the house-letting section of Glasgow's Housing Department is basically indistinguishable from any social security office. At times, people may have to wait hours before being called up to the glass-partitioned counter for a brief and usually unproductive interview. A common complaint among Gairbraid residents was that the clerks threatened them with eviction, told them wrongly that they were entitled to only one offer, that they would have to find their own accommodation and provided misinformation about the availability of houses. Even when not actually abusive, the clerks have anyway neither the knowledge nor authority to be of much use, as important decisions are taken by their superiors. As different clerks are usually seen on different occasions, on each occasion detailed case histories have to be wearily repeated. In short, the ordinary resident wishing to enquire, inform, request or complain at the Housing Department, has no real access to authority. The GHC, for its community, managed to by-pass the existing apparatus.

Residents wishing to be accompanied to the Housing Department approached committee members either in their homes or at the weekly GHC meetings. One member from at least half the families still in the area at the time attended one or more of the committee meetings and contact was regularly maintained with most of the rest. Anticipating that many of those who were least able to cope were among those least likely to seek help, the GHC initiated contact with old people living alone, families in rent arrears, single-parent families and others suffering under particularly difficult living conditions. The GHC provided an advocacy and advisory service for the community. For the most vulnerable section of population, committee members assumed rôles normally associated with those performed by professional social workers. A measure of the committee's success is that out of the 352 families in the area, the Corporation rehoused 319 and only 33 found their own accommodation. Calculated as a percentage of the 399 dwellings in the area which included the 47 vacant properties, 80 per cent were rehoused from Gairbraid. In contrast, the Glasgow Housing Working Party (1970:17) reported an average 60 per cent rehousing rate from the city's clearance areas. While many who find their own accommodation do so out of choice a substantial proportion, probably the majority, do so because either they cannot accept the terms offered by the Corporation, are disqualified from rehousing by official regulations, cannot cope with rehousing procedure or cannot wait for rehousing because of intolerable conditions in their clearance area. The presence of a community organization in Gairbraid ensured that the numbers forced to fend for themselves were kept to a minimum.

The advantages of the system adopted in Gairbraid were not all with the residents but the Housing Department also benefitted. Local knowledge was used to provide information of empty council houses of which the authorities were not yet aware and these were thus able to be let more quickly. It provided an opportunity for the official point of view to be explained and often compromises were reached between, on the one hand individual preferences and on the other, the availability of houses in particular areas. Arrangements were made to repay Corporation debts about which the residents affected were ill-informed and confused. Emergency cases, particularly where fires and flooding caused homelessness, could be dealt with immediately. The relative seniority of the official meant that offers of houses could be made then and there, thus increasing the chances of acceptance. The system ensured that proper regard was had for the individual's special circumstances which, in spite of what is assumed by the existing house letting procedures, do not necessarily remain stable over the usually lengthy period between the time they are noted by the Housing Visitor and when rehousing actually occurs. It created an avenue of flexible communication with officialdom, allowing the individual to be heard in the knowledge of the alternatives available and provided the opportunity for him to question the decisions made about

178

his future. In this way, it enabled large numbers of people to be quickly and satisfactorily rehoused. It was in full operation for less than three months and yet about a hundred families, roughly half the remaining Gairbraid population, were rehoused as a consequence.

A weakness of the GHC's position was that while the area was being rapidly depopulated, those remaining depended on the goodwill of the Housing Department. The GHC attempted to formalize the procedure so that, through practice, it would appear at least semi-official. For instance, lists of the people to be seen were issued so that the official could save time by having their files ready before-hand. A rota of committee members was also established to spread the commitment and to avoid the procedure becoming dependent on the relationship between the Housing Department and only one or two individuals on the GHC. Although not always possible, the GHC attempted to limit the numbers on each visit so as to decrease the pressure on the official concerned. The method adopted seemed to operate smoothly, certainly to the satisfaction of the Gairbraid residents. The authorities, however, changed their minds and abruptly ended the arrangement. While an interview was in progress, the official was ordered by his senior to stop seeing Gairbraid residents who it was said, would have in future to deal with the clerks: the committee member present was completely ignored and was given no reasons for the sudden change in official attitude. The authorities made no attempt at prior consultation with the GHC who were given neither warning nor explanation for the action taken. On this as on all other occasions, the GHC were granted none of the basic courtesies and were clearly not accorded recognition as an organiza-tion representative of their community.

Claims later made that the authorities did not know what had been going on are not credible. Even in the chaos of Glasgow's Housing Department, a middle-ranking official could not interview groups of people week after week, during which time significant numbers were rehoused, without anyone in seniority being aware of it; he must have had at least the tacit approval of his colleagues. One reason later given for ending the interviews was that rehousing is purely a private matter between the Department and the individual concerned which ignores the fact that the committee's presence was almost always requested by the residents themselves. The organized visits to the Housing Department were stopped in a most rude and bureaucratic manner, perhaps on the assumption that since so many had been recently rehoused, including six committee members, the GHC was no longer a force to be reckoned with. Although there were only about eighty families left in Gairbraid, the authorities calculated wrongly.

Protest in Gairbraid

Immediately the interviews were discontinued, a meeting with the Corporation's Housing Committee and the Housing Manager was requested and after an exchange of eleven letters and many telephone calls, it was finally convened some eighty-three days later. Each Glasgow councillor was also sent copies of a proposal for reform in housing policy which outlined the procedures that had been followed and suggested that rather than discontinue it in Gairbraid, it should be extended to apply to the whole city with a senior official assigned to deal with and be accessible to each treatment area. None of the councillors replied. Had the authorities agreed to the proposed meeting within a reasonable length of time and the position negotiated, then conflict could have been avoided. The GHC, however, was disregarded and therefore forced to take independent action.

Gairbraid was told to see the clerks like everyone else and this the GHC proposed to do, not individually but in mass. The idea was to use the system so as to expose it. A bus was hired to transport residents to the Housing Department, where, after posing for photographs and interviews with the press, a few remained outside with banners distributing leaflets, while the bulk filed upstairs. There they queued to request interviews and then overflowed into the waiting room until called by a clerk. Each resident when interviewed was accompanied by a committee member who insisted that details were fully noted. Mothers were encouraged to bring young children to overcome baby-sitting problems and, of course, to add to the bedlam. As only about eighty families still remained in Gairbraid, and the success of the action depended greatly on numbers, residents were recruited from a nearby clearance area in and around Oran Street. There rehousing had begun years before and Glasgow Corporation have the distinction of creating some of the worst living conditions to be found anywhere in Western Europe. People lived in crumbling buildings infested with rats, and most were without running water, functioning toilets or electricity. In addition to augmenting numbers, the inclusion of an Oran Street contingent in the demonstration realised the GHC threat of spreading organization to other areas. The press reported over a hundred present but this is probably a slight exaggeration.

The Housing Department was completely disrupted for a morning and the staff had obvious difficulty in coping. The demonstration was orderly and entirely in keeping within the Corporation's own rules of conduct. Nevertheless, the authorities felt it necessary to summon the police who could find no reason to intervene and who anyway were sympathetic to the local residents. Other people at the Housing Department, caught up in the demonstration by chance, expressed encouragement although it meant that they themselves were seriously delayed in seeing the clerks. The authorities later continued to accuse Gairbraid of wanting preferential treatment although the protest had called for reform in rehousing policy and practice to be applied throughout the city. The sincerity of this objective was manifestly shown in the presence of the Oran Street people and in the offer of support contained in the leaflet, to people in other areas. In terms of morale and the sympathetic and widespread press publicity obtained, the protest was locally viewed as highly successful. Within about three months, more than half of the remaining families in Gairbraid were rehoused compared with over twice that length of time taken to rehouse the last twenty families left in the area when the committee could no longer function effectively. Oran Street also claim benefit through increased rehousing. Other community groups have since followed Gairbraid's example of protesting outside the Housing Department. The GHC believe that the meeting finally achieved with the authorities would not have been held but for the demonstration.

Once the meeting had been agreed in principle, the lessons learned from the first encounter were applied. The community workers were excluded from the delegation and the atmosphere was much improved although bias from the chair was still evident. The GHC also insisted that the meeting be held at night to accommodate a delegation whose members worked during the day, although one member was actually on night-shift at the time. The purpose was to gain a psychological advantage in what had been diagnosed as a power game in which Gairbraid had very little to lose. The authorities reluctantly agreed to a night meeting and a host of senior councillors and officials assembled, after hours, to meet the GHC delegation. After lengthy and sometimes hostile discussion, the meeting ended in agreement being reached that the Gairbraid proposal be implemented for the whole city of Glasgow. As this recommendation was recorded in the Corporation minutes, it seemed that at long last Gairbraid had achieved a meaningful reform in housing policy. However, it was not to be. Months after, when the GHC had ceased to function effectively it was announced again in the Corporation minutes that on the advice of the Housing Manager the agreed changes were not after all to be made. No explanation was ever offered to the GHC nor was one asked—the committee had lost its power of protest. In that the proposed reform would have alleviated uncertainty and increased local control over decision-making, it was more than a mere administrative change. It is suggested that the reform was rejected once it was fully appreciated that it involved a real transfer of power to the community.

Consensus or conflict

During the Gairbraid campaign, the right to information and the right of choice, both of which embrace access to authority, were variously achieved at different times for different individuals, but at no time did Glasgow Corporation concede them as rights that could be claimed on demand and which were applicable to all. The denial of rights is so basic, power is so unequally distributed in favour of the bureaucracy, that a working class community such as Gairbraid, if it is to defend its interests, has no choice but to enter into conflict with the local authority. In these terms, concensus as a choice of action has no reality in clearance areas. Glasgow Corporation never considered the GHC as a legitimate expression of local opinion and even less conceived of the possibility of entering into negotiations with it. All the local activists are unanimous in their belief that the Gairbraid campaign far exceeded even their most optimistic expectations. In so far as the GHC was successful, this was achieved only in relation to the power, real or imagined, wielded by the community organization. Quite simply, Glasgow Corporation considered it more prudent to satisfy local demands than to engage in lengthy and possibly politically damaging conflict with the GHC.

The authors of the SNAP Report (1972:6), reflecting on their work in Liverpool, write that 'to depend entirely on local action seemed romantic'. It is suggested here that if this attitude prevails, professional community activists will not be the means of increasing local control but will become yet another vehicle through which outside solutions and blueprints are imposed on the working class. A consensus approach could conceivably have been attempted in Gairbraid but only if imposed from the outside. It is argued that if a working class community organization controls all decision-making, determines its own strategies and supplies its own leaders and spokesmen, conflict will invariably arise whenever it attempts to protect threatened local interests. Conflict is inevitable, not because the working class are more militant than professional community workers (the reverse is often true), but rather that while outsiders, whatever their rhetoric, may decide between consensus and conflict, communities struggling to survive have no such alternatives. In such situations consensus is usually only possible when one group of professionals attempts to negotiate with another like-minded group of professionals, that is, community workers talking to councillors and officials, and where agreement is only likely at the expense of the working class communities they purport to serve.

References Cited

Alinsky, S. D. (1970), *Rules for Radicals,* Vintage Books, New York.

Bryant, R. (1972), 'Community Action', *British Journal of Social Work,* vol. 2, no. 2, pp. 205-216.

Cable, V. (1972), 'A Councillor's Opinion', Glasgow News, no. 15, 5-18 June.

Coates, K. and Silburn, R. (1970), *Poverty: The Forgotten Englishmen,* Penguin Books, Harmondsworth.

Gans, H. J. (1972), *People and Plans,* Penguin Books, Harmondsworth.

Glasgow Housing Programme Working Party (1972), The Corporation of Glasgow and Scottish Development Department.

Hindess, B. (1971), *The Decline of Working Class Politics,* Paladin, London.

Holman, R. (1972), *Power for the Powerless: The Rôle of Community Action,* Community and Race Relations Unit of The British Council of Churches, London.

Radford, J. (1970), 'From Kinghill to the Squatting Association' in Lapping, A. (Ed.), *Community Action,* Fabian Tract 400.

Shelter Neighbourhood Action Project (SNAP) (1972), *Another Chance for Cities,* Shelter, London.

CHAUCER HOUSE TENANTS' ASSOCIATION: A CASE STUDY

David Thomas

February 1969—'The Chaucer House social worker said he could not see why normal lettings could not be earmarked for the homeless . . . however, he did not really have any constructive ideas as to how such a policy could be sold to councillors in the context of a long waiting list of 9,000 people.' (A community worker's report.)
March 1972—'No more "Cathy Come Home" families will be admitted to Chaucer House . . . In future families without a roof over their heads will be offered homes scattered throughout Southwark, if they are accepted by the council as genuine cases.' (South London Press 10.3.72.)

1. *Introduction*

The above quotations intimate that over a period of three years the London Borough of Southwark made a significant change in its policies for housing homeless families. This change was not 'sold' to councillors but was achieved by a tenants' association in Chaucer House, a block which the Borough used as a hostel for homeless families.

This paper provides an outline of the formation and development of the Chaucer House Tenants' Association, as it sought the demolition of the block and changes in the local authority's policies and procedures in respect of the homeless. The Tenants' Association used the resources of a local community work project and we shall describe some of the interactions between the Tenants' Association and the community workers at the project.

Chaucer House Tenants' Association (CHTA) has been chosen for this case study for a number of reasons. It provides a completed piece of community action which was recorded by workers at the Southwark Community Project. These workers helped CHTA from the preparation of the first informal meetings of tenants in 1970, to the rehousing of the last family from the block in December 1972. The block was itself demolished in 1973. Secondly, the change efforts of CHTA had an impact which was not only borough- and city-wide but also national. Its work led to a revision of the council's policy in respect of the homeless, it encouraged tenants' associations in other

185

parts of Southwark and south London, and a television documentary
of its work and the plight of the homeless had an impact at national
level which many observers thought as significant as that of 'Cathy
Come Home'. Finally, the predicament of families in sub-standard
Part III accommodation is a recurring problem in major cities throughout the country.

'Chaucer House', wrote the *Guardian* in 1970, is '. . . as attractive
as an open sewer . . . It is a hopeless, grim and depressing pile of
soot-blackened brick . . .' It was built in 1916 and provided accommodation for Southwark's homeless families since 1965. It was an
L-shaped block, of several stories arranged as open balconies which
overlooked a central courtyard. The yard contained open refuse bins,
pram sheds and car-parking space. There were 118 flats, two of which
were used by the Housing and Social Service Departments as offices.
The block was in a drab and depressing neighbourhood of mixed
residential and light industrial uses; it was bounded on one side by
a park, the centre-piece of a large estate of several thousand families.

2. *Southwark and its Homeless Families*

There were some 9,000 people on the Borough's waiting list in
1969. There were 143 families (662 persons) in homeless family
accommodation in March 1969, and an average of 13 families per
month were being admitted to Part III accommodation. 24 per cent.
of total admissions were a result of private landlord action, and some
9 per cent. a result of local authority actions. One of the most interesting figures relating to Part III accommodation was that, of total admissions, 50 per cent. were lone women and 50 per cent. were
married or cohabiting couples, all with children under 16 years old.
(Southwark Community Project, 1970.) Some 40 children were in
care at December 1969 because of homelessness.

There were a variety of attitudes towards the homeless in the
council's departments. In 1969, for instance, a senior housing official
felt that 'speaking of the social structure of Chaucer House, he did
not believe that there was any type of social breakdown there . . . The
arrears were rooted basically in bloody mindedness and a refusal to
pay . . . (he) thought that poverty as a factor in rent arrears was a
small one . . .' A Housing Department circular of that time stated
'that the majority of homeless families exhibit anti-social tendencies
of one form or another.' A more sympathetic view of arrears came

from a Welfare Department worker who said that 'people are living under such stressful conditions that they just don't feel motivated to spend their money on rent—it tends to be used for other things which will be of more immediate relief to the stress.' A local headmaster said of Chaucer children: '. . . it was not that the Chaucer House element in the school caused the trouble; they were more remarkable because they were sub-average, and they moved the school towards mediocrity . . . there was never a bright child from Chaucer House.' Another worker from a voluntary agency in the Borough was reported as saying:

> He believes that all the men in Chaucer House are unemployed and are playing bingo . . . he thought most of the families were immigrants . . . he felt that welfare benefits to families was wrong, that people ought to be given vouchers to spend in the shops . . . he thought that the rent arrears problem could be solved by painting the doors of people's flats at Chaucer in significant colours . . . and that tenants should be given tokens for their gas and electric meters to prevent stealing . . .

Chaucer House was administered by the Housing Department but admissions were the responsibility of the Welfare and, later, of the Social Services Departments. The Housing Department contributed to the prevention of homelessness through the detection and notification of families in rent arrears. The Childrens Department under Section 1 of the 1963 Childrens and Young Persons Act could make payments to families under the Rent Guarantee Scheme. This facility was not normally extended to families living in private rented accommodation, yet we have noted that 24 per cent. of total admissions came from that sector of the housing market. The Welfare Department had a crucial rôle in detecting families at risk of homelessness, yet this was not formally recognized in the Borough's 1967 policy statement on an early warning system, nor was the department represented on the Rent Arrears Sub-Committee.

Communication between the Housing and other departments was ineffective and often strained. For instance, when the Welfare Department closed a large Part III accommodation block called Newington Lodge, no extra housing units for large families had been agreed from the Housing Department. This led to more children coming into care amongst the homeless group. The opportunities for families to move out of Chaucer House were constrained by the usually latent but sometimes overt power struggle between Housing and Social Services Departments. This was particularly exemplified in the procedure for nominating families from Chaucer House into permanent council housing. The trading and bargaining between these departments in the nomination process emerges in the following account from the records of the Southwark Community Project:

> Although the Welfare Department decides who to nominate, the Housing Department decides when and whether it shall be, i.e. it has the right to decide whether to accept the nomination. Indirectly, crises of overcrowding in the reception unit may be factors which precipitate a family's rehousing from Chaucer . . . In addition to being sensitive as to whether the nomination is one which is likely to be acceptable to the Housing Department, the social worker has to be reasonably confident that the family will accept the accommodation offered by Housing, and that it will not incur future rent arrears. If either of these things happen, it tends to weaken the Welfare Department in its dealings with the Housing people.

The internal politicking between departments was set within the context of a local authority which had been held by the Labour Party for a great number of years. There were only a handful of Conservatives elected onto the council. Local people in the ward in which Chaucer House was situated showed little interest in local or general elections: at local elections in 1971 and 1974, for instance, the percentage poll in Chaucer Ward was 30 per cent. and 24 per cent. respectively. It was 31 per cent. and 27 per cent. for the Borough as a whole. A survey in 1969 by the Southwark Community Project on an estate near Chaucer revealed that of the 88 tenants interviewed only 3 said they knew a local councillor. Two of these were not able to name the councillor they knew. In a question about problems and complaints, no tenant mentioned going for advice to a local councillor. As far as residents were concerned, local councillors were not seen as particularly effective resources. The councillors, who were effectively regimented by a powerful Labour group, appeared to be more interested in 'Town Hall affairs' than committed to their constituency.

3. *The People of Chaucer House*

The Southwark Community Project documented the characteristics of the 112 families that were in Chaucer at September 1969. An examination of case files showed that the largest single reason for people being in Chaucer was the action of private landlords. The average length of time in Chaucer amongst the 112 families was between 1 and 2 years; of a sample of 32 families, three had been in Chaucer for 5 years and more, whilst 8 had been there for 2-4 years.

There were 336 children in Chaucer (September 1969) in the 0-16 age range; of these 120 were in the 2-5 range. 96 of the 119 children of primary school age had free school dinners. There was a constant problem of non attendance at school of children from Chaucer House.

Of the 112 families, over half were from England, Scotland and Wales, 19 from Ireland, 25 from the West Indies and the rest from Nigeria (3), Cyprus (2) and India (1).

A large number of families were in receipt of welfare benefits. Of the sample of 32, some 45 per cent. were receiving DHSS allowances. Of the men who worked, the majority were in unskilled and semi-skilled occupations.

The poverty of many families, and the stressful conditions of Chaucer, were revealed in the high number of families who were in rent arrears. Of the 112 families, 61 owed rent.

In addition to unemployment and the difficulties of income-maintenance, the problems of living in Chaucer included the overcrowding of families in their flats; a lack of privacy and too close contact with neighbours; insufficient play facilities for the large number of children; a deteriorating environment because of vandalism; an inadequate repair and maintenance service; feelings of depression and hopelessness amongst tenants the longer they stayed in Chaucer; and financial worries about rent, gas, electricity and hire purchase commitments.

One issue seemed to unite people at Chaucer House. This was their feeling of rejection by the surrounding neighbourhood. The following indications were mentioned by the community work project's report:

> Exploitation was occurring with one local shopkeeper who was able to charge high prices. Cases were cited of HP firms who would not give terms to families with a Chaucer House address and similarly of local employers who were reluctant to offer Chaucer House residents a job. One local school was reluctant to admit more Chaucer House children. In consequence families felt stigmatized and people living in Chaucer House felt that they were shown a lack of respect by casual passers-by. Some people felt they were being forgotten by the 'authorities'— 'we are treated as one, but we're all different.' (Southwark Community Project, 1970: 16.)

Residents had no illusions about how they were regarded by one particular 'authority' in the Borough. The chairman of the Housing Committee were reported in the *South London Press* as saying:

> We have a big problem in this Borough with homeless families. You all know the type of people that become homeless . . . These people are anti-social and wherever they are put they are going to cause great frustration among decent people.

David Thomas

The extent to which families could achieve change in this stigmatized housing situation was very limited. The primary opportunity for rehousing lay through the nomination procedure.

The capacity of families to move out of Chaucer through the nomination procedure assumed knowledge amongst tenants both of the procedure and the criteria for nomination. The survey carried out by the Southwark Community Project revealed that over 80 per cent. of tenants had either incomplete or no knowledge of how they were selected for rehousing. When tenants were asked what factors determined their rehousing chances, three quarters replied the regular payment of rent, one quarter replied clean flats and the remaining quarter were convinced that they would have to do 'time' after which they would be rehoused as a matter of course. Knowledge apart, rehousing through the nomination procedure could offer hope only to a small number of families—thirteen families were rehoused in 1968/69 and fifteen in 1969/70.

Although nomination helped individual families, it was often an anti-social factor and one which exacerbated housing stress in Chaucer. The rehousing of individuals meant that a flat was vacated to be occupied by another family from the reception unit. Where this family was, for instance, larger than the outgoing family, greater strain was put on the inadequate amenities of the flat and of the public parts of the estate.

4. *The Southwark Community Project*

Chaucer House lay within the target area of the Southwark Community Project, which had been established in 1968 by the National Institute for Social Work. The Project, which was funded for five years, employed three full-time community workers and supporting secretarial and administrative resources. It had been established to provide community work field placements for students at the National Institute, but it was stressed that the Project would make a worthwhile contribution to the neighbourhood in which it was situated. This contribution was to take two forms: firstly, the community workers were to help people identify their needs and take collective action in respect of them; and, secondly, to participate with statutory or voluntary organizations in thinking about how to develop their services in ways relevant to meeting community needs. The Project worked with a large number of local groups concerned with housing, play, redevelopment and a host of other issues. Over a thousand families were rehoused as a consequence of the work of tenants' associations who used the resources of the Project.

When the Project withdrew in 1973, community action continued in the neighbourhood: local parents continue to administer two adventure playgrounds with finance from the Urban Aid programme and the Inner London Education Authority; local groups have established a federation to maintain a community work base in the area; and the North Southwark Community Development Group has received urban aid funds for five years to provide a planning information service in north-west Southwark.

5. *The Origin of Chaucer House Tenants' Association*

The event which precipitated the formation of a tenants' association in Chaucer was the trial of a tenant for committing rape against a pregnant neighbour. A local curate gave evidence in mitigation for the man. The curate's evidence, together with the nature of the offence, led to widespread newspaper publicity of the conditions and residents of Chaucer House. A small group of residents subsequently called the curate to a meeting at which they explained that:

> they were not angry with him for bringing the attention of the press on Chaucer House . . . but the press had given a false picture and had suggested that all the residents had poor standards of home and child care . . . they were concerned that the residents themselves should improve the conditions of Chaucer House by forming a residents' association.

The curate helped them to arrange a public meeting for all tenants, and contacted the Southwark Community Project for support and assistance. A project worker attended the meeting, at which some 50 residents were present who proceeded to elect a committee.

The tenants initially came together to improve their public image and self-respect. They were concerned to balance the picture of them given by the adverse press comments. The field records of the Project worker do not show that the tenants had any clear notion of how an association would help in this task; nor was there any specificity about goals and tasks. At the public meeting, however, the tenants compiled a list of complaints concerning repairs, decorating, general maintenance and the facilities offered by the Welfare Department. The newly-elected committee was charged with taking up these complaints with the council and within three days the Chairman reported to the first committee meeting 'that the council were now taking notice of the residents and the council had already taken action on various points that the residents had mentioned.'

This meeting in March 1970 was the first and last of that committee. New elections followed and officers and members changed with unnerving frequency during the next six months (and, to a lesser extent, through the life of the Association). Officers were voted off for the most trivial of reasons ('a vote of no confidence was carried against the Chairman because he had given the rent office a list of shed owners unknown to the Committee'). Votes of no confidence were used to resolve conflicts and tensions which in most groups would be dealt with by amicable discussion.

Despite or through these internal conflicts, the committee developed in terms of its competence and confidence. Within a month, it had seen the Housing Manager and the Acting Chief Welfare Officer; by July it had participated with other local tenants' associations in a demonstration at County Hall about play facilities in the neighbourhood. There was a stream of letters to local MP's and to the Housing and Health Ministers about conditions in Chaucer. The first edition of the Association's newsletter appeared in June, and the committee organized jumble sales, visited new arrivals and took up the complaints of individual tenants with the relevant authorities. By this time, the Project worker had put them in touch with the Chairman of an association from a local tenement who talked to them about how best to organize for their struggle with the local council.

The community worker and the local curate had three major tasks in this early phase of the Association's work. They were:

—to assist individual tenants to come together as a collective, and to assist them to function as a committee. This involved helping the committee to work through and develop from internal conflicts and problems; and enabling individual members to take on leadership rôles and responsibilities, and develop in the tasks and skills associated with those rôles. These tasks would range from writing letters to the council, drawing up agendas, conducting a committee meeting, to face-to-face negotiations with council officers.

—to help the committee identify decision-makers with whom it would have to negotiate to achieve its change objectives. The committee had also to learn to whom these decision-makers were accountable, and to whose influence they were susceptible.

—to allow the committee to work at its own pace in the formulation of the goals of its change efforts. Thus the worker encouraged the Association as it developed through a series of objectives, namely, a concern to redress the public view of Chaucer residents; to effect cosmetic improvements to the buildings; to pressure the council to improve its services to the block; and to negotiate with the council for the closure of the block.

6. Development of the Activities of the Association

One event in September 1970 was responsible for a major contribution to strengthening the Association's confidence in its own status and power. The committee had written to Sir Keith Joseph, then at the DHSS about conditions in Chaucer. A meeting was subsequently arranged with DHSS officials, which the committee records describe as a 'major breakthrough'.

The sense of legitimacy and power which the Association derived from this meeting was soon reflected in a number of different ways by the Association's target system, the local authority. There occurred in the same month (September 1970):

—further meetings with the heads of the Housing and Welfare Departments;

—a rash of scurrilous comments in the local press from anonymous councillors who talked of 'large cars and T.V. sets' in Chaucer and who described the Council's policy towards the homeless as 'too soft';

—a press release from the London Borough of Southwark in which it stated that it intended to use Chaucer until March 1971; it would use patch-repair houses in redevelopment areas to rehouse families in Chaucer; and it would provide special family care units for families with severe problems. The Association responded with a petition protesting against these proposals.

The Association made its first contact with the mass media in October when Thames Television came to film a programme on homelessness in Southwark.

The Phoney War

1971 was the year of the letter. The committee's primary instrument of negotiation was the letter, and to a lesser extent, the telephone in the offices of the Southwark Community Project. There was little important face-to-face negotiation with the local authority, but the committee dispatched hundreds of letters to officials. These were largely about the housing situation of individual tenants, maintenance and repairs in Chaucer, clarification of the council's policy for closing the block, and letters to the DHSS about the way Chaucer tenants fared at its local office.

This was a phoney war, and 1971 was, from the perspective of the tenants' association, a period in which its negotiations about closure was less significant than other events and activities which helped to prepare its committee for the use of campaign and conflict tactics against the council in 1972. These included:

—the 'apprenticeship' of a chairman who was to lead the Association to the final demolition of the block.

—the committee diversified its interests—it opened a youth club in the block, explored health problems facing tenants, investigated the under-use of a neighbouring play-group, achieved the rehousing of individual families, effected changes in the way tenants received their monies from the DHSS and participated with other associations in neighbourhood-wide issues. The Association became what Alinsky has referred to as a multiple-issue organization—'An organization needs action as an individual needs oxygen. With only one or two issues there will certainly be a lapse of action, and then comes death. Multiple-issues mean constant action and life.' (Alinsky 1971: 77-78.)

—there were a number of incidents which galvanized the committee and which gave it opportunities to become proficient in public debate. First, the committee alleged on television that the Church gave a low level of pastoral care to Chaucer tenants. A controversy developed between the committee and the BBC on the one side, and the Bishop of Southwark on the other. Secondly, the committee discovered that a DHSS investigator had used an empty flat in Chaucer to spy upon single women in receipt of benefits. This provided the committee with the opportunity to take issue with the Housing Department about whether it had given permission to the DHSS of its investigator to use the empty flat. Thirdly, the chairman of the Housing Committee described homeless families as 'anti-social' and as 'a frustration among decent people.' This provided another opportunity for the committee to learn how to use the media to its advantage.

Each of these incidents (and there were many more of a less substantial nature) allowed the committee to develop its ability to negotiate with authorities, and its skills in utilizing other resources (the press, TV and sympathetic councillors and MPs) to strengthen its negotiating positions. At the same time, the committee continued to cope with internal problems about finance, leadership, personality conflicts and periodic bouts of depression about the possibility of successful outcomes of its work. Committee work was also constrained by the domestic and work problems of individuals—unemployment, marital disputes and trouble with the police affected most of the members of the committee.

1972: The Last Year at Chaucer

The year began with the Association's Annual General Meeting. Television cameras were present at the meeting. The BBC had approached the council for their help in producing a documentary on poverty. The Southwark Community Project did not accept an invitation from the council Press Officer to take part in an initial meeting to discuss this documentary. However, it welcomed the producer at the Project offices, and introduced him to the committee at Chaucer House.

The presence of the cameras at the AGM ensured a large turn-out of tenants. It enabled the committee to stimulate tenants who might otherwise have been resigned to bad housing and apathetic about the work of committees. Tenants may have come to see themselves later on television, but they took part in the meeting and enhanced their knowledge of the committee and its work on their behalf. New members were elected to the committee, and there was an over-whelming feeling of anger and bitterness as tenants realized that the council would not be able to meet its revised estimate for closure of the block of April 1st, 1972.

In the weeks after the AGM, the new committee prepared its plans for more militant tactics. The first of a series of demonstrations occurred in the yard at Chaucer in the middle of February. The demonstration took three principal forms:

—rubbish which had accumulated in the yard was set alight in the rubbish bins; the arrival of the police and fire brigade added essential drama to this event.

—cars that had been dumped in the yard were used as barricades between the block and surrounding streets.

—officials from the rent and welfare offices in Chaucer were excluded from their offices, which were subsequently boarded up with old timber.

The demonstration began at eight in the morning and carried on through the day. Television cameras and reporters from the local and national press were present, and the media coverage was crucial for the pressure it put on the relevant local authority departments. An unforseen consequence of the demonstration was open hostility between the committee and some tenants who suspected that Chaucer's stigmatization would not be helped by the publicity.

The committee followed up the demonstration with a request to the council to receive a deputation of Chaucer tenants. A meeting was offered with councillors and officers on March 6th, at which the council announced that there would be no admissions to Chaucer House after April 1st, and that it would be closed at the end of the year. A press statement to this effect was released jointly by the council and the Tenants' Association. The committee organized a further demonstration on March 13th to indicate that its activities would close only when the last family was moved out.

Families were subsequently moved out at the rate of two a week, and by December 1972 the last families had left. Chaucer House was eventually demolished early in the New Year. The BBC documentary on Chaucer, *The Block*, was televised nationally in September and December.

The period between the council's decision and the closure of the block was a difficult one for the committee. The council's decision meant that the committee had been successful in its primary change effort; after the March meeting it decided that it would, firstly, continue its activities so that the council were given no opportunity to back-track on the decision; and secondly, work to ensure that families were rehoused from Chaucer into adequate accommodation.

Chaucer itself deteriorated environmentally as families moved out. Flats were boarded up with corrugated sheets, and the level of services and maintenance to the block dropped even further. There was constant friction between tenants who remained; their anxieties about moving increased as they watched their neighbours leave. Disputes occurred between tenants and the committee, whose officers were frequently scapegoated by those tenants who were amongst the last to move. Tensions occurred within the committee, as members' enthusiasm and energies dwindled.

The Comunity Work Tasks

Because of staff changes at the Southwark Community Project, the Tenants' Association worked with two different workers from 1970 to the closure of the group. It is, however, possible to identify some of the major tasks which the workers were engaged upon in their work with the Association and its committee. These included:

(a) the continuing task of helping the committee strengthen its organizational structure and procedures. The workers, for instance, would stress the need and value of promoting task-sharing and participation in the committee; of recruiting new tenants and of 'training' members for officer rôles; and of adequate feed-back to the tenants of the committee's decisions and actions.

(b) work in planning and preparing for meetings, delegations, press conferences, television interviews and support in tasks like letter-writing, drawing up agendas, taking minutes, and keeping accounts. The workers also helped in introducing new resources to the committee that were relevant to a particular task. For instance, student volunteers to run the youth club.

(c) participation in the planning and execution of the committee's tactics. The Association moved through the categories of tactics identified by Brager and Specht, namely, collaboration, campaign and contest or disruption. (Brager and Specht 1973: 272.) The workers participated with the group in choosing the appropriate tactics for particular situations, and the criteria of 'appropriateness' included the scope of the desired change, the resources of the Association in those circumstances, the resources and attitudes of the target system, and the likely reaction of the media and local public opinion.

(d) participation with the group in its direct negotiations with decision makers. The workers were often invited to accompany the committee to meetings, and were usually given a low profile rôle. The worker was invited in this rôle for a number of reasons:[1]
—to support and encourage the committee by his presence
—to mediate between the cultures of the articulate and the inarticulate; that is, 'to help us make sense of the big words they always

197

use'

—to take notes of the meeting, to help the committee prepare minutes which would later be sent to the council for their concurrence, and to make sure the council 'dosen't get away with anything'

—to act 'as witness' to what the council would say; the worker's status as a reputable professional would help the committee to keep the council honest

—to clarify and analyse the content of the discussion with the committee after the meeting.

(e) helping the committee to come to terms after the council's decision of March 6th with the prospect of its own termination and dissolution. This largely took the form of helping the members of the committee understand how anxieties within the committee about termination, and stress in the block associated with the break-up of a community, lay behind many intra-committee, and committee-constituency tensions.

7. *The Sources of the Tenants' Association's Power*

There are two ways in which we can identify the sources of the Association's power in its efforts to close Chaucer House. First, we can search for sources of power within the characteristics of the Association itself; second, we can consider some features of the Association's target system (the local authority) which strengthened the Association in its work. We shall look at each of these in turn, and it is important to note that the Association's struggle with the local authority took place in a period of growing public concern about homelessness.

(a) *the Tenants' Association*

We shall examine factors which are more or less specific to this Association. We shall not, for instance, describe those characteristics which are present in most forms of organized collectivities which make the efforts of groups more potent in effecting social change than the efforts of individuals. These general characteristics of groups are described elsewhere,[2] and include a wider range of negotiating techniques and strategies available to groups, and the support, encouragement and invulnerability that a group offers to its members.

The factors which seem specific to the Chaucer House situation include:

—the availability of officers. Most of the Committee members were available during the day to carry on the work of the Association. About half the committee were women, who left their children with neighbours or brought them to the Project office. The men were available because they were unemployed, and two officers decided to remain unemployed in order to do their committee work.

—the quality of leadership. The Association in its last two years had a charismatic and skillful chairman who was able to keep the Association focused on its task despite the tensions and stress within which it operated.

—the fact that there was nothing to lose. The Chaucer residents felt they were at the end of the line in respect of their housing situation, and there was a sense of power which derived from the prospect of there being everything to gain from organized community action.

—despair and apathy about individual achievements. Few tenants believed they would ever get out of Chaucer through their own individual efforts. This despair cut both ways: it was difficult to get people to participate in the work of the Association; but it helped in overcoming tenants' resistance to collective action *per se*. There were a few tenants with delusions that the difficulties and responsibilities of community action could be avoided through self-assertion in the private or municipal housing market. In this respect, it was important that there was no councillor in the ward who had an effective constituency rôle; the work of such a councillor in pushing the interests of particular families might have sustained tenants' belief in the efficacy of individual petitioning for rehousing.

—the relationship of the committee to its constituency. The community workers and tenants often despaired at the seeming hopelessness of starting and maintaining a tenants' association in a block for homeless families. There was a continuing turn-over in the committee and in the constituency of individuals as they were rehoused, sent to prison, moved away or dropped out as a consequence of low morale and committee tensions. The committee was often criticized for its 'apartness' from the tenants it represented; but this was its response to the instability in the block. Yet the changing population in the block was also a source of strength: it meant that the population from which officers and committee members could be recruited was in a more or less constant state of renewal.

—the committee became particularly skilled at presenting its case through the mass media. It's exploitation of the media was tempered with care and discrimination: for instance, it refused to take part in a television discussion when its spokesman was found to be unacceptable to the programme organizers.

—the use of volunteer resources. The coverage of the Association by press and television, as well as the contribution of committee members to lectures and seminars in teaching institutions, attracted many helpers to the Association. The committee learnt how to use the skills and resources of these volunteers as and when they were needed for specific tasks.

(b) *the local authority*

The local authority was particularly ill-equipped and ill-positioned to do battle with such a resourceful group of tenants as those on the Chaucer House committee. It shared in what was a fairly general ambivalence to the block: on the one hand, people like those in Chaucer 'deserved' to be in Part III accommodation, and its low housing standards acted as a punishment both in the deterrent and retributive senses; on the other, Chaucer was the source from which emanated considerable work and pain for local authority and other services like the police, fire, probation, health and education. There was always something about Chaucer in the press (about miscreant individuals or the activities of the Association) and closure of the block would at least secure some 'relief' for the service providers. The extremes of affluence in the borough, and the punitive attitudes of local authority members and officers to the homeless contributed to Chaucer's newsworthiness, and attracted considerable support and sympathy outside the borough for the Association's activities. Local authority personnel were often so publically uncaring that it was not difficult for the Association and the media to portray them as 'the baddies'. The local authority was by no means united in its stance on the Chaucer issue; the tenants were able to capitalize upon rivalries and tensions between different groups of councillors. For instance, the Association obtained support from some of the group of younger, professional, house-owning councillors who were opposed on a number of issues to the policies and thinking that characterized the more paternalistic councillors who had ruled Southwark for a great number of years. At the same time, the Association benefited from the upheaval in the local authority which preceded and accompanied the implementation of the Local Authorities Social Services Act, 1970. During this period, Southwark lost the heads of its Children and Welfare Departments, acquired a new Chief Executive and Director of Social Services, and was anticipating the retirement in 1973 of its Housing Manager.

The tenants' association effectively exploited through the media the council's sensitivity about its attempts to meet the needs of those living and working in Southwark. The existence of Chaucer and the activities of its Association were a considerable embarassment to the council at a time when it sought public recognition of its work in the fields of housing and social services. Southwark ranked fourth out of 12 inner London boroughs in 1971-72 for its expenditure per 1,000 population in social services. And one of the first major concerns of its newly-appointed public relations officer was to publicize the council's housing programme —the return of houses under construction by London Boroughs on 31st March 1971 showed that Southwark was building almost two new houses for every one by the London Borough with the next highest total.

The council might have drawn comfort from the level of antagonism towards Chaucer tenants in north-west Southwark. Attitudes to Chaucer people were generally punitive and hostile, and other tenants' associations using the Southwark Community Project were also resentful at the relative success that the Chaucer Association enjoyed in its negotiations with the council. Other users at the Project often complained that the Project offices had been 'taken over' by the Association and that its officers monopolized the time and energies of the community workers. The council were unable, however, to capitalize on the anti-Chaucer feeling. The council was isolated from the constituency partly because of the ineffectiveness of the ward councillors in their constituency rôles; and partly because of the apathy and in-

David Thomas

difference of the electorate (reflected in the poll turn-outs). There were still other consequences to the council's remoteness from grass-roots or community politics. Most importantly, the local authority had developed little skill or experience in working with local groups. The authority particularly lacked skill and experience in campaign and conflict-type negotiations, and this was clearly revealed in 1970 and 1971 in their street and legal battles with the squatting movement. Southwark's politics were essentially paternalistic, rather than collegiate or participatory. Chaucer House Tenants' Association, like many other community groups in Southwark, faced a double challenge: not only had they to argue and demonstrate the validity of their demands; but they had also to effect a major shift in the way that Southwark viewed groups such as themselves. In its early days the Association detected a general feeling in the authority that representation of the interests of 'the people' was the responsibility of the elected members; by what right and authority did these community groups represent their constituents?

8. Conclusion

It has been feasible in this case study to attempt only a tabulation rather than a study of some of the major themes in the development of the Chaucer House Tenants' Association, and its relationship with the Southwark Community Project and the local and other authorities. The thematic priorities have in turn been determined by the fact that the case study appears as part of a book whose major conceptual thrust comes from the social sciences, particularly sociology, and not from social work. Thus the case study has not dealt with the process of the community work intervention; although we have explicated some of the tasks which confronted the community workers, we have not elaborated upon the methods, techniques and skills of their intervention. Nor have we described the personalities and interests of those involved in the community action; the people in the study deliberately remain cardboard figures because we have chosen to emphasize the systemic features of the Tenants' Association's struggle to achieve its change objectives.

Footnotes

[1] This is taken from *Organising for social change: a study in the theory and practice of community work* by David Thomas (1975), Allen and Unwin.

Chaucer House Tenants' Association: A Case Study

[2] David Thomas, *op. cit.*, chapter 5.

References Cited

Alinsky, S. (1971), *Rules for Radicals*, Vintage Press.

Brager, G. and Specht H. (1973), *Community Organizing*, Columbia University Press, New York.

Southwark Community Project (1970), *Report on Homeless Families in Southwark*, London.

GOSFORD GREEN RESIDENTS' ASSOCIATION:
A CASE STUDY

John Benington

1. *The Setting*

This is a case-study of a small-scale attempt at community organisation and political education in a non-crisis situation. The context is Coventry, widely regarded as a boom city. Its rate of growth this century has been among the fastest in the country. It has established a widespread reputation as a pace-maker for high-wage jobs, civic planning and architecture and local government administration.

Nevertheless even such a prosperous and progressive city has its problems of disadvantage and inequality. There are several groups and localised areas which have not shared in the general bonanza. For example, the older working-class area on the north of the city—with its dense industry, congested housing, decaying environment, outworn facilities and cramped open space, all enclosed within a triangle of railway lines—is in striking contrast to the attractive modern conditions which represent the 'planners' dream' Coventry. The better-off have largely moved out of this older segment of the city, leaving behind higher than average concentrations of unskilled workers, Asian immigrants, pensioners and other 'non-productive' or otherwise vulnerable sections of the population.

One of the less well-off areas, within a stone's throw of the modern city-centre, and lying literally in the shadow of the £14½ million inner-ring road, is Hillfields. Before the war, Hillfields was known as a well-established working-class community. The local paper called the people who lived there 'the salt of Coventry, the backbone of the city'. But since the war the area has been run down badly. It has not been neglected by any means, but the plans for redevelopment have been cut back or delayed so often over the past 25 years that for much of the time it has been like living in the middle of an enormous building site. The inner-core is now nearly fully redeveloped. However, there are still large tracts of land which have fallen waste where houses have been demolished and the Council's money has run out before new ones have been able to be built. Perhaps the greatest uncertainty affects the outer belt of Hillfields, where even the plans are still indefinite.

This case-study is about local action in part of that outer belt of Hillfields.

2. *The Community Development Project*

In 1970 Hillfields was selected as one of the pilot areas for the national Community Development Project (CDP)[1] —a government sponsored action-research investigation into small-area deprivation— and that experiment completed its five years work in Spring 1975. During the first three years the Coventry team's main thrust had been in social planning for institutional change. However from the beginning, part of our programme had been concerned with stimulating and supporting the processes by which local residents were able to represent their needs, and protect their interests, particularly in relation to key welfare state services. In this early period we helped to set in motion, and then to service, a number of new kinds of participative and representational mechanisms at the neighbourhood level.[2]

However, our experience[3] of trying to bring about policy change through this kind of experiment in communication and co-ordination gradually made us more aware of the political and economic structure within which decisions were made. It became clear that many of the factors influencing the conditions and quality of life in Hillfields operated in the private sector and lay largely outside local government control (e.g., the investment and employment policies of the car and engineering industries; interest rates on capital borrowed by the local authority; changing land values and the private housing market). Our early strategies had largely ignored this dimension, and had focused far too exclusively on the relationship between the Hillfields people and the local bureaucracy.

In the last two years of the Project, therefore, we not only tried to analyse in more detail the effects of political and economic forces upon the fortunes of Hillfields, but to understand better the relationship between such forces and the local state, and also to test out what potential exists at the local level to bring the situation more directly under the control of local people and their representatives.

3. *Our Framework of Aims and Strategies*

We therefore tried to express our overall aims for the last two years of the Project in the following terms:

(a) To try to service interest-groups of the worst-off sections of the working class with information, analysis and hard skills, in order to develop greater consciousness of the nature and sources of inequality and to encourage collective struggle against oppression.

(b) To try to develop connections and alliances between the Project, 'worst off' groups and the organised sections of the labour-movement (the Labour Party, the ward parties, shop-stewards committees and the trade union branches) on issues of inequality and their eradication.

(c) To try to use whatever opportunities the CDP framework provides to lodge propositions about the needs of people living in disadvantaged urban areas, and to contribute to wider movements of political debate and action demanding:

(i) major increases and redistributions in public and private investment, and

(ii) increased levels of and new forms of control over such investment.

We decided to concentrate our work in the final phase into three main programmes:

(i) Legal and Income Rights
(ii) Housing and Environment
(iii) Private and Public Investment.

Legal and Income Rights

In addition to advice and advocacy on specific problems this programme has attempted to disseminate information about, and understanding of, the issues underlying our income maintenance system, through information leaflets and teach-ins aimed at both community groups and the trade unions. We have offered the services of a solicitor and a welfare rights expert in the following ways:

(a) to individuals who call at weekly surgeries in four neighbourhoods;

(b) to community groups who are helping claimants and others with legal and income problems;

(c) to pensioners' rights groups in the city;

(d) to trade union groups, helping their members to claim their full rights at times of short-time working or strike.

Housing and Environment

We have been able to offer the services of a housing team comprising a planner, a public health inspector, a solicitor and a community worker. This has enabled groups to prepare reports on collective demands, alternative plans for general improvement areas and action areas, and has helped other groups collect data about their areas to inform and support their particular campaigns. This has involved work with neighbourhood groups concerned about the following range of issues:

(a) the effects of the Local Authority's Comprehensive Development Area and Action Area plans for particular small areas;

(b) campaigns to get streets declared as General Improvement Areas or to influence the kind of improvements which take place once such areas are declared for GIA treatment;

(c) action to achieve the scrapping of a major road proposal for the city which had blighted an area of 600 houses for the last 10 years;

(d) groups concerned with more general problems affecting their housing, e.g. spiralling house prices through speculative dealings in the area; the intrusion of industry and other non-conforming uses into residential areas; homelessness and the loss of family houses as a result of change of use by landlords; and environmental nuisances such as derelict buildings and land;

(e) this work has led to the setting up of a tenant controlled housing co-operative and a feasibility study for a Common-Ownership House Improvement Company.

Private and Public Investment

We worked in conjunction with a small team of economists and sociologists from Warwick University to begin an analysis of—

(a) the patterns of private industrial investment (particularly capital concentration and technological change) in the four main industries in Coventry and their consequences for different sections of the work force (particularly the unskilled, semi-skilled, working women, and the immigrant) and hence for different geographical areas of the city.

(b) the pressures and constraints imposed by central government, private industry and the wider money markets upon the overall level and pattern of investment (particularly the capital programme) in Coventry.

Within these broad programmes we have tried to offer residents' groups, and (in some cases) trade union groups, 5 inter-related services:

(i) Information and intelligence—help to residents in the gathering of information about their own situation (e.g. household surveys, census analyses) and about how decisions affecting their lives are made (e.g. housing finance; local government structures and procedures).

(ii) Hard technical skills—a pool of expertise to be drawn upon by residents and their representatives on a 'hire or fire' basis; the range of skills include those of a solicitor, planner, public health inspector and income and welfare rights specialist. The aim is to present the knowledge which such specialists have in a clear and understandable form and to share it as openly and widely as possible, to reduce the dependency of groups on outside experts.

(iii) Community organisation—helping groups and individuals to identify and define the problems they wish to tackle, to organise and develop a constituency, to keep their supporters informed and involved throughout the course of a campaign, and to draw on the experience of other organised groups, both nationally and locally, who are involved with similar issues.

(iv) Adult education—encouraging mutual learning, by reflecting on the experience of action, and by sharing our own analysis of the concrete issues around which the groups are working.

(v) Administrative support and practical resources—help in the preparation and presentation of news-letters, reports and campaign material plus access to typing photographic and other resources.

4. A Low-Key Beginning

In many ways the case-study which follows is not the best example of how we tried to put these grand aims into practice. It is a relatively small-scale piece of work, which did not even arise directly out of the CDP programme. It sprang initially from the fact that I and my family were living in the Gosford Green Area (which is on the outer edge of the Hillfields project area). This is generally regarded as one of the better provided parts of Hillfields. The terraced houses, though built at the beginning of the century, are slightly larger than those in the main core of Hillfields, and they have small back gardens. Lying outside the comprehensive development area there was no immediate threat to the future of the area, though a good deal of uncertainty and vague rumour. In the three years that we had been living there a number of grievances had kept cropping up in conversation with neighbours—particularly the nuisance caused by the Coventry City football ground at the end of the street, the disruption and damage caused by visiting football crowds, and the general uncertainty about road and redevelopment plans rumoured for the area. Some of these affected our own family life, and so I began to talk with some of my neighbours about the possibility of organised action to tackle the situation collectively.

There were two possible starting points. The CDP Team had done some research about the 1973 revaluation of the rates. We had discovered that the older working-class areas of the city had come very badly out of this, compared with the better-off areas on the south of the city (and even worse compared with industry and commerce). The CDP Team had wondered about the possibility of collective rates appeals as a means of challenging this inequality. The other possible starting-point was with general, but immediate grievances. I began to talk with the people who lived in the house on either side and opposite my own. Together we decided it would be better to start with general local grievances than with a collective rate appeal, as the latter might attract owner-occupiers more strongly than the many tenants in the area. We prepared a leaflet calling residents to a public meeting at a local school to get a local action group started.

This case-study will try to decribe the experience of what followed over the 12 months from the inaugural meeting on 4 July 1973. It will not take the form of a process-record, but of a selective diary of events interspersed with tape-recorded discussions of those events by members of the residents' committee. Finally I will try to assess what took place, in terms of : —
  (i) the material changes achieved
  (ii) the development of organisation and political consciousness
  (iii) the contribution made by myself and other members of the CDP Team.

5. *The Foundation is Laid*

The main themes the original group put forward in a leaflet circulated to about 1,000 houses in the area immediately around the football ground, were :

— rumours about roads and redevelopment plans;
— vandalism and nuisance from the Football Ground;
— proposed expansion plans by the Football Club. (The local paper had announced the previous December that the Club planned to build a £1 million super-stadium which would be linked with the Corporation's plans for a 6-lane road.)
— the inadequate play facilities, and the unsafe nature of those which were provided, for the children of the area.

Between 50 and 60 residents attended this first meeting (held in a local school hall) and it was quickly suggested from the floor that we should constitute ourselves as a proper action group. We decided on the 'Gosford Green Residents' Association' taking the name of a nearby landmark.

Many individual grievances were raised and others told of previous attempts they had made to get improvements in their situation, mostly without success. However the spirit of the meeting was one of excitement, and at the end a committee was formed of residents from the main streets in the area. This was done fairly informally, people in the hall suggesting the names of friends and others they knew in the area.

It was agreed that the Committee's first steps should be:
— To let the Parks Committee know the residents' views and to ask for a statement of their plans for the two parks in the area;
— To suggest to the Football Club that they should provide insurance against damage to houses and shops caused by their fans;
— To write to a local MP requesting stiffer penalties for vandalism;
— To request the Council to clean up the streets sooner after each football match;
— To request the Council and the Football Club to provide alternative parking for visitors to the Club and that parking in the streets around the ground should be prevented by a bye-law;
— To invite the Planning Department to a public meeting to explain their plans for road and redevelopment in the area.

Finally, it was agreed that there should be frequent public meetings to report back progress and discuss developments.

6.   *The Pen is Mightier than the Sword?*

In some ways the Committee which had been elected to carry out these jobs was a very mixed bunch of people! In addition to the CDP Team member, it included a pensioner who had lived in the area all her life; four people in their 20s and 30s who were clerks in central or local government departments in the city, e.g. employment office, tax office, local authority (one came from a family with long-standing roots in the area, but the others were more recent to Coventry and to Hillfields), a young single man who had been sick and unemployed for some time, and a Ugandan lawyer who taught at the Polytechnic.

This residents' committee was much more varied than most of its kind in Hillfields. To some extent this reflected the cosmopolitan mixture of long-standing residents, more recent arrivals, students and others in this part of Hillfields. The major group not properly represented on the Committee was the single men from rooming houses in the area—many of them immigrants from Ireland or Scotland who were working in the car factories or in the building industry.

For the first few months the Committee seemed to spend most of its time establishing its identity and writing letters. An imposing Constitution was prepared, headed notepaper was ordered, and the Committee as a whole sat down to compose letters to the Planning Department, the Parks Department, the City Transport Committee, the Town Clerk's Department, and the City Football Club. In each case the letters recorded the complaints made at the public meeting, and asked for improvements, or for a meeting.

The results weren't very encouraging. The local authority mislaid two of our letters about a residents' parking scheme, and the Committee did not get a reply until 11 January, 1974. Exactly six months after the first one was sent.

Between August and November six or seven letters were exchanged with the Town Clerk's Department about the Association being represented on a special committee set up to tackle the problem of vandalism. Finally, the Town Clerk promised to put our request to the next meeting of the Committee and to write to us again.
— We never heard from him again.

A letter to the Planning Department in July 1973 was followed by an exchange of 12 further letters before arrangements were finally agreed for a public meeting on 30 January 1974.
— Six months to make even the first move forward.

The tone of the Committee's letters got more and more sharp as the delays and frustrations got greater. We might still be writing letters, and getting buried in a mountain of paper, if it hadn't been for a tragedy which hit the area in October. A 12 year old girl from a nearby street died after falling from one of the swings in the local park. We had already begun to campaign to get improvements in the local parks, but her death spurred the Committee into more determined action than just writing letters.

7. *A Stronger Lead is Given*

The Committee had written to the Parks Committee in July expressing the residents' annoyance and dissatisfaction with the general maintenance and safety in the two parks in the Gosford Green area, and with the serious lack of equipment provided for the larger number of children in the locality. The Council replied to the Committee nearly six weeks later.

Generally, the explanation given was that the lack of finance prevented sufficient staff being employed on clearing rubbish and glass, repairing railings and hedges, maintaining the surface of the footpaths or providing full-time supervision. But the Parks Department equally blamed the high degree of vandalism which they said existed in this particular area. Any danger from the electricity substation in Primrose Hill Park was not their responsibility and

'any lack of play equipment is probably due to the fact that money has not been allocated to this purpose.'

Again, vandalism was blamed for increasing the damage to existing equipment.

Then in October, the young girl died in Primrose Hill Park from a fall from the swings. A teacher from the school she attended asked our Association's support in raising public questions about how and why this tragedy occurred.

The Committee wrote to the local paper informing them of our unsuccessful efforts to get the Council to improve conditions in the park and of our concern that unless there were improvements in at least the safety conditions, there would be more accidents.

The paper reacted by saying that they would not give too much publicity to lack of safety provisions in case it caused panic reaction among parents.

The Committee wrote angrily to the *Daily Mirror* requesting their support. In spite of an encouraging reply there was no further response.

At this stage the Committee decided we had to take a stronger lead in mounting a campaign about the whole question of conditions for children on the north of the city.

8. *A Better Deal for Highfields Kids*

The Committee drew up a leaflet for distribution to all residents. With the help of photographs taken one weekend with Instamatic cameras, we drew attention to the fact that while Hillfields contributed its share to the Council's budget via the rates, there was a startling contrast in the way the Council were able to allocate money to parks in other better-off areas, and to projects such as a £¼ million golf course and clubhouse, while at the same time saying that it was lack of finance which prevented them from providing suitable play facilities in Hillfields, or even providing a safe play area. As our leaflet said:

> 'Half our homes on this side of the city still don't have hot and cold running water, or a bathroom or inside toilet.
> Our streets are narrower and the houses more crowded together than in the better-off areas.
> Instead of big houses and gardens our kids have to play in small back-yards and bomb-sites.
> They've knocked down more houses than they've built, and the sky-scrapers that have gone up are DEATH TRAPS for children anyway.'

The Association called a public meeting for 9 January specifically to ask local people to help them demand a better deal for Hillfields kids and that the area be made safer for their children. One of the local ward councillors attended this public meeting and agreed to present a petition to the Council on behalf of the Association. Although the councillor told the meeting that there were long term plans to develop play areas, the residents were adamant that improvements were needed now.

The meeting was very badly attended, in spite of full leafleting of the area, some days in advance, and a reminder on the night via a loud-hailer from a car driven round the area from tea-time onwards.

Cold, foggy weather was part of the reason, and also probably a poor choice of meeting place—a church hall in the middle of waste-land, some distance from Gosford Green.

However, another part of the reason was certainly the mixed feelings in the area about a campaign for improved play provision for children. Some of the more elderly people whose houses backed on to the park feared an increase in nuisance and damage to their houses from a play area.

However, the small group who did attend the meeting took an active part from the floor, and at the end of the meeting three more people were co-opted on to the Committee—a working mother with a family of school-age children, a factory worker nearing retirement, and the wife of a student teacher who had already been active in campaigning for improved play provision in Hillfields.

This enlarged Committee then set about a systematic door-knocking of every house in the area, to get suport for our petition demanding:

— a full-time play leader in Primrose Park with a first-aid qualification,

— improved play equipment and facilities for children of all ages in Primrose Park,

— safety tiles around all play equipment.

This was a long, hard slog but it brought the Committee face to face for the first time with a large number of residents in the area, and door-step discussions gave us a chance to pass on information, to listen to reactions and above all to begin to build up more widespread backing for our campaign than was possible through public meetings. Eventually we had collected 732 signatures and made plans to present this to the City Council at their monthly meeting on 12 February.

9. *A Turning-Point for the Committee*

A leaflet was put around the area inviting residents to walk down to the Council House with us to hand in the petition. Apart from the Committee, only a handful of people turned up but spirits were high as the little group walked down through Hillfields. One carried a small banner:

'730 residents demand a better deal for Hillfields kids'.

The press had been invited to photograph the petition being handed over to the ward councillor, and the group then went up into the public gallery to hear what happened to it.

The experience proved to be a turning point for the Committee.

They felt that much of what went on in the Council meeting was a childish charade. They heard councillors laughing, shouting and jeering, and felt that none of the business was being treated at all seriously. Eventually the time came for the Gosford Green petition. The Committee were quite pleased with what the ward councillor said in support of it, but were angry when the Lord Mayor immediately cracked a joke about the Football Club, which seemed to reduce the whole thing to a laughing matter. We all trooped out of the Public Gallery and one member of the Committee felt so angry that she wrote a note of complaint about his behaviour and rammed it over the aerial of the Lord Mayor's car which was parked outside. Another

Committee member propped our banner up against his bonnet to drive our point home further.

10.   *The Petition Disappears into the Machine*

Two representatives from the Association were invited to attend the Recreation Committee on 8 March 1974 when our petition was discussed. It seemed to get more serious attention in this Committee than in full Council.

Councillors decided that representatives from the Recreation Committee, the Education Committee and the Public Consumer Protection Sub-Committee would make a joint visit to Primrose Hill Park to meet the Residents' Committee. This took until April to go through all the Committees, but the Association was hopeful that at least some of their demands would be met in due course.

It was decided to prepare for the the councillors' visit to the park by preparing detailed plans of the improvements we suggested, and to make sure these had full backing from local residents and from other residents' associations in the surrounding area. We also decided to ask officials in the Education Department about a grant to help us run a summer play scheme as a safeguard in case the demands of our petition had not been met by then.

The City's Youth and Community Adviser promised this as part of the Department's usual summer programme. He encouraged us to think of developing more permanent play activities and facilities on self-help lines. We rejected this and re-emphasised that, as ratepayers, we were arguing that the Council had an obligation to provide at least as good facilities for childen in Hillfields as in other better-off areas. We asked him to try to speed up the councillors' promised visit to the park to meet us.

In April the Committee sent its detailed plans and diagrams for improvements to Primrose Hill Park to the Chairman of the Recreation Committee, the three ward councillors, and the Director of Education. It was not until 2 July that the delegation from the Council Committees eventually visited the park.

The Council visit took place in the middle of the afternoon so our Committee was not able to turn up in full strength. Our representatives pressed the councillors hard for a definite decision about the demands in our petition, but they were still very non-committal. They said they would ask their officers to cost the schemes that we had put forward, and would consult us further, but there was not much money available next year, let alone this year. They mentioned that other residents' groups in the area were also competing for money for improvements to play facilities.

11. *One Year on and Still a Lot to Learn*

We began to feel that we were going to be fobbed off again. The Committee decided to keep pressing, but also to go ahead with the safeguard arrangements for a summer play-scheme. This would not only be better than nothing for local children; it could also help us to build up our case for play provision all the year round.

The Education Department had provided summer play activities on a small scale for some years in different parts of the city including Hillfields. We decided to try to make the best of this opportunity.

In July, a temporary summer play-scheme began in Primrose Hill Park. The play leader was a student teacher paid for by the Education Department. We also got a grant of £150 for coach trips and other play activities from the Hillfields Community Association, which acted as an umbrella for a number of community activities and which got an annual grant from CDP. The play scheme was a great success while it lasted. But there was still no sign of real progress over our demands for a full-time play leader; permanent improvements to play facilities in the park; or safety tiles.

A full year had passed since the beginning of the Association. Public meetings had been held. Literally scores of letters had been written. The Committee had met many times with individual councillors and officials. A strong petition with a lot of local support had been put in to the Council. We had met the Council Committee to discuss our demands. Hopes of success had been raised but time was dragging on, and we still seemed no nearer to getting our demands met. We obviously still had a lot to learn about how to get things changed.

12. *We're Learning as We go Along: We're Still Teething Aren't We?*

It may be helpful to break the story for a bit, to take stock of what the Committee feel they learned from the Play Campaign. This was tape decorded at a discussion at the beginning of October 1974 which I was not able to attend because of another engagement. Parts of the discussion show the benefit of hindsight, as it followed the campaign against the Football Club which is described later. However, it also shows how much more we still have to learn about working together to get things changed.

George:	What is your impression of our fight for improvements in the park ?
Kate:	Well, we've fought, fought hard and we haven't achieved anything yet.
Pat:	Due to lack of support from the local ward councillor . . . inactivity on his part.
Angela:	I wouldn't say that.
Kate:	About 20 of them turned up at the park.
Angela:	I think it is the red tape.
Kate:	What have they done? Nothing!
Pat:	We asked our local ward councillor, at the last public meeting—in public we asked him to press the Council to do something, urgently . . . and let's face it, he hasn't. We haven't had his support.
George:	I don't know whether we should condemn him so strongly.
Pat:	No, I wasn't condemning him then. I was just saying what I think the facts are. He just hasn't done anything has he?
George:	Well, what more did we expect him to do? He presented our petition, right? He attended our public meetings. He's spoken very strongly for our Association. I don't know how much more he could have done. What do you think, he could have done?
Pat:	At the last public meeting we asked him to look into it again, didn't we?
Karen:	I don't think he really did. He wasn't dedicated to the idea at all.
Phil:	They keep saying Hillfields has had its quota, but what about Gosford Green? They've done nothing at all there, have they?
Kate:	Yes, they promised to cut that hedge to 18 inches, for the safety of the children so that people could see what was happening, and they haven't done that. And that's only a small thing.
Angela:	That was at the public meeting.
Pat:	In fairness to the councillor, I think I should point out that we asked him to enquire as to the routine maintenance of the park—why wasn't it swept and kept in a state of good repair. He just didn't even do that. It wasn't a major financial project like we were asking for at the last meeting. It was just whether he could get the place swept up, more or less.
Kate:	At the meeting in the park we asked if that toilet could be fenced off for the safety of the children, because men were trying to entice children in there. Oh yes, they were going to get that done. 'That was the first thing'. 'The most important thing'. And they haven't even done that!
George:	But can we blame our ward councillor alone?
Kate:	I blame the whole Council.
Pat:	No, not alone, but I think we must realise that he is our representative, isn't he? If he won't do something about routine maintenance such as sweeping up—if he won't do that, it is an indication of the sort of chap he is. If he won't do that, what is he going to do on the major issue?

Gosford Green Residents' Association: A Case Study

Kate: But he did say that there was a park keeper there who was supposed to keep it in good order.

Pat: We asked him to see about that as well if you remember. He has done nothing. He has been inactive since the last public meeting.

George: That's the latest thing, but earlier on he was very enthusiastic, wasn't he?

Pat: Yes, but I think if we look at what he has done now to date and reflect on the earlier issues, it could give an indication as to why things haven't been happening.

Angela: I think perhaps at the beginning he thought that we were going to be a flash in the pan. Enthusiastic one minute and then it all die off so all we got was promises, promises. And he's surprised that we keep pushing.

Kate: Can we point to just *one* thing that he has forced.

Pat: There isn't.

George: I like Angela's analysis of the situation: that in the early days the councillor was very enthusiastic because he thought we would just last for a few months.

Angela: He practically told me that when he came to see me the other week about when he couldn't come to the meeting. He said that as a residents' group the Council had got more than they had bargained for. That we were very forceful. And he said that we had achieved a lot for such a short flung group, going for such a short time.

Kate: Such as?

Angela and George: Publicity?

Surinder: It hasn't done the Council much good, all this in the paper, has it. It hasn't made them look like saints has it—all this publicity? That's what we've achieved. We haven't achieved anything solid but we've achieved something in the press.

Angela: I think it will take a long time before we do achieve anything. I think we are trying to rush things. Because it does take a long time.

Alan: We've not exactly rushed have we!

Surinder: I thought this was supposed to be an action group . . .

Angela: The point is we've tried to cram a lot into the last 18 months. We have. And the Council just doesn't work that way. I mean they take things as it comes.

Pat: The Council just *won't* work that way.

Angela: You've got to keep pushing.

Surinder: We've got to push through the councillor. We can't really go up there every day.

Angela: We are pressuring our councillors all the time, aren't we?

George: Do you think we could have achieved more if we had had more public support? If more residents had come to our public meetings, if our petition had been signed by more?

Kate: I don't think we could have got more than we did, when we got 700 names.

Angela: I mean we got good support on our petition.

Kate: But people don't seem much for meetings do they? Because at the HCA AGM the other week there were only about 70 people there, and they were all elderly people. No young people among them.

219

Surinder: Well they think the same as the Council, that it is just a flash in the pan. They're here for two weeks and they're gone after that. You never hear from them again.

George: Going back to the park, what about the play leader? Was that an achievement.

Karen: No, we would have got one anyway.

Surinder: There was one last year wasn't there?

Angela: Although I think this summer was more successful than previous years.

George: Didn't we get more kids coming because of the Association's publicity?

Kate: Oh, I think that had an effect on it.

Angela: Yes, Kate went round and Harry went round, taking the news.

Slim: I think the play leader was able to do his job because he had the support of you lot. A guy is terribly isolated on his own and finds it much more difficult.

Surinder: He's got nobody. If the local people don't help him, who does he go to? . . . He can only talk to the kids, and that's it really.

George: So to that extent the Association was useful.

Karen: Yeah. I think so.

George: On the park, do we feel disillusioned or do we feel that the fight has been worthwhile?

Karen: Well the fight hasn't begun yet!

Kate: The fight's been on—but we haven't won anything.

Angela: I think we've got to put on more pressure.

Pat: I think it is significant that it is a *fight*. Why should it be? Why should it be a fight?

Karen: You mean we shouldn't have to fight for it?

Surinder: But it is our right, that's it surely.

Pat: Maybe we should have to ask . . .

Angela: When you look at the other side of the town—yes.

Surinder: You can compare it with Finham Park or Stivichall—those areas —you don't get kids running round in the roads playing football. You get proper amenities. Why not here?

Kate: And another thing, they have got bigger gardens. They are not like the kids round here. The gardens are not big enough to play in.

Angela: So by right we should have more play areas.

George: Do you think the the response we've had from the Council makes you think that we have turned our fight into a right? Do you think they look upon it now as a right?

Angela: No, not at all. I think we still have to battle for anything we get.

Pat: They'll take their time too. If they want to do it, they'll do it. That's it. If they don't want to do it they'll probably just sit around watching us lot jumping up and down.

Angela: So, we've got to create as much fuss . . .

Alan: I don't think we can sit around and wait for them to decide what they want to do. It's got to be the other way round because they're just not going to do that. It's got to be us deciding what we are going to do, and how we are going to get it. The important thing is how we apply pressure on the Council to get it. At the moment as regards this park, they've just been satisfied to give summer schemes not only in this area but all over the town, with all the publicity in the world—kids out to Coombe Park, trips on the canal—while the rest of the year nothing happens. And they've done that for years now.

Surinder: Of course they get a big spread in the Telegraph any time they do anything. But when they don't do anything, nobody ever hears at all.

Kate: All that seems to matter to the Council is to have lovely parks on the main bus routes. That park is off the bus route and it just doesn't matter to them.

Pat: The play leader was able to achieve a lot more because the Gosford Green Residents' Association got some funds from the HCA for him to dip into apart from the Council grant.

Angela: Don't they have that every year though or is this the first year?

Karen: This is the first year they have given that amount of money away.

Angela: That's because you had the cheek to ask for it!

Alan: We were lucky to have an HCA in the area then, or else even that wouldn't have happened.

George: Do you think then that what we have learned from our experience convinces you that you should go on fighting?

Pat: We've got no choice have we really? If you don't do anything more, you're giving up the fight that you've started. And if you give up on that, every issue you bring forward they'll say they'll give up on. See if we keep on going with one issue, from all the issues we've started, they'll take notice. But if we keep dropping off our issues, they will think—well they've forgotten that one. In another few months they will forget that one, and that one . . . and you know we've got rid of them.

George: So we're even more determined to continue fighting.

Surinder: Yes, we've got to. There's no other thing we can do.

Alan: We've got to ask ourselves how we are going to do it though. Surely we've learned over the past . . . we've been fighting. (The word is a bit strong I think really—with all this letter writing nonsense that happened early on—which people laughed at then—I was at the second public meeting before I was on this Committee and they were going about all this letter writing to the Football Ground and I got a mouthful from a guy who was the secretary at the time about 'Oh we're going to write some letters and see how it works out you know.') But I think experience shows that we have to question the whole kind of way in which we apply pressure.

Angela: *These are the things we're going to learn as we go along. We are learning. We're still teething aren't we?*

13. *An Unfriendly Match*

During the summer play-scheme another issue came to a head which taught us all quite a lot. We discovered that the City Football Club had plans to demolish four houses in King Richard Street to make way for a carpark for the club's directors and vice-presidents. Our attempts to stop this were another important milestone for the Committee.

Although we did not realise it at the time, the kick-off for this unfriendly match had taken place at our inaugural public meeting back in July 1973.

Here is the action replay of the key moves by both sides:

4 July 1973—Inaugural Public Meeting
Among many complaints about the Football Ground, an old age pensioner from the top end of King Richard Street by the football stand, said that an agent from the City Football Club had come round pressing her to sell her house and she felt under considerable pressure. She said, with quite a lot of emotion, that nothing would ever get her to move out of the area. Other residents at the meeting complained about the number of houses which the Football Club seemed to be buying up and turning into ticket offices or storerooms for the Football Club. Doubts were voiced about whether they had planning permission for all these changes of use. It was agreed to first meet the Manager of the Club to press for more information in a friendly atmosphere and to base future decisions on the Club's reaction.

July to December 1973
Correspondence with the City Football Club was followed by meetings with Mr. Plumley, the secretary, and later with Mr. Joe Mercer, the manager. The Committee were told by both of them that lack of finance would prevent the City Football Club for some years from developing the schemes which had been publicised in the local paper for a double-decker stand, a concert hall, clubroom and other social facilities and a car park to hold 10,000 to 15,000 cars.

In fact, however, we later discovered that during this very period while we were in discussion with them the city football club had actually applied to the city council for permission to demolish numbers 76 and 74 King Richard Street and to develop a small car park on that site.

30 January 1974
A public meeting was called by the Association to get information on road and redevelopment plans for the area. It was attended by the Chairman of Planning Committee, Chairman of Housing Committee, the Deputy Lord Mayor and other councillors and officers.

Residents protested again about the rumours of expansion by the Coventry City Football Club. We were told that the City had not got or even applied for planning permission to build the £1 million super stadium which had been described in the Coventry Evening Telegraph in December. However, residents had evidence that the Club were still buying up houses in the area and feared that they intended to demolish them. We were told by Council Officers that there is no law which can stop the City Football Club buying up houses and no law to say that they cannot pull them down. But they must have planning permission to build anything after that.

5 February 1974

A letter was sent by the Residents' Committee to the City Architect and Planning Officer asking for copies of any plans put forward for the development of Coventry City Football Club and for the Stoke Conservative Club on the corner of Walsgrave Road and Grantham Street.

His reply, dated 19 February, invited the Association to call at the Department of Architecture and Planning to inspect the plans.

13 March 1974

The Committee wrote to the Patron, the President and each of the Directors of the Coventry City Football Club Ltd. asking for a statement about the rumours around the area that the City Football Club planned to pull down a number of the houses that they owned at the top end of King Richard Street to make way for a bigger car park for the directors and vice-presidents.

25 March 1974

Reply from the General Secretary of the City Football Club.

His letter gave no definite answer to our question but seemed to accept that the Directors were acquiring property in the area for the eventual extension of the Club's facilities (including car parking) but that lack of finance would limit the progress of this for some years to come.

But the very next day . . .!

26 March 1974

Coventry City Council refused an application which had been made by the City Football Club in November 1973 to demolish numbers 76 and 74 King Richard Street, and use the land for a car park. One of the reasons given for the council's refusal is that the houses in question could continue to be used as family accommodation, of which there is a current shortage in the City.

14. *One Law for the Rich . . .*

During May, residents told the Committee of further strong rumours that the Football Club were planning to shortly demolish a block of four houses at the top end of King Richard Street to clear space for an open car park. Although they had been refused planning permission to do this for 76 and 74 King Richard Street we knew that they had recently bought number 70 and that the old age pensioner who was sandwiched in the middle of these houses at number 72 (and who had complained at our first public meeting about the Football Club's pressure to sell her house to them) had eventually sold up to the City Football Club.

We heard that the Football Club was preparing a flat at number 89 King Richard Street, which they own on the opposite side of the street, to re-house the present occupant of 76 King Richard Street, who is the widow of a former employee of the club.

Although the council had refused planning permission to build a car park, nothing could stop the Football Club knocking the houses down and using the empty site for car-parking.

Over the years, the Football Club had done a number of things in the area which seemed to flout normal procedures.

> Their new stand was built 9ft higher than people had been led to believe; this caused poor T.V. reception in the area and cost the most nearby residents £30 each for extra high aerials. It also created wind current so that smoke blew back down their chimneys. The Football Club had also turned a number of houses into ticket offices or store rooms, either without planning permission, or after planning permission had expired.

In view of this the residents' Association Committee decided to circulate a leaflet about what was going on and to organise a petition to save these houses. Our leaflet produced quite a lot of local publicity.

The Committee invited the Chairman of Housing Committee, who is also one of our local ward councillors, to meet to discuss the possibility of the City Council buying up the houses by compulsory purchase.

He called to see our secretary before the meeting and said he was unable to attend, but that he had the problem in hand. He said publicity might spoil what he was trying to do, and advised the

Association to keep quiet and leave it to him. He said that he was also looking into the possibility of making the whole area a General Improvement Area.

The Committee decided we could not rely on these kind of informal promises in view of the evidence that over the years the Football Club seemed to have been able to do what it wanted with or without planning permission.

15. *Beds Before Bentleys*

June 1974

We went ahead with our information leaflet and began to do quite a lot of door knocking in the area, to get support for our petition. We decided to hand this in to the ward councillors the night before the full Council meeting, when the controlling Labour Party held their party group meeting.

We wrote to the councillors telling them of our intentions and lobbied other Labour councillors with leaflets as they entered the Party meeting, on 10 June.

11 June 1974

A petition of 540 signatures from local residents was presented to the City Council by one of the ward councillors on behalf of the Residents' Association.

The petitioners asked that in view of the growing housing shortage in Coventry, the City Council use their powers:

1. To stop the Directors of Coventry City Football Club from buying up any more houses in the area for use other than as family dwelling houses;
2. To put an immediate stop to all plans the Directors of the Football Club have to demolish houses in the area;
3. To compulsorily purchase the houses which have already been bought by the Board of the City Football Club, and to convert them back to ordinary dwellings;
4. To ensure that the City Football Club compensate the residents of Mowbray Street for the hardship and inconvenience caused by the Club.

The petition was later submitted to the Housing and Planning Committees who decided to send representatives to meet the City Football Club and the Residents' Committee. They were advised by their officers, however, that it might be difficult and lengthy to use the compulsory purchase powers.

The Residents' Association Committee decided to call a public meeting to decide what more we could do to press the issue.

We also considered asking Trade Union branches and other organisations in the city to give us support, and decided to invite representatives from the Trades Council and from the Housing Action Group (a squatting group concerned with homelessness and the housing problem in Coventry) to meet us for discussion.

17 June 1974

The Housing Action Group sent two representatives to describe what their group did. They had done a survey on empty property in the city last December and had come across the Football Club's empty houses in King Richard Street then.

At this stage they did not plan any action over these houses and would wait to see what local residents decided.

The Residents' Committee decided to call a public meeting on 3 July to discuss with residents the possibility of some kind of demonstration against the Football Club. A small group of Committee members was asked to think about various kinds of direct action that we could put forward to the public meeting for their decision. Two members of this small sub-committee got involved in further discussions with the Housing Action Group and came to the conclusion that the best thing would be for homeless families to squat in the empty houses. They argued to the rest of the Committee that this should be done *before* the public meeting in order to give a definite lead in the area. Others on the Committee argued that no action should be taken until after the full discussion with local residents at a public meeting.

9 July 1974

This division of opinion came to a head the night before the public meeting. Two of the Committee members announced that there was a homeless family waiting to be moved into one of the Football Club's houses that night. They pressed the Committee to support this action and to ask for the public meeting to 'confirm' it the following evening. After a lengthy and painful discussion it was decided that anything that the two Committee members chose to do before the public meeting could not be in the name of the Association but would have to be in their personal capacity or under the auspices of the Housing Action Group.

The following morning these two Commitee members with support from the Housing Action Group entered number 70 King Richard Street and began to prepare the house for occupation by a homeless family.

The City Football Club immediately boarded up numbers 72 and 74 King Richard Street.

10 July 1974
Annual General Meeting of Gosford Green Residents' Association

The Committee had done quite a lot of door-knocking to encourage people to attend the public meeting, and at tea-time went out with a loud hailer to remind everyone. The attendance was disappointing. This time neither the weather (fine) nor the place (the local pub) could be the explanation. At one stage there were more representatives from the Housing Action Group in the hall than local residents. However, numbers slowly built up and eventually reached 35 to 40.

As it was the AGM members of the Committee reported progress in the various campaigns being carried out by the Residents' Association. These reports suggested that little success had resulted so far from either 'reasonable' letters or discussions with the appropriate bodies, or from working through the established machinery of councillors, petitions, and so on.

When it came to the issue of the houses threatened with demolition, members of the Housing Action Group told the meeting that they had occupied one of the houses that morning and were preparing it for a homeless family to squat.

Residents had a lot of misgivings about the HAG squat and expressed a number of prejudices about homeless and 'problem' families.

However, members of the Committee spoke out in support and finally the discussion centred on what action we as an Association should take over the Football Club's creeping control over the area. A vote was taken which gave the Committee full support in organising any direct action that might be necessary in an emergency to prevent the four houses actually being demolished. There was little realistic dicussion of how this could be done in practice, but some kind of 'sit-in' was favoured.

16. *Direct Action*

21 July 1974

The Residents' Committee was informed by the Housing Action

227

Group that the family squatting in 70 King Richard Street would be leaving for more permanent accommodation at the end of the week. The Committee decided to call an emergency meeting of all those who had attended the previous public meeting.

23 July 1974

The Committee told the emergency meeting that the family who had been squatting was going to move into more pemament accommodation. The Committee feared that as soon as the house was empty the Football Club would board it up and even strip out the inside. The Committee suggested we could stop this in one of three ways:

(i) occupying the house and using it as a day centre for old people;
(ii) using it as a play centre for local children;
(iii) that Committee members should occupy the house with the support of local residents on a rota system.

After discussion, the third suggestion was agreed by all present, with only one vote against.

During the above discussion the local ward councillor visited the meeting. He confirmed the previous hints from the Chairman of the Housing Committee that the area might be declared a General Improvement Area. He said that once this was done the Football Club would not be able to demolish any more houses. (We later discovered that this is not strictly true, as houses can be pulled down in a General Improvement Area.)

We asked the councillor how long it would take to make our area a GIA. He said it would probably come up at the next Council Meeting in September but could not give an exact date. Residents disapproved of this because of the need for urgent action over the houses and the risk of a change of policy after the next elections, which could put us back to square one.

A planning adviser from the CDP Team reminded the meeting that the Council had powers to compulsorily purchase the houses under section 19c of the 1957 Housing Act. Councillor Richards said he did not know of this, but invited the Chairman of the Committee to go with him to discuss this possibility with Council officials.

After the Councillor had left, the Committee decided to make an appointment to see the local MP; to ask the Trades Council to pass a resolution urging the City Council to compulsorily purchase the houses; and to put out a leaflet to all local residents asking them to come on Sunday afternoon to an open air meeting outside the houses which we feared were to be demolished.

Sunday, 28 July 1974

There had been a lot of controversy both in the area and on the Committee about the Housing Action Group squat at 70 King Richard Street. This had produced a lot of personal tensions and the Committee's spirits were fairly low when we went along to the open air meeting. A handful of a dozen or more people had gathered outside the house, and a bit of door-knocking around surrounding houses encouraged two or three more. There was a general air of uncertainty and hopelessness around, but everyone agreed that it would be scandalous if the Football Club managed to get away with the demolition of the houses after all this. The Committee told the group of its proposal to try to stop this by getting up a rota of residents to occupy 70 King Richard Street, as soon as the family squatting there moved out the following day. After some discussion, a few people offered their names and times, including at least one resident who had voted *against* direct action of this kind at the Annual General Meeting on 10 July.

29 July 1974

The family moved out and the Residents' Association rota of occupation began. This was done on an hour by hour basis, throughout each day and evening, with the temporary play leader, from the summer play-scheme, sleeping there every night. Keeping the rota going involved Committee members in a lot more door-knocking and perhaps for the first time there began to be some sense of the Committee being in touch with and getting active support from a wider group of local residents.

Easy chairs, a radio and magazines where brought in, and cups of tea and coffee were kept brewing. The house began to feel like a small community centre, with neighbours getting to know each other better. A feeling of real solidarity developed against the Football Club and a determination to put up resistance this time.

30 July 1974

The County Court granted the City Football Club possession of the house but the order was made in the name of the individual who had first occupied the house on 10 July. The Residents' Association put a notice in the window of the house explaining that no person of that name was now there and that the Association was now occupying the house and must be dealt with through the Courts.

A notice inside the door reminded those in occupation not to give their individual name to any enquirers, but always to say that they were acting on behalf of the Residents' Association.

The rota of occupation continued on a 24 hour basis for over 300 hours and involved 35 separate local residents. The day time was covered by mothers with their children, old-age pensioners and people on shift-work. On odd occasions it wasn't possible to get anyone to fill the rota. When this happened the radio or the lights were left on in the house to keep up the evidence of occupation!

17. *The First Signs of Victory*

2 *August 1974*

The Committee went by appointment to see the local MP to ask him (in view of the housing shortage in the city) to press the Council to use their powers to compulsorily purchase the houses. He began by suggesting that the Football Club should be asked to re-let them as ordinary dwellings. But the Committee argued forcibly that the Football Club had a bad record of doing what it liked in the area and of flouting planning permissions and so on.

He accepted the Committee's arguments and agreed to make a statement to the press supporting their case. (The Committee had taken the precaution of telling the press of their visit to the MP beforehand so it had already been announced publicly that he would be making a statement.)

His statement in support of compulsory purchase of the houses was duly reported the following day, together with his promise to tell the Lord Mayor and the Leader of the Council of his views.

5 *August 1974*

A statement appeared in the local paper that the City Football Club had abandoned their plans to pull down the four houses and were willing to negotiate for their sale to the City Council.

18. *How Much Did We Really Achieve?*

This was not a final or straightforward victory for local residents. First, the City Football Club had only said that they were 'willing to negotiate' with the City Council for the sale of the houses they had planned to demolish. Even by October those 'negotiations' were still not finished, and the houses were still unoccupied. Second, it emerged that although the statement had not appeared in the press until Monday, 5 August, it had actually been released by the City Council on *Friday* (2 August) and so had come out before the Committee had met the MP and gained his public support. Thirdly, we later discovered that in March 1974 central government had asked for an enquiry into the control of demolition. The report of this enquiry was not published until September 1974 but the local authority may well have heard rumours that it was going to recommend that demolition without planning permission should be made an offence.

However, there is no doubt that the Gosford Green campaign made a big contribution to the rescue of King Richard Street houses. On top of this, the Committee had certainly learned a lot more about how to organise to bring about changes. The following tape-recorded discussion took place in October when the Committee's spirits were a bit low again, but it shows up some of the things we have learned.

George: I think Alan you said we hadn't achieved anything. My own opinion is that we have achieved something as far as the houses are concerned.

Angela: Well, I think we've stopped them pulling them down.

George: Yes, they haven't pulled them down. I noticed that that house we were occupying has not been boarded up. Which is something. I think they feel it is no longer necessary—their case is almost lost so there is no point in doing it.

Angela: I think we have achieved something in that field.

George: What do you think?

Alan: The houses are still there. But why did we want them to not knock them down? Surely we wanted them to not knock them down so that people could move into them, not so that they could stand there being boarded up, or not being boarded up, and stand there empty! So we haven't actually achieved anything yet.

Angela: We've stopped them from pulling the houses down, which they admitted when they offered to sell them.

Pat: That's an achievement, isn't it?

Surinder: It's a step in the right direction.

Kate: That's all.

Surinder: Yes, but I mean you can't take these things straight off.

George: It takes time. I mean we couldn't say well tomorrow we'll put in residents and we have achieved something.

Kate: It will take months when they've got them, before they move anyone in.

George: They'll have to renovate them and decorate them and so on first.

Angela: When we first started occupying the house, we couldn't see ourselves keeping the house open from one day to the next but we've
managed it so far. So I think we have achieved a lot. By just keeping those houses open we've proved something to our councillors.

George: What did you think was our main ammunition in that? The
turning point?

Pat: The MP.

Angela: No, I think the squat. I think it was already decided to sell them
to the Council before the MP . . . Because we went to see Wilson
on Friday and it was announced on Monday and I don't think
they took that decision over the weekend.

(N.B.: We were told later that the statement was in fact released on the
Friday).

George: One interesting feature of the housing issue was the number of
residents who came to support us and were amazed that we could
have achieved so much. They were not so interested before, when
they thought we were fighting an irresistible force. When they saw
the statement in the press a lot of them turned up as volunteers to
support us.

Surinder: Another point was that the Committee went to the doors and asked
people rather than waiting for them to come.

Angela: And the public meeting we had in the street the day before we
occupied and we went round banging on the doors—I think that
was a lot to do with it.

Alan: I think people are definitely attracted by some kind of action within
the locality.

George: Do you remember at our public meeting we invited people who
were prepared to come and sit down if possible and to stop the
bulldozers pulling these houses down. And we had so many volunteers, including women and kids.

Surinder: Well this is it you see. It involves them. It really involves them
round this area. In national issues they can't do anything about it
but when it is local they can actually see something happening, and
once you see something happening you want to do something about
it. But if it doesn't really involve you then you don't really think
about it.

Alan: I think we would have done even better if—I stick to the point I
made when the decision was taken, that we wouldn't open the
place to old people and kids. I think we would have done even
better if we had done that now. I think it would have been more of
a focus, more a centre of attraction.

Kate: I don't think so really.

Surinder: I don't see what that would have achieved really.

Alan: I am just saying that the sort of reaction people had when something was on, people came along and sat there for an hour in the
the house and did their bit on the rota. Even that meeting we had
in the street, that caused a bit of a stir in the street you know. And
I still think that we would have done better had we opened
it for the kids as a play centre.

Mr. Beech: But that was going to be difficult. If you started an old people's
club or got kids in, the Council would not have considered buying
them because they would call them tenants wouldn't they?

Gosford Green Residents' Association: A Case Study

Angela: Let's face it if we had put anyone in there they would have called them tenants. No matter what we were doing.

Pat: No, it goes against trying to achieve our objective to keep them as dwelling houses.

Alan: I'm not talking about a permanent thing but given the fact that we had play leaders up at the park . . .

Kate: But look at the disappointment you are going to have to give to children that have been playing there when you tell them the Council have bought this, you can't come any more. Old people get involved with older people and you tell them you can't come you can't come any more. I think it is the wrong thing.

Alan: I don't know Kate. We've been looking at those two problems as well and probably many more. Why isn't there somewhere in the area where kids can go?

Kate: We want somewhere in the area but not in that way, when we want the Council to buy them. I think we should . . .

Angela: But we'd have shown the Council that we do need something if it was supported well.

Surinder: But maybe people now would be prepared to do a litttle bit more because they would have been disappointed with what had happened so they would have wanted to carry it further on.

George: But I think on the whole the housing issue so far anyway has been going our way. I feel we have achieved something. Not much but it was something to be proud of and it sort of rekindled the spirits of the residents because we had been fighting—this was something positive to show and they were more prepared to support us.

Kate: And I think it is a pity that we stopped the rota. Because it showed we were still interested. Now it looks as though the interest is lost since we finished the rota.

Slim: What are people saying in the streets about the houses now?

Kate: Nothing.

Surinder: They seem to think the fight is won and that the Council are going to buy it.

Alan: I still think though Kate that if we had tried to keep the rota going it would have died in the state that it was because there was nothing happening there. It was a novelty for a bit.

Kate: I think it began to be a bit of a social centre. We didn't want it in that way but it would have carried on for a while until they bought them.

Alan: I don't think we would have kept it going that long.

Kate: I think we would, because more and more people were coming in weren't they?

George: Especially elderly ladies who were coming to chat.

Kate: Without making it an old people's meeting place, it was a place where they could come and talk about things in the area.

George: I think we went as far as we could have gone. Having reached the stage where there are negotiations between the Council and the Football Club, short of compulsory purchase, there is nothing else we could have done and if we continued making a noise about it, then perhaps the Council might have said look what you complaining about? After all we are negotiating to buy the houses . . .

233

George : The other thing I think is that for a long time the residents in this area haven't complained, at least not collectively. As far as I know, ours was the first collective group that came out of this area—I mean in this particular region of the area. When I have talked to councillors they say that before your Association started in that area, it was very peaceful . . . and now you have these militants coming in and causing a lot of trouble.

Angela : That could be because a lot of the people in this area are older people and the younger people don't stay long so you know that could be something.

Kate : Of course there aren't many places that have got garages and most people have got cars and the young people move out.

Angela : It's a dying area.

George : It's a dying area—yes I think that is a good description.

Angela : It *was* a dying area!

Pat : What about the GIA?

Angela : What *about* the GIA?

George : I think it was one of the bribes the Council wanted to give us!

George : Is there anything we have learned from our experience. Is there anything we would have done differently if we had known what would happen?

Angela : I thing in future campaigns we will realise that we have not to be fobbed off by the Council. We have got to push and fight for everything we get from the start and no more letter writing, being polite, waiting for replies. We've got to take the bull by the horns and go straight in and ask for what we want. Demand it, not ask. Demand.

George : It doesn't pay to believe in their promises.

Angela : No, not all all. Unless you've got them in writing, actually signed, sealed and delivered.

Alan : We can talk about demand and push and all the rest of it, but how are we going to do it? You are not in a position to make any kind of demands unless you've got some kind of power at your finger tips. You can't demand anything of anybody let alone the Council.

Pat : Obviously you've got to organise something like a demonstration.

George : What is our power then?

Angela : Surely bad publicity for our councillors; passing a vote of no confidence like we talked about before.

Alan : We're not going to get the Council bad publicity in our local rag though, are we?

Pat : No.

Angela : They could have given us more support over those houses.

Kate : I don't think they've treated us badly. We have had as much coverage as most of the groups.

Angela : We haven't had support from them.

Pat : They should have taken our side and they didn't.

Kate : I don't think they take sides.

Alan : They take sides all right, Kate.

George: The Telegraph always had something on us. It may have been non-committal, but at least it kept the issues alive.

Angela: But they should have committed themselves, especially over this housing situation. But of course they've got shares in Coventry City Football Club.

Pat: They're the second largest shareholders aren't they?

George: Has any of us ever thought the Committee worthless. Who have no enthusiasm . . .?

Kate: Just lately I've got a bit depressed. We seem to have achieved nothing. Everything has gone dull.

Angela: Oh Kate enjoyed the squat.

Kate: I want to see things happen.

Angela: I felt a bit down just before we started the squat because I thought we couldn't do it, and I didn't see what we were going to do or anything. But the sun shone the next day!

George: Have any of you ever thought 'well this is really too much'? Alan I know for you without action, we're doing nothing.

Alan: It's not a case of action or nothing. I still don't think we've got down to talking about it. I think what we've really got to discover is what threat we pose to the Council. What power we've got as a residents' group. Unless we've got some kind of power we can use against them . . .

George: We really have not discovered what our power is and unless we have power, really we are not achieving anything.

Alan: Basically, it is whether we have got power or not. Not whether we have discovered what it is.

Pat: Stopping those houses coming down—it may not be a lot in your eyes—but it is something. I know you don't think it is a lot; I don't think it is such a lot, but it is something.

Kate: But there's such a lot of little things they could have done.

Alan: You see, it seems to stick out like a sore thumb to me that this whole thing has been going on over 18 months or whatever and I am sure most people have said tonight that we have achieved next to nothing . . .

Slim: (a community worker) What I would like to ask him is where does he see power coming from in this sort of situation? Because I can remember conversations that we've had about things like, does this committee give a lead, particularly at the time when there were all those troubles about were we going to squat a family or not. There were all sorts of different arguments being put forward as to what was the most powerful way of making the point about those houses. What do you think? Where do you think the power lies and how can a group of people organise to get and maintain that power? It is all very well to say we don't understand where the power is but I suspect that you have some ideas about what power means and how it can be used.

Alan: Really to be honest I think it is a very tricky position as a residents' group because I don't see us having so much power, and without some kind of threat behind us . . . with something to back you up. At work the situation is very simple. All the guys at work . . . if they want to effect a change at work in conditions or wages or whatever, they talk and they might write letters to their

235

	employers the same as we do, but they won't do anything until the blokes walk out the gate. They say we are not going to make your cars for you. That is the time when people start sitting up and taking notice.
Kate:	But what could we do in that way?
Alan:	Quite. That's the point. They have the power in that they do produce something. The guy that runs that car plant can't work, can't make his money if his workers walk out on him.
Slim:	The workers can only walk out in that situation if they are solidly organised.
Angela:	So our power lies with the people in the area . . .
Slim:	So two guys can't just decide up and out.
Alan:	True, but the point is the possibility is there. The power is there . . . if you know how to use it. What I am questioning is whether the power is here.
Karen:	You mean if we had all the residents behind us . . . would that be power then?
Slim:	How do you demonstrate you've got a threat? Karen says let's have a rates strike . . .
Alan:	Well that is maybe a bit of a threat.
Pat:	So what do they do? They take a couple of test cases. They take them to court and prosecute . . .
George:	The only power I can identify belonging to a group like ours is public pressure. Publicity, embarrassing . . .
Alan:	That's not where the power is, though George, is it?
George:	It means for example lobbying the Trades Council, lobbying the groups that have power. Certainly publicising the issues involving residents, having demonstrations, having squatting, as we have. That's the only power we have as far as I can see.
Alan:	You just mentioned approaching groups that have power but say if you haven't got power, and we seem to know that we haven't got any power, and we approach the Trades Council that have got power, against the City Council. That is something we haven't done, is it? That may be a good thing to try and do.
George:	We attempted to do it over the housing issue, if you remember. We did write to the Trades Council . . . and while things were moving I think the decision was taken that they were negotiating to buy the houses . . . But I think that is the only power we have.
Slim:	What are your ideas about power and the number of people involved. How do you see that sort of solid organisation that you have at work being developed here? How do you see that sort of organisation being developed at home, in the way in which it is at work?
Alan:	It's very tricky. I don't really see it but if you want to succeeed I think you've got to develop some kind of power—let''s put it that way . . . We've got to find it from somewhere and we haven't got it at the moment.
Angela:	We've got to find out who supports us in the residents. That's where our power lies—with people in the area. That's the only way we are going to get anywhere. It's got to get full backing of every resident in the area.

Alan: But don't you see my point? What does that mean in effect? Even if you get every resident in the area to stand up and say we want, I don't know, a new swimming bath planted in the park over there.

Pat: Even if you did have the backing of them and everybody had a rates strike, it wouldn't come to much. It's like you said, we've got to tap off something like the Trades Council that's got real power.

George: I don't know really . . . I still feel that people still have the hope and they can use that as a threat. If you can mobilize the residents to demand and say unless you are prepared to support us, we are going to withdraw our votes and we are going to put up another candidate.

Slim: That's right George, but like the rates strike, that depends on a total commitment by everyone.

19. *Assessment*

When set against the broad aims we outlined for our group, the Gosford Green experience is certainly a very small-scale, and low-key piece of work. The conditions in the area were not of the most gross kind; the issues tackled by the residents association were not the most acute forms of oppression; the numbers involved in the action were relatively small; the contribution made by the C.D.P. Team members was fairly unsystematic. Nevertheless, there are perhaps as important lessons to be learned from this amorphous kind of experience as from those situations where the political issues present themselves more starkly. It is certainly part of our belief that the consequences of capitalism are experienced not just at the level of macro-economics and the political structure, but also in the here-and-now relationships of ordinary day-to-day living, both at work and at home. I will try to assess the Gosford Green experience in terms of

(1)   the material changes achieved

(2)   the development of political consciousness and organisation

(3)   the contributions made by ourselves as workers.

20. *Material Changes Achieved*

The main material change that the Residents' Association has seen is undoubtedly the stopping of the possibility that four sound terraced houses would be demolished by the Directors of Coventry City Football Club Limited, to make way for a car park for their Directors and Vice-Presidents. The City Council would probably claim that they had already opened negotiations to buy these houses from the Football Club and that the Residents' Association campaign and occupation made it harder for them to pull this off. It is true that the City Council at the time had a policy of buying up private housing in the older areas, and so that Residents' demands represented pressure to *implement* an existing policy, rather than a challenge to existing policy. Futhermore the City Council's 'municipalization' policy was backed by Central Government policy and finance. In that sense the residents demands did not even amount to pressure for new or extra resources but only for their use in a particular direction.

The Directors of the Football Club Limited were also subject to pressures not to demolish their houses, from other sources than simply the Residents' Association or the City Council. Central government had recently ordered a top-level enquiry into 'development control', and although the Dobry report was not published until September 1974, it was rumoured some months earlier that one of the main recommendations was to be that demolition without planning permission should be made an offence.

These three factors mean that it cannot by any means be claimed that the Gosford Green campaign was directly responsible for stopping the houses being demolished. However it is more certain that the residents actions changed the *way* in which that decision came about. The Gosford Green campaign meant that the reversal of the Football Club's intentions could not be limited to an internal temporary procedural change, but was forced into becoming a public, irreversible shift of principle. The issue could not any longer be dealt with as an isolated local matter, but was debated in relation to wider questions about the size of the housing waiting-list in Coventry, the constraints on public house-building, and the relative influence of commercial and voluntary organisations.

The other issues—conditions for children and play provision in the local parks—was ostensibly less controversial. The City Council never disputed that what residents were asking for was reasonable. However, in practice, the demands for a fulltime play-leader and more extensive imaginative and safer play facilities, represented pressure for creation of a new policy and investment of extra resources. The Councillors kept arguing that if they provided these facilities in Hillfields there would be a precedent for similar demands from other areas. It was difficult for them to reject the validity of the demands as such, so after a long period of energy-sapping non-decision making, their response was that the scope of the demands was over-ambitious and financially unrealistic. They were gradually whittled down to the costing of some minor improvements in hedging and fencing, but even these concessions were lost when central government imposed further cuts on local government expenditure at the beginning of 1975. The only material change in the conditions or the facilities in the two local parks by Spring 1975 was the cutting of the hedges down to half their previous height. The Chairman of Recreation Committee offered this to reduce the risks of children being importuned (following worries by residents) but it later emerged in the local press that hedges were being halved in height at a number of parks, to reduce the costs of maintenance. In material terms the Parks campaign was a complete failure. However, the aims we expressed for our work were not only concerned with material change, but with political learning. It is this that I will now try to assess.

21. *Developments in Political Consciousness and Organisation*

One of the main problems of political organisation in an area like Gosford Green is how to build a movement out of a variety of cross-cutting interest groups (e.g., long-standing owner-occupiers, short-stay tenants of rooming houses; English, Irish and Asian; students, deviants and respectable working-class). Before the initial public meeting, I had discussed with the other people in the sponsoring group the possibility that we might try to work through some kind of mass meeting rather than the traditional Committee. This was very quickly scotched at the first public meeting by demands that before we discuss any issues at all we should constitute ourselves as a 'proper Association' with officers. Given that the public meeting had failed to attract some of the interest-groups with most pressing problems (e.g., tenants of single rooms; single pensioner householder), the people who got elected on to the Committee tended to be those who expressed a concern for 'the area' in general and sometimes abstract terms, rather than those with an immediate self-interest.

The Committee realised very early on that its strength and credibility depended not upon the passion of the letters we wrote, or the comprehensiveness of our constitution, but upon maintaining a broad power-base in the area. At first the Committee acted as if it could take no initiative at all without being instructed by a public meeting. It soon became clear that public meetings were not giving the

Committee any clear directives, and that residents were looking to the Committee for a lead. Gradually the Committee moved from seeing itself purely in terms of simple 'bottom-up representation' and began to take responsibility for exercising leadership and trying to build up a constituency of support around initiatives that it was prepared to suggest. It saw its mandate coming from having checked out such initiatives with as wide a group as possible, beforehand. Sometimes this was done at public meetings, but (as attendances were generally poor) increasingly through petitions, door-knocking, news letters and on two occasions emergency action mettings. The Committee and a small constellation of supporters learned some important lessons about solidarity and accountability, particularly at the time of occupation of the Football Club houses. One long-standing resident showed his understanding by allowing himself to be bound by a majority decision with which he had personally disagreed and voted against. More painful issues were struggled through by the Committee in deciding how to react to the Committee member who had chosen to act as an individual, without the Committee's support, in occupying one of the Football Club houses *before* the public meeting had mandated this kind of action. When interviewed by the local press he gave a false name but allowed himself to be photographed and quoted as a member of the Committee. He refused the Committee's request to resign and the Committee eventually asked authority from a public meeting to dismiss him from the Committee. The issue was confused and emotionally-heated, but, whether or not in the end the best decisions were made, there was a deep exploration of the questions of political discipline and collective responsibility.

The Committee also learned a good deal from its encounters with the formal representative system of councillors, Committees and M.P.s By chance the three Ward Councillors were all also either Chairman or Vice-Chairman of important local authority committees (Housing, Education, and Social Services). The Residents' Associations' two campaigns fell heavily within these Committee responsibilities, housing committee being responsible for the purchase of older housing and for General Improvement Areas, and education committee for the financing and appointment of play-leaders. The Residents Committee found the Ward Councillor presenting himself as a representative of local neighbourhood interests. Although his advocacy of our interests in public was unexceptionable, it was clear that there was a conflict between his roles as representative and as Manager—between his responsibilities to the Gosford Green Residents' Association on the one hand, and to the Education Committee on the other. Because this ambiguity was not openly acknowledged by many councillors, the Committee experienced it as a betrayal. The final loss of trust of this representative machinery came when after months of discussions and half-promises, the Recreation Committee (including our Ward Councillor) were reported in the press as saying that our proposals were wildly unrealistic. Members of the Gosford Green Committee felt this to be a means for the Councillors to save face by making us look fools in public.

Although this loss of confidence in the formal representative process began quite early on in the GGRA campaign, the Committee remained strangely transfixed by it right till the end: the Committee's rhythm was largely determined by the Council system, waiting for a decision from such and such a Committee, or a costing from such and such a Department. Although at many points in the campaigns the Committee's actions were challenging or even defiant, the only occasion when the *initiative* was really gained by the Committee was during the occupation of the Football Club's houses. At this point residents had opted out of the traditional negotiating machinery, and had shifted the game onto their own ground rules.

Somehow this was sensed by the Committee to be a liberation. In contrast to the despairing frustration of most Committee meetings, the mood quickly became manic, and play-ful. The underlying solidarity within the Committee spilled over into more easy social relationships. The sense of fun was obviously felt by outsiders to the Committee also, as we found residents getting involved much more actively and enthusiatically than in any other part of either campaign. Furniture and supplies of tea and biscuits were brought into the occupied house, and the place began to operate as a kind of small social centre. Door-knocking produced a lot more people willing to take part in the rota, and others who clearly saw our action as an important symbol with which to identify.

Yet, when the battle for the houses was won, the Committee seemed unable to *transfer* this experience to other issues. As the campaign for improved play facilities dragged on through the Autumn

241

and Winter of 1974 and into the New Year, the Committee was still in an impotent defeatist mood, resigned to waiting for the Council to make its tortuous and long-delayed decisions. We somehow failed to get the initiative back on our side, in spite of a number of discussions about how we could do this by building our own Adventure Playground in the park and setting play schemes in motion that would be difficult to stop and which would reinforce the need for proper provision. Part of the reason may be that we failed to consolidate the learning from the occupation in the collective consciousness of the Committee. Although we often referred back to the experience we had not made enough space to think through the theoretical implications of what we had been through. This is apparent in the tape-recorded discussion, about the sources of power in the community situation, as opposed to at the work-place. Much of the learning which is articulated in that discusion is not about much more than techniques of pressure group politics. Yet I have argued above that the Committee and about 20 other residents actually experienced something more radical than that during the occupation.

It is probably significant that the first initiative to occupy the houses came not from the GGRA Committee, but from the Housing Action Group. The Residents' Committee might well have never taken the leap of direct action if the lead had not been given by another group—not by verbal exhortation, but by their own action, based upon their own more explicit political analysis. The Committee found the impulse to take this new knd of action when confronted by a clear and immediate threat from outside—the probability that the Directors of the Football Club would repossess and board up their houses, as soon as the Housing Action Group squatters left. A similar kind of active leadership might have ben exercised within the GGRA Committee by the CDP workers but this was consciously shunned, in favour of a more accountable back-up rôle. The advantages and limitations of this contribution will now be discussed.

22. *The CDP Contribution*

I admitted earlier that the Gosford Green case-study is not the most representative or flattering example of our Team's work. In fact at the beginning my involvement in the Association was more clearly as a local resident than as a member of the CDP Team. The failure to clarify that ambiguity in the early days led to a number of confusions. For example I was asked more than once to act as Chairman for the Association. My reasons for declining were not very clearly thought out, and were probably not very credible. I felt that it was right to be more fully involved in the decision-making and in giving leadership than would be traditional in the community work rôle. But I was reluctant to be fixed in such a definite leadership rôle as Chairman. The decision was almost certainly right, but for the wrong reasons. I was helped to handle some of these ambiguities a bit more clearly when joined in working with the Association by another member of our team, Slim Hallett. This at least helped to clarify that I was not simply a local resident, but also a member of a Team which offered particular services to organised campaigns of this kind. Although not offered as systematically or as rigorously as in other parts of the Team's work, we were able to make some distinctive contributions. We fed in relevant information about the local authority's machinery and operations: the minutes of Committee decisions: the breakdown of expenditure between different schemes and between different Committees: and about the finances of and shareholdings in the City Football Club. We were able to make use of our Team's specific technical skills to advise the Committee about the powers of compulsory purchase available to the local authority; about the pros and cons for residents of becoming a general improvement area; and about the effect of the 1973 revaluation of the rates upon the area, and the mechanisms for collective appeals.

We were also able to provide access to hardware like off-set litho for leaflets, instamatic cameras, video equipment, loud hailer and so on. Our limitation was probably in the very areas that we regard as the raison d'etre for everything else: political education and organisation. Our contribution was relevant enough in terms of tactical learning (e.g. the most effective way of gaining support for a petition and where and how and when best to lodge it) but much less satisfactory in terms of strategy. Our analysis of the politics of the situation probably drew too much from other groups we were working with, who were campaigning to change or gain more control over various forms of planning intervention. We were less worked out in our analysis of the areas where there was no immediate threat of special public sector intervention, and where the demand was for public control over the operations of the private sector (e.g. the Football

Club). We were also not clear enough about the strategies that need
to be adopted in a 'no growth' situation, to avoid equally needy groups
being forced into competition against each other for a fixed amount
of resources, instead of being able in some kind of alliance to challenge
the overall amounts allocated for sharing out. The Gosford Green
group were aware that they shared a common interest with many
other sections of Coventry as far as improvements in their housing
and environment was concerned. After the occupation they looked
to our Team to suggest a strategy for working in alliance with other
Residents' Associations, trade union groups or other coalition federa-
tions, or ad hoc action committees. We failed to give that kind of lead,
partly I think because of lack of clarity about our analysis of the
overall housing situation in the older areas, and partly because of uncertainty about the implications of negotiating, alliances between
groups, outside the traditional representational process linking residents, through their Ward Councillors to the formal decision-makers
of local government.

GGRA may have been able to extend their political learning if the
CDP workers had been able to offer the kind of leadership unwittingly
provided by the Housing Action Group. This might have encouraged
the Association to find ways of regaining the initiative, of strengthening its power-base by associating with a broader constituency of
interest, and even of engaging in self- conscious political education.

Footnotes

[1] CDP is an action-research investigation into small-area deprivation,
sponsored and financed by the Home Office as part of the Urban Programme,
in conjunction with 12 selected local authorities and 8 Universities. In
each locality a small team is appointed (some members attached to the local
authority and some to a nearby University or Polytechnic). The Project Team
has no formal executive powers, but is expected to operate catalytically. It
is provided with an annual budget to undertake its own action and research,
or to stimulate new programmes in collaboration with other agencies, government departments or voluntary bodies. It is accountable at the local level to a
management committee which is normally the central Policy Committee of
the local authority, with added representation from the Home Office and
voluntary bodies. The Coventry Project completed its allotted period of
five years in 1975.
Although in the first three years the main thrust of the Coventry Team
had been social planning for institutional change, from the beginning, part
of our programme had been concerned with stimulating and supporting the
processes by which local residents are able to represent their needs and to
protect their interests, particularly in relation to key welfare state services.
In the first three years we had helped to set in motion and service a number
of new kinds of machinery: a resident-controlled shop-front Information

and Opinion Centre: consumer-representation on the Management Committee of the nursery centre and play centres; annual grants of 'seed money' to a local Community Association which acted as an umbrella body for a federation of more particular local interest groups; a new organisational coalition to act as an independent employing body for a community worker to work with residents' associations.

[2] For example, a resident-controlled shop-front Information and Opinion Centre; consumer-representation on the Management Committee for the local day nursery, nursery school, and play centre; annual grants of 'seed-money' to support new initiatives, administered by the local Community Association which acted as an umbrella body for a federation of more specific local interest groups; a new organisational coalition to act as an independent employing body for a community worker to work with residents' associations.

[3] See Coventy CDP Final Report, Part I available from:
Infomation and Intelligence Unit,
Mary Ward House,
5-7 Tavistock Place,
London WCIH. 9SS.

[4] The original and main purpose of writing up the diary and discussion of our campaigns was to help the Residents Committee to take stock and assess experience. They are reproduced here with the Committee's permission. The interpretation of what took place is entirely my own responsibility, though it obviously owes a lot to discussion with my other colleagues in the team, particularly Slim Hallett.

acta
sociologica

OFFICIAL JOURNAL OF THE SCANDINAVIAN SOCIOLOGICAL ASSOCIATION

ACTA SOCIOLOGICA is published quarterly in English. Subscriptions are by one volume only. The subscription price, payable in advance, is Danish kr. 132.– (total US $25.–). Orders should be made to Munksgaard, 35 Nørre Søgade, DK-1370 Copenhagen K, Denmark. Other correspondence should be addressed to the Editor, Acta Sociologica, Work Research Institutes, Gydas vei 8, P.o.box 8149, Oslo-Dep., Oslo 1, Norway.

as

Volume 18 · No 2-3 · 1975

VERONICA STOLTE-HEISKANEN — The population problem and underdevelopment

WALTER KORPI — Poverty, social assistance and social policy in postwar Sweden

Special section on women's sociology:

BERIT ÅS — On female culture

ROLV MIKKEL BLAKAR — How sex-roles are represented, reflected and conserved in the Norwegian language

IRJA ESKOLA & ELINA HAAVIO-MANILA — The careers of professional women and men in Finland

ERIK GRØNSETH — Work-sharing families: — Adaptations of pioneering families with husband and wife in part-time employment

JO FREEMAN — Political organization in the feminist movement

Current projects in the nordic countries

Sociological encounters

Summaries in Russian - Book Reviews - Publications Received

American Journal of Sociology

Publishing the latest analysis, research, and debate on a variety of issues:
community and group structure, social change, institutions and social
organizations, personality, population, methodology, and social theory.

Articles in 1975

Ralph Underhill, Economic and Political Antecedents of Monotheism
Edward A. Tiryakian, Neither Marx nor Durkheim . . . Perhaps Weber
Claude S. Fischer, Toward a Subcultural Theory of Urbanism
Harvey Molotch and **Marilyn Lester,** Accidental News: The Great Oil Spill
as Local Occurrence and National Event
Ivan Light and **Charles Choy Wong,** Protest or Work: Dilemmas of the
Tourist Industry in American Chinatowns
Victor W. Marshall, Socialization for Impending Death in a Retirement
Village

Published bimonthly by The University of Chicago Press
Charles E.Bidwell, Editor

American Journal of Sociology

Please enter my one-year subscription:
☐ Institutions $20.00   ☐ Individuals $15.00   ☐ ASA Members $12.00
☐ BSA Members(GB)$12.00   ☐ Students $12.00 (with signature of professor)
Countries other than USA add $1.50 to cover postage

Please mail with your check or purchase order to **American Journal of
Sociology,** The University of Chicago Press, 11030 Langley Avenue, Chicago,
Illinois 60628

Name _____
Address _____
City _____ State _____ Zip _____

MSR

The Canadian Journal of Sociology
Cahiers canadiens de sociologie

The Canadian Journal of Sociology is published at
The University of Alberta. Individual subscriptions are $12.50
per year. Subscriptions from institutions and libraries are
$25 per year. Requests concerning manuscripts,
advertising and subscriptions should be sent to
The Canadian Journal of Sociology, Department of Sociology,
The University of Alberta, Edmonton, Alberta, Canada T6G 2E1.

SOCIOLOGY

THE JOURNAL OF THE
BRITISH SOCIOLOGICAL ASSOCIATION

Editor: Gordon Horobin   Review Editor: Rex Taylor

Some Recent Articles

PETER HILLER	The Nature and Social Location of Everyday Conceptions of Class
CHARLES TALBOT GILLIN	Freedom and the Limits of Social Behaviourism: A Comparison of Selected Themes from the Works of G. H. Mead and Martin Buber
STEVE CHIBNALL	The Crime Reporter: A Study in the Production of Commercial Knowledge
KRISHAN KUMAR	Holding the Middle Ground: the BBC, the Public and the Professional Broadcaster
ROY WALLIS	Scientology: Therapeutic Cult to Religious Sect
H. M. COLLINS	The Seven Sexes: A Study in the Sociology of a Phenomenon, or the Replication of Experiments in Physics
STEVEN LUKES	Political Ritual and Social Integration
PETER HILLER	Continuities and Variations in Everyday Conceptual Components of Class

MEMBERS of the British Sociological Association and of the American Sociological Association may subscribe at reduced rates. Enquiries about membership of the B.S.A. should be addressed to the Hon. General Secretary, 12 Endsleigh Street, London, W.C.1.

For NON-MEMBERS the annual subscription (for 3 issues) is £10.50/$31.50 post-free; single issues £5.00/$15.00 postage extra. Orders may be placed with booksellers or sent direct to: Journals Manager, Journals Department,

OXFORD UNIVERSITY PRESS
Press Road, Neasden, London NW10 0DD

Social and Economic Administration

EDITED BY R. A. B. LEAPER

Volume 9 Number 3   Autumn 1975

ROD BALLARD

Knowledge for Use in Social Work Practice: Some Problems of Application

G. P. MARSHALL

Sex Discrimination and State Responsibility

MICHAEL RYAN

Hospital Pay Beds: A Study in Ideology and Constraint

J. L. BAXTER

The Chronic Job Changer: A Study of Youth Employment

R. C. L. HEMMING

The Net Resource Distribution of Two Parent Low Income Families: A Regional Comparison

Reviews

The journal is published three times a year, in Spring, Summer and Autumn, by BASIL BLACKWELL in association with the UNIVERSITY OF EXETER. The annual subscription is £4.50 ($13.50); single issues £1.75 ($5.25). Orders and remittances should be sent to: Journals Department, Basil Blackwell & Mott Ltd., 108 Cowley Road, Oxford, OX4 1JF, England.

The Monographs of the Sociological Review

Edited by Paul Halmos

University of Keele
KEELE
Staffordshire, ENGLAND

Title	*Price including postage*	
Sociological Studies in British University Education. 1963. Vol. 7.	£1.90 U.S. $5.70	
The Development of Industrial Societies: Proceedings of the 1964 Conference of the British Sociological Association at Nottingham. 1964. Vol. 8.	£1.90	$5.70
Sociological Studies in the British Penal Services. 1965. Vol. 9.	£2.50	$7.60
Japanese Sociological Studies. 1966. Vol. 10.	£1.75	$5.20
Latin American Sociological Studies. 1967. Vol. 11.	£1.75	$5.20
The Foundation Year in the University of Keele. 1968. Vol. 12.	£1.75	$5.20
The Sociology of Mass Media Communicators. 1969. Vol. 13.	£1.75	$5.20
Sociological Studies in Economics & Administration. 1969. Vol. 14.	£1.75	$5.20
The Choice of Work Area of Teachers. 1970. Vol. 15.	£1.75	$5.20
The Sociology of Sociology. 1970. Vol. 16.	£2.15	$6.30
Hungarian Sociological Studies. 1972. Vol. 17.	£2.50	$7.60
The Sociology of Science. 1972. Vol. 18.	£2.15	$6.30
Stochastic Processes in Sociology. 1973. Vol. 19.	£2.50	$7.60
Professionalisation and Social Change. 1973. Vol. 20.	£2.50	$7.60

S.R. Monographs Vols. 1—6 are now available from: Kraus-Thomson Organisation Ltd., 9491 Nendeln, Liechtenstein.